CAPE TO CAPE

A 1,250-mile backpacking walk from Cornwall to Cape Wrath in Scotland

CAPE TO CAPE

JOHN SUTCLIFFE

Published by Crescent House, Sheffield

A 1,250-mile backpacking walk from Cornwall to Cape Wrath in Scotland

CAPE TO CAPE

JOHN SUTCLIFFE

First published in Great Britain in 2018 by Crescent House.
Crescent House, 228 Psalter Lane, Sheffield S11 8UT UK.

This book is a work of non-fiction based on the life, experiences and recollections of John Sutcliffe. The author has stated to the publishers that, except in such minor respects not affecting the substantial accuracy of the work, the contents of the book are true.

A CIP catalogue record for this book is available from the British Library.

ISBN: 978-1-909461-55-0 (Paperback)

 Design and production by Ryder Design – **www.ryderdesign.studio**

Crescent House is committed to printing on paper from sustainable sources.

Printed and bound in Europe by Latitude Press Ltd.

CONTENTS

List of Maps

*To my family and the friends
I made along the way.*

MAP 1 - CAPE TO CAPE

PREAMBLE:
GETTING READY FOR THE OFF

On a chilly late April morning in 2014, I set off to walk from Cape Cornwall in South West England to Cape Wrath on the north-west tip of Scotland. The 1,250-mile-long backpacking trek was planned as a pre-retirement celebration of my fast approaching 70th birthday. It was to be an amazing journey that would take me through some of Britain's finest hill country and wilderness areas.

During my last two or three years as a Peru-based exploration geologist, I had started to plan a route using online detailed mapping software, often working until late in the night to take advantage of faster night-time internet speeds. The basic parameters of the walk were simple: to devise an end-to-end walk of Britain keeping wherever possible to upland areas, taking full advantage of the country's splendid network of long-distance trails.

The route that I eventually settled on started out from Cape Cornwall along the Cornish cliffs, and then cut inland across Devon and Somerset to Glastonbury and Bath and on to the Severn Bridge. I would then follow the delightful Welsh Borders to Clun in Shropshire and cross the English Midlands by way of Wenlock Edge and Cannock Chase, and on through the Derbyshire Dales to the start of the Pennine Way. This grandfather of Britain's long-distance trails would take me along the crest of the Pennines for 250 moorland miles with a final climb up on to the Cheviot Hills and into the Scottish Borders.

From the end of the Pennine Way, I would then follow St Cuthbert's Way to the glorious River Tweed and cross the Southern Uplands and the Pentland Hills. After skirting around the former industrial heartland of Scottish Lowlands on canal towpaths, the John Muir and West Highland Ways would lead me into the Scottish Highlands and on to Fort William to clock up 1,000 miles. From here a short ferry crossing would take me across the Loch Linnhe narrows, leaving behind the trappings of 'civilisation' as I headed across the wild, remote and sometimes desolate lands of Ardgour, Knoydart, Torridon and Sutherland. This would make a splendid and unforgettable 'dare to imagine' 250-mile-long grand finale for my 100-day Cape to Cape adventure.

A frequently asked question from people I met along the way was: why did I start the walk at the little-known Cape Cornwall (which one off-the-planet guy actually confused with Cape Canaveral!) and why did I not head to John o' Groats, 'like everyone else'?

I decided to start at Cape Cornwall, located just four miles to the north of Lands End, because it is a beautiful place and, thanks to the custodianship of the National Trust, it remains unspoilt.

At the top end of the walk, Cape Wrath is one of the most remote places on the north coast of mainland Scotland. It is not its most northerly point, but then, for that matter, neither is John o' Groats. Furthermore, a person heading to John o' Groats would miss out most of the remote North West Highlands and have to settle instead for mile after mile of dreary moorland terrain underlain by dreary Caithness Sandstone – an ugh for any 'hard rock'[1] geologist. Cape Cornwall and Cape Wrath are the only true capes in the British Isles, and joined together, if nothing else, they make for a splendid book title!

I don't think anyone, except perhaps the amazing Nepali Sherpa, would enjoy lugging a 40-45lb pack[2] for 1,250 miles with sections of fairly rough terrain. The neck pains started on the first day of the walk and daily doses of Ibuprofen soon became the routine.

So 'why lug all that clobber?' was the next question some people asked. Perhaps I could have trimmed the weight a little, but backpacking, with a home on your back, is the only practical way to undertake an off the beaten track walk like this, for it gives the walker the flexibility to roam and vary the route and itinerary according to weather and whim. There is also a safety consideration. For a lone walker getting on in years, the tent on your back gives a degree of reassurance when crossing the more challenging terrain, miles from anywhere.

I mostly wild camped[3], but had no qualms about upgrading to a youth hostel or a B&B for the occasional touch of comfort, Internet access, and a splash of hot water. In the southern counties I aimed to camp in woodlands, hidden from sight in the company of the hooting and rustling creatures of the night. In the northlands I would often camp on open moors with curlew and skylark singing from aloft as I ate my porridge. In the North West Highlands of Scotland, the excellent bothy[4] network is a veritable godsend for any backpacker who dares to venture into Highland midge country during the peak midge months of July and August.

I completed the walk in 99 walking days, camping for 56 nights, and spending 17 nights in

---

1 Meaning hard igneous or metamorphic rocks such as formed most of the Scottish Highlands, as opposed to the 'soft rock' sediments that underlay much of Britain.   **2** Half his normal load!   **3** Meaning not a designated campsite.   **4** A bothy is a basic, wonderfully midge-free shelter left open for anyone to use, mostly found in the Scottish Highlands.

bothies, with the balance spent in hostels and B&Bs. I averaged 12.6 miles per day. I had no fixed timetable, seldom knowing in advance where I would spend the night, the uncertainty adding to the adventure as the evening wore on and the shadows closed in around me. If I came across a cosy woodland glade with a rushing stream a little earlier in the day, I would gratefully drop my pack with a 'This'll do.' This is the essence of wild camping: the freedom to roam off the beaten track, exploring special places and overnighting where, within reason, the fancy takes you. Believe me, it is worth all the Ibuprofen!

I carried a full set of mountain-rated camping gear as detailed in Appendix 1. When you see it spread out on the spare bed, as I did, week after week in the run up to the walk, it's an awful lot of stuff. In the comfort of my Yorkshire cottage I found it incredibly difficult to whittle it down, weighing this against that, and then sometimes taking both! Once the walk got under way, however, my favourite pastime was listing the kit I thought I might dispense with, and I posted off three lots of surplus – and sometimes stinky – kit to my eldest daughter Penny. (That, I hope, will not be her only inheritance from Dad.)

My pack and basic contents weighed about 17 kilograms, (38 lbs) but in the North West Highlands of Scotland, I took on an additional three to four kilos of extra rations and fuel to carry me over the six or seven day remote sections. I posted off three food drops to strategic locations by prior arrangement, finding the Scottish hotel and shop owners very happy to hold these for me.

I will just mention a few bits of kit that I really loved. First my 70-litre Osprey Aether pack, bought en route in Bath for its larger capacity and excellent waist belt, which helped take some of the weight off my shoulders. Next, my freestanding Hilleberg Soulo tent was an excellent bit of kit and reassuringly gale-proof. The fly-first, self-standing design means you can erect just the outer fly and quickly get in out of the rain. If the weather is bad in the morning you can, with a bit of calisthenics, take down the inner tent and do most of the packing under cover. I slept in a faithful Rab Quantum 400-gram down-filled sleeping bag with a silk liner on a Thermarest sleeping mat. In the southern counties I cooked with a butane camping gas stove, switching to a tried and tested Trangia one-man meths stove for the Highlands[5].

For navigation I used a Satmap 2 GPS with full country 1:25,000 scale OS map coverage, switching to 1:50,000[6] from Fort William, for longer battery life. A reassuring bit of kit was my Spot two-way satellite tracker device, with emergency SOS call-up capability, which allowed my family to track my progress on a daily basis. Unless otherwise indicated, all photographs were taken by the author with a Panasonic Lumix LX7 camera, with a Leica 1:1.4 lens – a great bit of kit.

By early April 2014 I had completed the planning and arranged a four-month sabbatical with my company. Finally, it was time to get going and, on 21 April 2014, I caught the train from Leeds to Plymouth and on to Penzance for the start of my Cape to Cape walk.

This is the story of my incredible adventure.

---

5 Prior to setting off I conducted innumerable tests comparing weight of stove, fuel bottle/gas cylinder weight, and fuel consumption to boil one litre of water. The Trangia performed best when extended fuel autonomy was required.   **6** Also, once you leave walls, fences and footpaths behind, I find the 1:50k mapping is quite adequate, with shorter start-up and wake-up times, key when trying to conserve battery life.

Cape Cornwall with chimney stack from the old tin mine, Day 1.

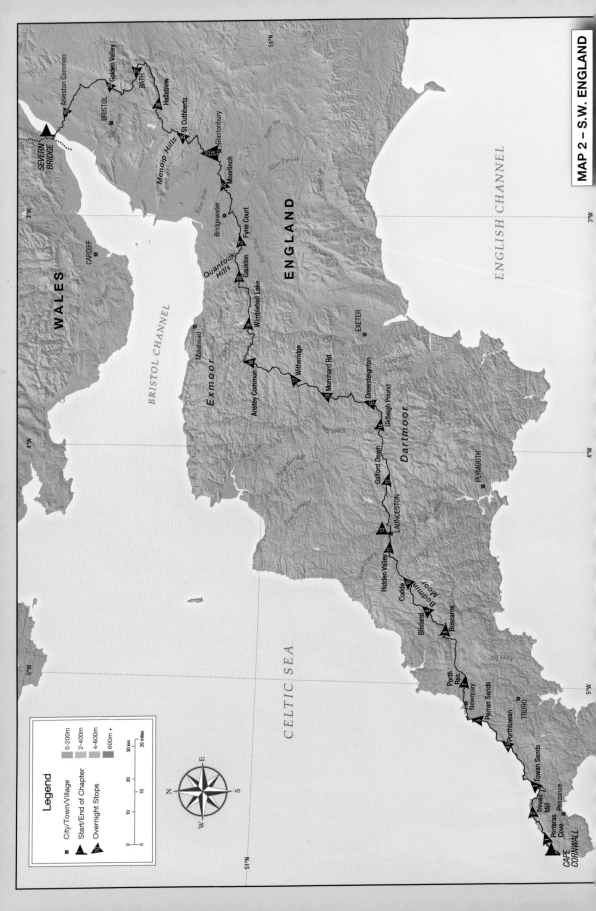

MAP 2 – S.W. ENGLAND

1

CORNWALL TO THE TAMAR

*Starting out at Cape Cornwall near to Land's End, I follow the South West Coast Path
along the stunning sea cliffs through Cornwall's historic tin and copper mining district.
At Newquay I turn inland to cross Bodmin Moor, sleep among the dead at Brisland
and almost get invited to a wedding in Launceston on the border with Devon.
I clock up my first 100 miles.*

DAY 0: 21 April, 2014   Train Journey from Yorkshire to Cornwall
Miles this day: **0**   Miles to date: **0**

The 10.10 a.m. cross-country train from Leeds to Plymouth and on to Penzance was an inauspicious start to my amazing adventure. I hadn't exactly been expecting a fine 15-carriage intercity named train like the *Cornish Riviera* or the *Devonshire Rambler* with a posh dining car and stewards in starched jackets offering grilled Dover sole with a glass of Chablis, but neither had I expected this uncomfortable bus-on-rails CrossCountry contraption for the 400-mile journey, with barely enough space for my knees and no sensible place to stow my rucksack. Bring back British Rail – almost all is forgiven.

The train rocked on through endless tracts of green countryside passing scattered towns and villages for the best part of the day, covering in an hour what would take me a week to walk – a scary thought as the hours ticked by. I had been up half the night with final preparations and I kept nodding off, but in my waking moments I fired up the Satmap to peruse the route and follow the train's progress. The train pulled into Penzance just after 6 p.m. where I was greeted by an unfriendly wind that blew swirls of cold drizzle into my face. I had thought about overnighting in the town and treating myself to a pre-walk seafood feast, but I was tired, and didn't fancy trailing around the town looking for somewhere to stay in this foul weather. I decided to continue on to St Just, a small market town some six miles to the west and closer to Cape Cornwall – the starting point for my walk. The cheerful taxi driver from some other continent amazingly seemed to know just about everyone in Cornwall and made a quick phone call to the Commercial Hotel before we set off.

Formerly a coaching inn, the Commercial Hotel was solidly built of hand-dressed grey granite, looking out over the market square. It looked the perfect spot for the last night before the walk.

Until Cornwall's mining industry went into decline in the 19th century, St Just had been a prosperous town and the inn would have done a busy trade. Merchants selling timber and gunpowder, steam engine fitters and fettlers, mine surveyors, assayers, ledger-keepers and top-hatted mine owners, as well as prospectors with hazel dowsing sticks, would all have lodged at the Commercial in the boom times when the St Just and Pendeen mines were producing a significant share of the world's tin and copper.

After a so-so steak pie supper I wandered over to the Star Inn, a lovely old pub where a Cornish ceilidh was in full swing with a group of my-age musicians knocking out a stream of lively music from an assemblage of banjos, violins, guitars and flutes. With the start of the walk now just hours away, I had been feeling a bit apprehensive but the jolly music and a celebratory pre-walk malt whisky revived my flagging spirits.

DAY 1: 22 April   St Just to Portheras Cove
Miles this day: **5**   Miles to date: **5**

Day one of the walk kicked off with a splendid 'Full Cornish' breakfast served in the hotel conservatory. Whilst lingering over several cups of coffee, I fired up the Satmap to peruse the route, wondering where I would be spending the night and what I would see on the way.

Apart from a couple of people out and about with their dogs, the town was deserted. It was dry but overcast but with the vague promise that the low cloud and the dusting of coastal mist would clear later. A narrow lane led me to an ancient granite gateway where I caught

St Just, setting off on Day 1.

Granite gateway to Cape Cornwall, Day 1.

my first glimpse of Cape Cornwall. The walk that I had been planning for the past two years was about to start, a thought that filled me with a mix of excitement and a healthy degree of trepidation.

Before leaving, I took some time to explore Cape Cornwall's rocky headland that H.J. Heinz had bequeathed to the nation to celebrate 100 years of profitable bean making in Britain. I am not normally a bean eater but they were included with the all-in breakfast and I thought I might chance some.

Disappointingly, there was not much evidence of the tin mine that had operated there until the middle part of the 19th century. The handful of mine buildings had long since been converted to dwellings, but the elaborate chimney for the mine's steam engine had survived as an aide to coastal shipping and made a fitting starting post for my 1,250-mile Cape to Cape walk.

After following a winding path through the heather over to the steep western side of the headland, I found a small half-hidden coastguard station that looked out over the green-blue Atlantic. It seemed to be unmanned; perhaps the seals had taken over the coastguard's duties to save money. I sat for a few minutes to absorb the view. The sea was in one of its quieter moods with the steady swell breaking on the jagged outcrops of black slates in a final dash of foam and spray, momentarily drowning the cries of the gulls. In stormy weather the cape would take a hammering, but these black rocks, called 'killas' by Cornish folk, had been tempered and toughened with the heat shed off from molten granite, to which the cape owes its prominence.

Making my way back to the car park, I looked over the fields towards Porthledden House, a large granite-built mansion that looked a bit out of place and unloved sitting alone in the middle of a broad expanse of green fields and gorse. Francis Oates, a native of St Just, built the house in 1909. He had worked underground at the nearby Balleswidden tin mine from the age of twelve. Later, with the Cornish mining industry in decline, Oates headed off to seek his fortune on the newly discovered gold and diamond fields of South Africa, eventually taking over from Cecil Rhodes as chairman of the world's largest diamond company. He kept his ties with Cornwall, and in 1909 returned to build this house modelled on South Africa's famous *Groote Schuur* mansion, the house where Nelson Mandela and F.W. de Klerk signed the famous accord that ended the apartheid era.

For a minerals geologist like myself this is a fascinating area, with the coastal path running along cliffs that are honeycombed with ancient mine workings. The narrow lodes[1] of tin- and copper-bearing minerals were formed during a continental collision that took place around 300 million years ago, when life on the planet was restricted to primitive life forms that shuffled and swam in the deepest oceans. Silty sediments that had accumulated on the seabed over millions of years were compressed and melted to form the granites that today underlay the upland moors of Land's End, Carnmenellis (Camborne), Bodmin Moor and Dartmoor. As the granite cooled, hot metal-rich fluids escaped through fissures to form the rich mineral veins of tin and copper that played a vital role in Britain's Industrial Revolution, just as they had during the Bronze Age revolution some 3,000 years earlier. If you followed the BBC's excellent *Poldark*

---

1 A mineral-bearing vein or ore shoot.

Twin Crowns Tin Mine, Day 1.

series that was filmed in these parts, you may have noticed that tin- and copper-bearing veins can be fickle, with fortunes won and lost quicker than at the gaming table.

After a final dawdle over a coffee in the just-opened kiosk in the car park, I set off along the dramatic sea cliffs, testing the weight of the pack with each step as I made my way towards the iconic Twin Crowns engine houses.

Built on the cliff edge of local granite, the Twin Crowns once housed the giant steam engines that powered and kept dry the deep tin and copper mine workings that extended far out under the seabed. I stopped briefly to envy the seagulls soaring in the updraft and then diving at breakneck speed in a stunning display of effortless fun. Their cries were barely audible above the noise of the wind and sea – were they laughing at me lugging the huge pack, I wondered.

Salvaged from an old calendar that I had cadged from some hardware store, I had stuck a picture of the Twin Crowns on the inside door of a kitchen cupboard in my Yorkshire cottage to serve as a daily reminder to get on with the preparations for the walk, and later to urge me on with the writing of this book!

The highlight of that first day was a visit to the National Trust's Levant Mine museum with its unique working 1840s steam-driven beam engine. Until the 1850s, Levant had been one of the world's largest copper mines with tunnels extending out under the seabed for more than a mile. During stormy weather the miners could hear the shingle moving to and fro on the seabed just above their heads. Eventually the sea broke in and flooded the workings, but by a godsend, at a time when all the miners were up on the surface.

Levant Mine workers circa 1920, note candles on some of the miners hats! Day 1.

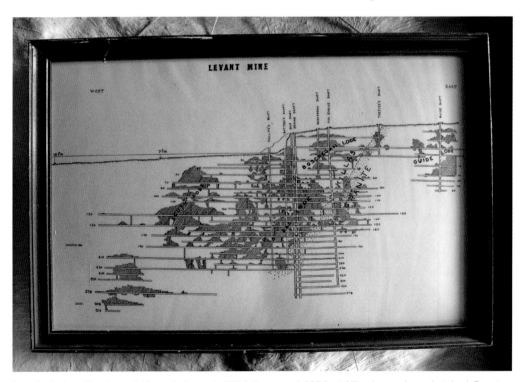

Longitudinal section, Levant Mine, shafts up to 278 fathoms or 1,390 feet. Mined area shown hatched. Day 1.

First tent pitch, above Portheras Cove, Day 1.

The Levant miners descended into the mine via a 'man engine', a fiendish German invention, rather like an oscillating ladder, that had been developed for use in the deep silver mines of the Harz Mountains. Mine cages, similar to modern-day lifts, had not yet been invented, hence the Cornish miners' reliance on *Vorsprung Durch Technik*.

On the 20 October 1919, just as 130 men and youngsters were making their way up to surface, the top coupling broke and the 1,800-foot string of connected timbers, along with its human cargo, crashed down the vertical shaft. Some lucky ones managed to leap off to safety, but 31 men and children died in this tragic accident – the worst in Cornish mining history.

When competition from overseas forced many of the mines to close in the latter part of the 19th century, the Cornish miners left in droves for the New World. Some headed for the booming Mother Lode district of California or to the frozen Canadian Yukon, with others sailing for Australia to work alongside ex-convicts in the gold fields of Bendigo/Ballarat, or the newly discovered gold and diamond fields of South Africa. For many years these Cornish miners were the county's last great export. The mining industry and the prosperity it brought has long since disappeared, with just a few ruins, spoil heaps and untended graveyards marking the passing of an era. Hundreds of feet below the moorland, there are tunnels where miners once sat on wooden planks for their mid-shift pasty by candlelight, laughing and cracking jokes and teasing the young lads. They are now filled with stagnant black water sealing off the memories of a bygone age.

Continuing on the cliff path, I found some of the steep climbs hard work, with the pack getting steadily heavier as the day progressed. My neck, injured in a road accident in Venezuela many years ago, was beginning to play up and sharp pains were starting to spread across my shoulders. I dosed up with 800 milligrams of Ibuprofen: this was to become my mid-morning elevenses for much of the walk.

I camped that first night on the grassy clifftops overlooking Portheras Cove, a campsite that offered little in the way of mod cons but with an ocean view to die for. Relieved of the pack, I felt like I was floating, an uncomfortable sensation standing so close to the cliff edge. My tent, a geodesic Hilleberg Soulo, was up in no time and I sat on the grass for a while enjoying the evening as the sun slipped below the horizon.

A simple packet pasta meal prepared me for the next day's walk, before I snuggled down in my sleeping bag with a hot chocolate, courtesy of the Commercial Hotel, to read a few pages of Hilary Mantel's *Bring Up the Bodies*. I had only covered about five miles on this first day but put this down more to the geological distractions than to my old bones. Anyway, I had allowed myself a week to ten days to work up to reach my 'cruising target' of 20 kilometres (13.5 miles) per day.

I was tired and, lulled by the magical sound of the waves breaking on the rock far below, soon fell asleep.

DAY 2: 23 April   Portheras Cove to Trevail Mill (St Ives)
Miles this day: **9**   Miles to date: **14**

I awoke several times in the night to the sound of heavy rain lashing the flysheet, adding extra cosiness to my comfy sleeping bag. Up before 6 a.m., I got underway with the packing-up chores, enjoying the freshness of the morning as I trundled around the wet grass in bare feet.

Boots on, packed up and ready to go, I sat for a few minutes enjoying the early morning sunshine as I completed the previous day's log, perused my planned route for the day on the Satmap, and took a few minutes to soak up the ocean views. Despite my seemingly endless kit lists prepared on planes and trains and sitting up in bed in Yorkshire and Peru, I discovered that I had somehow forgotten the tea bags. Counted, carefully weighed and ready packed in a Ziploc bag, they were probably now hiding under the bed in the front bedroom back in Yorkshire. You can't have breakfast without a brew, and, anxious to be off, I decided to skip it and grab something along the way.

Off by about 8.30 a.m., I made my way along the cliffs to Lower Porthmeor then cut across the fields to the Gurnard's Head at Zennor for a late breakfast of plaice and chips. Enjoying a good sit down, I made a list of all the surplus things that the Ibuprofen was already telling me I could probably dispense with – an ancient green radio (that would rejoin me later on the walk), a back-up GPS (that I would later sorely miss), a spare travel towel and a shirt and vest.

Cliffs at Trevean, Day 2.

During the first two months I would post off three parcels of unwanted items to Penny, the eldest of my three daughters, including a too-small rucksack.

The South West Coast Path is largely based on old coastguard paths that were initially made to check out hidden bays for smugglers, and I soon found the steep climbs up and down to the shoreline tiring, and so decided to try a shortcut by traversing the steep slopes just above the cliffs. As sometimes happens with my shortcuts, this one seriously backfired

Cornish-style cattle grid, at Treen on Day 2.

Cornish-style cattle grid, near Zennor on Day 2.

and I soon found myself hemmed in by chest-high gorse and brambles. Trying to clamber over a wall, my water bottle slipped out of the side pocket of my rucksack. The Platypus bottle, loved for many years, disappeared into the mass of brambles, puncturing in three places. I fished it out with my walking pole and after several attempts managed to repair it with superglue and an improvised patch.

I made camp a few miles west of St Ives, on a wide but secluded grassy track that teemed with frisky rabbits chasing each other around in circles, it being that time of year. With their guard down in the chase they would have made easy prey for a swooping buzzard.

DAY 3: 24 April   Trevail Mill (St Ives) to Towan Sands
Miles this day: **10**   Miles to date: **24**

After an unhurried start to the day, enjoying the beautiful spring morning and feeling in excellent spirits, I sorted out the surplus gear in readiness for posting. I decided to head over the open fields to St Ives rather than backtrack to the official Coast Path, and on the way there, I reworked an ancient ditty:

As I was going to St Ives
I met a cat with seven lives.
Each life had seven years,
And each year he'd seven wives.
If each wife had seven kits
With kits and cats and all the wives
How many were coming from St Ives?

The town was buzzing; the colourful narrow streets crammed with brightly painted pie shops, contented pie munchers, strumming street musicians and artists. It was a lovely town and, as I was in no hurry, I took time out for a relaxed lunch at the Union Inn. Afterwards I shopped for supplies, putting back on most of the weight I had just posted off!

Passing the historic Sloop Inn overlooking the harbour, I read that in the aftermath of the pro-Catholic Prayer Book Rebellion of 1549, the visiting English provost marshal had invited the warden of the port to join him for dinner at the Sloop. Whilst dining, the provost asked the warden to have a gallows erected which they later went round to inspect. The warden was then ordered to mount the steps and was promptly hung on his own gallows for his alleged part in the rebellion. I thought that was very mean.

The glorious weather held as I made my way to Hayle some three miles further along the coast. Hayle had recently received World Heritage recognition as one of the great engineering centres of the Industrial Revolution and I had looked forward to an interesting visit. By the time the award was made, however, much of the town's industrial heritage had disappeared

Turnstones at St Ives, Day 3.

Seals at Godrevy Point and pink sea thrift flowers, Day 4.

under modern housing developments and rather dreary shops, and is remembered only in a few street names. The town's 'modern' quay was constructed in the 1740s, and in 1758 the Cornish Copper Company set up a copper smelter on what is now the Copperhouse Creek, at the eastern end of the harbour. Cornwall was then booming as the world's largest copper producer.

As the shallower mines were depleted and the workings got progressively deeper, special attention had to be paid to keeping the deep workings dry. Steam driven pumps helped with this task but the early 'atmospheric' engines were inefficient. A Hayle blacksmith, John Harvey, perfected a technique for making boilers that could withstand much higher pressures, and mining engineer Richard Trevithick teamed up with Harvey (and then with Harvey's daughter!) to make the world's first high-pressure steam engine in 1799. The Hayle foundry soon became the world's leading manufacturer of powerful steam engines.

In 1801, Trevithick built the first steam-powered locomotive and the whole town turned out to see the inauguration of this amazing steam-belching 'Puffing Devil'. Appearing to run backwards, the steam-driven cart carried several men up nearby Camborne Hill on its inaugural run, inspiring the popular folk ditty:

Goin' up Camborne Hill, coming down
The horses stood still;
The wheels went around;
Goin' up Camborne Hill, coming down …

Eventually Trevithick travelled out to Peru on a Cornish whaler to help with the dewatering of the world famous Cerro de Pasco mine where, as a student about to graduate, I had been offered a job. The mine, which is still operating, is located in the high Andes about six hours' drive east of Lima – the city where I did much of the planning for this walk.

Arriving at the nearby Towans beach resort, I called in at a beach bar called The Bluff to take on water for the night's camp. A chap in the bar kindly bought me a gin and tonic to wish me well on my journey. Looking to take on water for supper and breakfast, I then discovered that I had somehow lost the second of my two precious Platypus water bottles. The pub gave me an unwieldy replacement that served until next morning when it was replaced by a one-litre refreshment bottle that I scavenged from a waspy rubbish bin. It lasted all the way to the top of Scotland in a marathon recycling endeavour.

Continuing up the beach for a mile, I made camp on a grassy path in the middle of the dunes just out of sight of some holiday huts. A man came by and offered to charge up my iPhone and Satmap batteries and return them the next morning.

OPPOSITE: Godrevy Point and lighthouse, Day 4.

DAY 4: 25 April Towan Sands to Porthtowan
Miles this day: **13** Miles to date: **37**

I awoke to another lovely sunny morning, and my batteries were duly returned to me. A girl came by with an out-of-control nosy dog that tried to get into my tent having sniffed out my precious food stash. She told me about a chalet-style cafe at the north end of the beach at Godrevy that sounded rather nice, so I decided to get going and breakfast there.

About two miles beyond Godrevy is a place called Hell's Mouth, apparently a popular suicide spot, for a plastic card nailed to a wooden post gives a telephone number for those in need of last-minute counselling. I did wonder if a person intent on jumping off a cliff would have brought along a mobile phone ... perhaps for a very short call on the way down. I continued along the clifftops, letting my mind ponder on this interesting thought experiment.

A nasty storm blew in off the Atlantic as I made my way towards the old mining village of Porthtowan. For the last mile or two before reaching the village, the path ran alongside the perimeter fence of the former Ministry of Defence establishment of Nancekuke, with rusting notices posted at regular intervals warning me to keep out because of 'non-ionising radiation'. I wasn't too sure exactly what that was but I didn't like the sound of it.

The storm brought with it an onslaught of icy rain. Passing a surfers' restaurant-bar and bunkhouse called The Unicorn, I went inside seeking temporary respite from the storm. It was warm and cosy and I got a very friendly welcome from Molly, Heather, Dom, Sam, Innes and Jorma. I decided to stay the night, and enjoyed a surprisingly good steak and eventually got used to the very loud music.

John at St John's Shaft,
Tywarnhayle Copper Mine,
Porthtowan, formerly owned by the
Royal School of Mines, Day 4.

OPPOSITE TOP: Wheal Charlotte Mine
workings near St Agnes
Head, Day 6.

OPPOSITE BELOW: Looking back to
Wheal Charlotte Mine workings
near St Agnes Head, Day 6.

DAY 5: 26 April   In Porthtowan
Miles this day: **0**   Miles to date: **37**

The cold stormy weather showed no sign of easing and I decided to stay for a second night. I had a long way to go but a day or two here and there would make no difference in the long run. Anyway, the village of Porthtowan was something of a special place for former students of the Royal School of Mines (RSM) so I really needed no excuse to linger a while.

Later in the morning the rain eased and I made my way up the valley to the remains of the 19th century Tywarnhayle copper mine that the RSM had purchased in 1906 to use as a field centre for instruction surveying and later for geophysics and geochemistry. The old mine was a fascinating place, with several granite-built engine houses and an adit[2] that followed a twisting and turning vein of copper ore deep into the hillside.

When we came here as students in the winter of 1964 for a three-week surveying course it was bitterly cold and we had struggled to focus the theodolite with eyes watering in the biting wind. We were shown how to survey the narrow adit and a steeply inclined under-ground stope[3] whilst hanging on to chains and grotty hemp ropes. The survey part was straightforward but then we had to burn the midnight oil on diabolical triangulation calcula-tions, using Brunsviga hand-cranked calculators and a huge book of six-figure logarithms. We did manage some time out to master the subtleties of Liar's Dice down in the pub, as well as for sorties to the Flamingo dance hall in Redruth to track down the legendary Cornish girls.

---

2 A horizontal mine tunnel.   **3** A mine extraction chamber.

These were sometimes followed by the painfully long walk back in the bitter cold, trying to hitch a lift.

Some 40 years later I would team up with two of these fellow students, John and Roger, to launch and then work together on a South American-based gold exploration company called Mariana Resources – but that's another story!

DAY 6: 27 April	Porthtowan to Penhale Sands
Miles this day: **10**	Miles to date: **47**

The storm eased overnight. I was well rested and ready to go. There was still a nip in the air and the cold wind threatened rain as I

Sea cliffs with mine workings and blue copper and red iron staining, St Agnes mining district, Day 6.

made my way along the cliffs and past the old Wheal Coates mine workings, heading towards St Agnes Head. This section of the coastal path is quite spectacular, overlooking the wild Atlantic and following an old mine road past the old Wheal Charlotte mine workings. The weather improved as the morning advanced, with the thin cloud cover giving way to blue sky.

The coastal path skirts around St Agnes' small natural harbour and then continues past the Blue Hills mining district, with spectacular reddish iron and blue-green copper-arsenic stained cliffs with exposed mine tunnels.

And so on to Perranporth, another popular surfers' town. The Penhale sands, located just to the north of the town, are one of the largest dune areas in the South West, extending for a good two and a half miles. Thinking the dunes might make a good place to camp, I filled my water bottle at the coastguard station before heading to the northern end of the dunes where I had noticed an area marked 'caves' on my Satmap.

As I had suspected, the caves turned out to be old mine workings, probably forming part of the old Perran iron mine. As students, we had tramped around the sand dunes just to the east of here trying to track the concealed vein using geophysical surveying techniques. I pitched the tent on a small grassy area in front of the entrance to the mine that was partly submerged in a pond of stagnant greenish water. It was an eerie place, reminding me of a scary part of the *Lord of the Rings* where the fellowship, struggling to open the Doors of Durin, awaken the terrifying multitentacled Watcher of the Lake.

Settling down for the night with my head full of fire-breathing Balrogs, I turned my mind

Dunes on the Penhale Sands, Day 6.

away from Moria and thought about the vast expanse of sand dunes surrounding my tent, recalling a true story from classical antiquity called the 'Sand Calculator' that I had come across some years ago pondering on the 'why something rather than nothing' riddle of the universe's existence.

Archimedes, one of the great philosopher-engineers of ancient Greece, had been asked by his friend King Gelo of Sicily (that at the time belonged to Greece) to work out how many grains of sand it would take to fill the 'known universe'. This delightfully silly two-stage task involved first calculating the size of the universe and then inventing some mathematical way to handle astronomically large numbers. To calculate the size of the solar system, (the 'known universe') Archimedes had used the new heliocentric model that had been proposed by another clever Greek, Aristarchus, who placed the sun, and not the Earth, at its centre. Archimedes went on to calculate the universe as having a diameter, in modern notation, of about four light years, which we now know to be about the distance to our closest star, Proxima Centauri. It wasn't such a bad estimate, given that it predated the first Italian telescope by some 2,000 years.

Aristarchus' heliocentric model for the solar system did not gain general acceptance and the Earth remained at the centre of everything for another 2,000 years until the Polish-born polymath, Nicolaus Copernicus, revived the heliocentric model. He was a gifted astronomer as well as mathematician, physician, economist, lawyer, jurist, four-language linguist, classics scholar, artist, Catholic cleric, governor and diplomat. In 1503, after spending many years travelling around Europe, he returned to his native Poland and, well beyond the reach of the Roman Inquisition, set to work developing his heliocentric theory of the solar system.

ABOVE: Wide expanse of Penhale Sands. **BELOW:** Ancient iron mine at the north end of Penhale Sands, Day 6.

Some years later the Naples-born Dominican Friar Giordano Bruno took the Copernican heliocentric theory to a revolutionary new level, concluding that the sun was in fact a star. He also conjectured that the universe was unlimited in size, and threw in the possibility of many inhabited worlds – ideas that have gained support from cosmologists in recent times. He was denounced for his 'plurality of worlds' belief and in 1593 summoned to the Roman Inquisition for his denial of 'core beliefs'. Imprisoned during his seven-year trial, he refused to recant. Pope Clement VIII eventually threw in the holy towel and declared him a heretic and had him burnt at the stake on the 17 February 1600.

Sixteen years after Bruno's death, the Italian astronomer Galileo Galilei went to Rome to try to persuade the church to accept the 'new' ideas on the solar system. He had developed an amazing new tool called the telescope and went armed with new observational evidence that clearly supported the Copernican theory. The same Cardinal Bellarmine who had 'grilled' Bruno interrogated Galileo, pressing home the point by conducting the interrogation in the very same room. Galileo sensibly reached a plea bargain with the church by agreeing not to discuss his theory further but spent the rest of his life under virtual house arrest.

In 1835 the ducat finally dropped in Vatican City and Galileo's book was removed from the *Roman Catholic Index of Prohibited Books*. In 1992 Pope John Paul II acknowledged that the Catholic Church had 'committed errors' during the Galileo incident, but the statue to commemorate the 400th anniversary of Galileo's first telescope – promised by Pope Benedict in 2008 – has still not been erected in Vatican grounds.

DAY 7: 28 April   Penhale Sands to Porth Reservoir
Miles this day: **12**   Miles to date: **59**

Slipping quietly past the sleeping watcher the next morning, I headed off towards Newquay where I had two awaiting missions. The first was to try to get my iPhone fixed as it was no longer picking up my work emails, and the second was to look up a chap that I had worked with in Venezuela in the late 1980s. A bright young Asian lad, working out of a scruffy back street shop fixed my iPhone in a few minutes. He said there was no charge for the help but accepted a tip when I insisted.

I then met up with Peter in a central pub. The passing years (he was now 82) had left their mark and he did not look a well man. I reminded him that the last time I had seen him, some 35 years earlier, he had driven me back to the town of Puerto Ordaz in Eastern Venezuela after a visit to the Botanamo gold prospect. Several days of heavy rain had turned the 60-mile laterite track into a quagmire but fortunately the Toyota Land Cruiser had an electric winch and Peter, then a very fit wiry man, jumped out every 20 or so yards to hook up the winch cable to some tree to pull us out of the bog. This epic journey took us most of the day instead of the usual 50 minutes.

I spent almost four years in Venezuela running programmes exploring for gold in the eastern

Bolivar province adjoining the former British colony of Guyana. It is a truly amazing country, with pristine rainforests that go on forever, and Lost World mesetas that rise majestically out of the steaming jungle.

The coastal section of my walk terminated at Newquay and it was now time to head inland to cross the moor country of Bodmin and Dartmoor. I said goodbye to Peter and headed quickly out of the town to find the night's camping spot. The next time I would see the sea proper would be at Sandwood Bay – just a few miles from my journey's end at Cape Wrath in three months' time; the next time I would see Peter we could both be recycled molecules mingling in the Earth's atmosphere.

I camped in a small patch of woodland about four miles east of Newquay, pitching the tent on a crunchy bed of bluebells. These, I discovered, make a really comfortable base layer for the tent, keeping sticky mud off the groundsheet. I slept well apart from being woken several times by some creature of the night rattling round in the undergrowth. It sounded fairly big, possibly a fox or badger.

DAY 8: 29 April   Porth Reservoir to Boscarne Junction
Miles this day: **16**   Miles to date: **75**

It was a chilly grey start to the day, with a dank earthy smell of rotten wood and squashed bluebells, but the birds were up and about singing their breakfast songs. I joined in, whistling back at them as I got my porridge underway. The tent was dripping with condensation so I hung it up in a tree to dry off the worst.

After a brew, I headed off along the pretty tree-lined lanes towards St Columb. The onset of spring had turned the south-facing banks into a mass of colour, but the high earthen banks restricted the view over the fields from which pheasants on the hunt for a better-late-than-never mating partner called out from time to time. By mid-morning the narrow lanes were surprisingly busy. Some of the speeding motorists gave me just a foot or two of space and, after a few scares, I tied red flagging tape on my walking poles and shook them at the worst offenders, raising the occasional rude gesture from the driver.

The sun came out later on adding a cheer to the day. I was clean out of water but I spotted a spring on the Satmap and tracked it down, giving me the chance to try out my new MSR ceramic water filter on the muddy seepage. It worked a treat.

South of St Wenn, I came across an old gentleman sitting in a walking frame looking out over the fields. Curious to know how he got there, I crossed over to say hello and recorded the ensuing conversation on my digital voice recorder. He spoke with a lovely Cornish accent – in fact I think he was the first native Cornishman I had encountered on the trip so far.

Gordon Furken was 83, and just about every day his good lady brought him to this crossroads, to look out over the fields that he had once farmed.

Asking who farmed the land now, he replied, 'My son-in-law.'

'Is he any good?' I asked.

'No, bloody useless. Look what an old farmer could do back then boy, 'ee could shear a sheep, lamb a ewe, break an 'orse, plough a field, build a mow, make a gate, cut 'n lay 'edges. I cut 'n laid 'em all', he said waving to the hedges opposite.

Asking what I was doing, I told him I was working in Chile. He listened, and asked, 'What ee bin doing there then?' adding, 'aye's only bin across the Tamar into Devon five times in 83 year.' Bidding him goodbye, I asked him to remember me in September when I would be up in Scotland. He was a grand old chap and I hope he is still out and about monitoring his fields.

During the course of the morning, I decided I would make a push into Bodmin for a steak supper, and perhaps overnight in a B&B. I still had eight miles to go but could make it if I got a move on and stopped rambling so much.

At Tremorebridge, I turned north on to a disused railway track that had been conserved to form a splendid foot and cycle path along a tributary of the River Camel. It joined the main river at Grogley Moor some two miles away, to form a very sizable swift-flowing river that hurried off to join the sea at Padstow, some ten miles distant. I love rivers and this was a

Boscarne Junction, Bodmin, Day 8.

good one, the low-slung branches overhanging the lively dark waters where otters would play and chase the silvery spring-run salmon. In the clear rivers of Southern Chile I have watched them in a playful mood running loops around the fish as if dancing around the dinner table.

On the way to Boscarne Junction railway station, now a tourist attraction, I stopped to chat to a couple that were making for the Bridge Inn on the outskirts of Bodmin. They kindly invited me to join them for dinner.

Afterwards I made my way back to the station as darkness fell and put up the tent just beyond the end of the platform, discovering that the flat turf was only half an inch thick and had been laid on a bed of concrete, making for a hard bed.

DAY 9: 30 April   Boscarne Junction to Blisland
Miles this day: **7**   Miles to date: **82**

Conscious of my high visibility I was up at 5.30 a.m. A few runners and cyclists were also up and about, some waving and shouting a greeting, unfazed by the green tent parked by the railway track. Setting off into Bodmin after a cup of tea and some leftover pub peanuts, I made for Sainsbury's for a wonderful sit-down breakfast with toasted teacakes and scrambled eggs.

Leaving the rucksack in the care of the store manager, I headed into town to hunt around for a hat to replace the one dropped somewhere along the way, and then checked out the town's infamous jail. A noticeboard said that a total of 32 hangings had been conducted here between 1802 and 1909, mainly for the murdering of husbands, wives, girlfriends and business associates. I noticed that the list on the wall included a 21-year-old lad who was hanged for setting fire to a hayrick, which seemed a bit harsh.

Having dallied away the best part of the day, I set off out of Bodmin, doubling back towards Boscarne Station to rejoin the Camel Trail. It was a beautiful morning, with the sun struggling to penetrate the archway of coppiced trees that lined the former railway track. The woods were alive with birdlife: songbirds, tits, finches, goldcrests and hidden pheasants, all out and about celebrating the arrival of spring and with it, the hide-and-seek of the mating season. On the way I stopped to talk to a local lady who showed an interest in the walk, suggesting I might depart from my planned route to take in the village and pub at Blisland.

The Blisland Inn overlooked the tree-lined village green and seemed a promising place to remedy the world's worst steak of the night before. Relishing the prospect of a late evening, I first looked around for a place to camp after the pub closed. Pitching the tent in the dark with a headlamp is no problem, but finding a suitable site in the dark with a limited headlight beam can sometimes be tricky. Just across the green was a lovely old church fashioned from Cornish granite. The graveyard would do nicely, I thought, after checking it out.

The pub had recently been awarded the CAMRA National Pub of the Year Award and was bustling with contented real-ale drinkers. Offloading my rucksack in a corner I settled in for the evening, enjoying first a gin and tonic followed by an extra-garlicky mushroom starter, and then a superb steak with a glass or so of good red. It was quiz night and I was invited to team up with a friendly couple. One of the questions was to name the sacred bird of Peru. Having lived there for over ten years and worked in the mountains watched by the condors, I took this to be a clear sign that Peru's Pachamama, the guardian of Mother Earth, was still backing me.

It was getting dark as I left the pub to head over to the graveyard where I camped next to Philip Hawking who, the gravestone said, 'fell asleep' in 1891. I fell asleep shortly after a hot chocolate.

Blisland – a hot chocolate to end Day 9.

Cornish wall garden near Blisland, Day 10.

DAY 10: 1 May   **Blisland to Bodmin Moor**
Miles this day: **8**   Miles to date: **90**

The overnight rain had eased to drizzle and I moved into the church porch for my morning tea with a nice porch slab to sit on. A chap arrived to repair the church roof and was quite unperturbed to find a lodger in the porch, cooking porridge, and we chatted for a while before I set off. Despite the turn for the worse in the weather, I was in excellent spirits. I was about to cross Bodmin Moor, my first taste of wilderness on the walk.

From Blisland I headed northwards on to Pendrift Down and then across the Kerow, Lady and King Arthur Downs before getting on to Bodmin Moor proper. This was very different country. The dramatic sea cliffs, meadows, woodlands and quiet lanes were now replaced by heath and moorland. There was not a soul about, just the noise of the wind and a high-flying skylark to add to the mood of the new landscape. The path led me past a number of hut circles, cairns and old field systems. Again I felt the vibes of past civilisations; perhaps imagined, perhaps not.

Bodmin Moor campsite on the River Fowey, Day 10.

Gorse bushes and colourful wild flowers were now replaced by brown tufted bog-grasses and mosses. The higher ground in the distance was capped with tors of sombre grey granite. My progress between Brownwilly Downs and Butters Tor was hampered by innumerable standing pools and deep ditches of sluggish brown bog water, which required care. This was a place where you could easily slip from sight with a foolish step. The landscape here showed subtle signs of man's intervention with irregular mounds and linear watercourses, and then it dawned on me: I was probably crossing terrain that had once been dredged for alluvial tin.

Alluvial tin accumulates from the weathering of the tin-bearing veins, but as far as I know there are no known veined tin occurrences on Bodmin Moor. Perhaps the presence of these old tin placers suggests that there could be concealed veins cutting through the granite awaiting some future discovery, perhaps in the next Bronze Age. Eventually I made it on to firmer ground. I had been very careful to avoid getting water over the tops of my boots, but both boots had now started to leak and squelched with bog water. This was a serious concern as wet feet can lead to blisters, especially when one is carrying a heavy pack.

Once off the moor, I camped on the eastern edge of Codda Downs, finding a lovely sheltered spot amongst the gorse bushes next to a tributary of the River Fowey. After hanging up

Boot drying in the Hidden Valley near Launceston, Day 11.

my socks to start the two- or three-day drying process, I went to fill my water bottle from the deep and fairly fast flowing stream. Leaning over the bank I dropped my MSR ceramic filter and it floated off downstream, bobbing up and down as it waved goodbye, disappearing into the overhanging undergrowth. Panicking, I tried to follow it on hands and knees but prickly gorse bushes blocked the way. The filter was a key bit of kit so I resumed the search later, luckily finding it some distance downstream, hiding under a bank.

This splendid first day on the moors ended with a chicken curry and couscous followed by a quick bedtime read.

DAY 11: 2 May   Bodmin Moor to Hidden Valley, (Launceston)
Miles this day: **9**   Miles to date: **99**

After a lazy start, I set off through the gorse thickets to discover I had actually been camping on a large island with an even larger stream blocking my intended route. Once over, I headed across the grassy expanse of Hendra Downs along an ancient drove road past innumerable settlements and stone circles similar to the downs of the previous day.

A sad peacock after his peahens were eaten by foxy, New Mills Farm near Launceston, Day 12.

The downs eventually gave way to fields as I made my way towards Launceston, and I camped in a bluebell wood near the Hidden Valley Discovery Park. The muddy ground sloped down to a small lake so I excavated a small platform with my toilet trowel, throwing leaf mould on to the sticky clay to keep the worst of it off the groundsheet.

DAY 12: 3 May   **Hidden Valley to Launceston**
Miles this day: **4**   Miles to date: **103**

Just before leaving, I listened to a pair of low-flying geese coming in to land on the lake, a short landing strip for such a big bird. They were honking away on the difficult approach and I wondered if one might be giving instruction to a less experienced mate or sibling.

'Steady there – final approach, 200 feet, veer left, flaps down, wing tips up.
Full flaps, honk honk, bank right, steady as you go, 100 feet, level wing tips, Steady now,
watch the trees, steady as you go, 50 feet, closing and 25 feet,
Flap to brake, flap to brake, shut beak, brace neck,
And 15 feet, splay feet, fast flapping, touchdoooown. Splooooosh …

A passing invitation to Ania and Darren's wedding, Launceston. **PHOTOGRAPH BY:** *Rob Frost Photography.*

Honk honk! Nice landing.
Just in time for tea with medals and watercress!'

Heading towards Launceston, I stopped off for a coffee at the New Mills Farm Park, where a huge Indian peacock with spectacular iridescent blue and green plumage cautiously approached me. His minder told me that he was a bit out of sorts because a wicked fox had recently eaten his peahens.

On the way into town I passed a large wedding group in front of the town hall. I could not resist joining in, and photobombed the scene. The wedding crowd roared with laughter and some weeks later Ania and Darren later kindly sent me a brilliant photograph that was taken by wedding photographer, Rob Frost.

This was a special day for me also, as I had clocked up my first 100 miles and was now just half a mile away from the historic Devon border. This called for a bit of a celebration and a shower. I was lucky to find a £30 room with breakfast at the White Hart, a fine traditional market-town hotel right in the town centre. ●

2

DEVON AND SOMERSET TO
THE SEVERN BRIDGE

*After crossing the River Tamar into Devon I head across Dartmoor and Exmoor,
then turn east towards Glastonbury and Bath where I get a free pair of boots and buy
a new rucksack before crossing into Wales on the 'old' Severn Bridge.*

DAY 13: 4 May   Launceston to Galford Down
Miles this day: **12**   Miles to date: **115**

The River Tamar rises just five miles from the Cornish peninsula's northern coast and flows
south to join the English Channel at Plymouth Sound. It forms the historic border between
Devon and Cornwall for much of its 65-mile length.

Making my way down the steep lane towards the Polson Bridge, enjoying the last mile of Cornwall on this glorious spring morning, I was on a high and sat on a wall, telephoning my three daughters to celebrate the crossing of the Tamar and completing the first leg of the walk.

My jubilation was rather short-lived for, just beyond the bridge, a large group of unfriendly fly fishermen primly dressed in matching Town and Country green and brown outfits said, talking in unison, that the public right of way had been diverted. They directed me instead along a nonsensical detour, across muddy fields with long wet grass that left me with wet feet from my now seriously leaking boots. The public right of way had been diverted so as not to pass in front of Welltown farmhouse, as it would have done for the last several hundred years, leaving me wondering if the farm owner and Chairman of the Parish Council were not fly fishermen. Several times during the walk I had come across this rerouting of ancient rights of way. It drives me up the wall as the new diversion, as likely as not, leads you off on three sides of a big square, just out of sight of the inconvenienced dwelling.

I pushed on into Devon following the Two Castles Trail until the strains of jolly organ music that came floating across the fields. Dingle's open-air fairground museum was conveniently placed next to the trail and was free, so I had a quick look around. The brightly painted exhibits included a 51-key Dutch organ as well as several colourful roundabouts. A shop with cafe provided me with a welcome sit down and a cold beer until the non-stop roundabout music pressed me to move on.

Shortly after Dingle's Fairground I passed Lewtrenchard Manor hotel, a potential source of drinking water. Set back from the road it looked rather posh, a place where 24/7 vagrants like myself might not be made welcome.[1] I carried on and, half a mile further on, passed a lovely old cottage at Lew Mill just as an elderly gentleman was emerging from his front door. He seemed a bit confused when I asked if I could have some water and he beckoned me inside to speak with his wife. They were a lovely old couple, well into their eighties, who spoke with a lovely soft Devon accent.

A stony track by the cottage climbed up the steep eastern slopes of the Lew valley on to Galford Down. A blister that had developed on the heel of my left foot was now giving me grief so the big green field at the top of the hill was as far as I got that evening.

DAY 14: 5 May   Galford Down to East Dartmoor
Miles this day: **13**   Miles to date: **128**

Awoken just after 5 a.m. by the sound of munching cows just a few feet from my head and the rousing breakfast birdsong, I made a brew and planned the day's walk, still tucked into my cosy sleeping bag. On the Satmap I spotted the Dartmoor Inn at the western edge of

OPPOSITE: A medieval bridge just outside Launceston, Day 13.

---

1 To later discover it was owned by the family of a good friend!

the moor, the perfect place to try a 'Full Devonish' breakfast treat before tackling the long trek across the moor. I was dying for some fruit, so perhaps a grapefruit to start, followed by crispy bacon with two, or even three soft-fried eggs, plus lots of whatever else was on offer and several cups of black Colombian coffee.

Excited at the prospect I packed up, brushed my beard and headed off towards the hotel. From a distance I saw the empty car park and the peeling paintwork, blowing away the promised breakfast treat. Making do instead with a handful of nuts to take away the remembered taste of bacon and tomatoes lingering in my mouth, I headed up the track in the direction of Dartmoor but was quickly brought back to reality when two Jack Russell terriers came bounding down the grassy track towards me, followed by their two owners out for a spring morning walk. The smooth haired of the two dogs took my mind back to my childhood.

I would have been about ten years old and Grandma was on her annual visit to Yorkshire from 'Down South'[2]. I could tell something was up as soon as I landed home from school. Everyone assembled in the kitchen, and Mum was grinning as if she had finally won something on the Littlewoods football pools. Then, looking around, I spotted a tiny head peering over the cut-away side of a small cardboard box parked next to the Rayburn stove. After a quick tickle around the ears, she jumped out of the box, with everyone laughing, and Trixie and I began a friendship that would last all through my teenage years. My mum ran a sweets and tobacco shop in the village and, through a young farmer (who was chasing after my elder sister) had made the acquaintance of the local vet who was looking for a home for the puppy.

Trixie joined me on long walks over the moors to Attermire Scar and Malham Cove, the Ribble Valley and elsewhere. She would chase around the fields until she finally ran herself into the ground and then jump up at the back of my legs to ask for a carry, and I would pop her into the front pouch of my scruffy brown anorak. From this high vantage point, she would scan the countryside on the lookout for rabbits, and let out a little squeal when she spotted one, her jaws chattering. Like all terriers Trixie was a born hunter, almost always with her head stuffed down some ratty hole as we ranged far and wide on rambles through the north-west Yorkshire countryside.

When she was a bit older I would take her ratting in the cattle auction mart just over the road from where we lived, before it was pulled down to make room for a housing estate. After everyone had gone home and the place was dark and deadly quiet, we would creep in by torchlight, the warm humid air rank with animal smells. Stealth was essential so I would hold Trixie under my arm, tapping her on the nose and waving a warning finger to put her on guard. A number of shippons, used for holding livestock in the daytime, led off from the central corridor and the rats would squeeze in through the gaps behind the heavy sliding doors to help themselves to the cattle feed.

Tiptoeing up to a door, I would put Trixie on the floor, her jaws trembling, and slide it open. Flicking on the light, all hell would break loose as Trixie shot across the floor like a loaded spring, rats scattering in all directions. Some would jump up on to bales of hay and in

---

2 Tidworth if I remember correctly, where she ran the YMCA.

desperation try to run up the smooth cement walls but Trixie would nab them in mid-air and dispatch them with a quick flick of her jaw. Her ratting skills became famous and we soon became the unpaid village rat catchers.

Sometimes, when the moon was just right, I would take her duck shooting, crossing Arnford Moor over to the River Ribble. The curious sheep would crowd around us with my feeble Eveready torch picking out the glint of 50 pairs of eyes. Some would get uncomfortably close and stamp their feet because of Trixie's presence, and it took an effort from both of us not to get scared. The best nights were the crisp, late autumn evenings with a full moon illuminating a thin veil of cloud[3] that silhouetted the ducks as they flitted across the night sky. With Trixie running around my feet, I would listen for the 'shew shew shew' of beating wings that gave me just a second's notice before they flew overhead and disappeared into the night sky. Trixie was a hopeless retriever, but that was no great problem, for I was a pretty hopeless night shot.

When I headed off to university, Trixie and my Greener twelve-bore shotgun 'retired' to my sister's nearby farm. Some years later I took Trixie and the twelve-bore for our last hunt together. Trixie was now an arthritic old lady with her face flecked with grey and her eyes starting to mist over, and the poor old Greener now had a long-neglected pitted barrel. I spotted an old buck rabbit over a wall munching away at the long summer grass. I didn't have the heart to shoot it like a sitting duck, so I picked up Trixie, holding her under the chin, and pointed her head towards the rabbit. Her jaws started to quiver, just like in the old days. Dropping her over the wall, she ran round and round in random circles puzzled by the confusing criss-crossing scents, until the old rabbit finally scampered off. Walking back to the farmhouse, I felt sad, knowing this had been our last hunt together.

My route across Dartmoor took me just to the north of Brat Tor. It was a grand morning, with no indication of the foul weather that was to land on me a short while later in the day. The track petered out somewhere near the headwaters of Rattle Brook just beyond the ruins of Bleak House. Here I struck a bearing across pathless moors and into the Okehampton Firing Range, taking my chances with the notorious quaking bogs. The OS map warns walkers to call an 0800 number to check the status of the range before crossing, but as today was a public holiday I figured I would be fairly safe. I made slow progress, testing the boggier ground with my poles and tripping over the wobbly tussocks, some as big as footballs.

The wind was now getting up, bringing with it black clouds, and it started to rain. I estimated I was covering no more than one mile per hour and, starting to tire, began to wonder if I would clear the moor before nightfall. This would not be a problem, carrying a home on my back and surrounded everywhere by marshy but drinkable water.

By mid-afternoon the wind had steadily increased to reach somewhere close to gale-force strength. The driving rain stung my face and the back of my jacket rucked up under the pack

3 A hunter's moon.

A Dartmoor mire with the dreaded purple bog grass (*Molinia caerulea*) on Day 14.

letting in the rain, and my boots eventually filled with peat bog. I no longer bothered to avoid the really boggy sections and, to add to my woes, the Satmap's screen started to flicker, either through the penetration of moisture or an indication that the battery was about to expire. Changing the Satmap's rechargeable batteries in this weather was completely out of the question. It is a fiddly job at the best of times.

Struggling to see properly with my spectacles now useless, I reached the top of a tor-capped ridge to find a small tower-shaped granite building sitting in the middle of nowhere. Thinking that it might offer shelter from the foul weather I walked around the circular perimeter, but the only way in was a small window-sized opening about five or six feet above moor level. Curious, I climbed up and saw that the stone outer wall was lined on the inside with modern red brickwork, with a painted pipe and a stopcock sticking out of the peat floor, perhaps something to do with the army presence on the firing range. The floor was about two feet below moor level so climbing inside with the pack was not feasible. I never figured out what the building was – perhaps an unfinished Bronze Age toilet.

Dropping down from the window, I got the scare of my life when a tall young man carrying a huge rucksack suddenly appeared right in front of me, as if from nowhere. He wore thin cotton army fatigues with neither hat nor waterproofs and, despite being completely soaked, had a big silly grin on his youthful face that I found a bit disconcerting given the appalling weather. His skin had a strange waxy aspect with the rain trickling down his cheeks like it does off glass. Recovering from the initial shock of this uncanny apparition, he explained that this was his army day off and he was just up on the moors to get fit. He was a big strapping lad who looked like he could have run non-stop to Cape Wrath carrying both our rucksacks! After a minute or two, he said he needed to get going and disappeared off into the horizontal rain.

It was a very strange encounter, and later I would wonder if it had really taken place. He reminded me of my youngest son, Will, who once went through a phase of running round the school playing field in all weather with a heavy pack to train for the army medical corps that he had set his sights on. He never joined in the end, but still heads out in foul weather as a doctor with the Llanberis Mountain Rescue team.

I started to get cold and headed off, with the rain now at my back. My logbook entry shows I reached the Boundary Rock by the Gartaven Ford at 6.30 p.m. I had about another mile to reach Gidleigh on the eastern edge of the moor and it was mostly downhill, a blessing as I was rapidly running out of steam after a ten-hour slog on half a bag of nuts.

Coming down off the exposed moor, the wind and rain eased and I found a sheltered place to camp in woodland near a place called South Creaber. I had just dropped my pack ready to get cracking with the tent when a dog came by, followed a few minutes later by its owner. He said he couldn't believe I had crossed the moor on a day like this, and then showed me a better place to camp, closer to a small stream – and further away from his septic tank. Moving to the new site, I set up the tent and crashed out after washing and drying my sore feet in the stream and making a simple meal of spaghetti with Tesco's bolognaise sauce.

DAY 15: 6 May   East Dartmoor to Drewsteignton
Miles this day: **7**   Miles to date: **135**

The neighbour from the previous evening dropped by as I was in the final stages of packing up, to see how I was faring. The storm had passed, the sun was already out and we chatted for a while. We were standing, he explained, in what was formerly the Gidleigh Pound, a walled-off area that had once been used by the Duchy of Cornwall to impound seized cattle when the owner had defaulted on payment of grazing dues. He also added that the mother of King Harold had lived hereabouts after the defeat of 1066. Dropping off the moor the previous evening, I had noticed a number of granite gateposts half hidden in the undergrowth and again I felt vibes of ancient history.

After a late start, I finally set off at about 11 a.m., heading off towards Chagford following the Teign Valley through lovely wooded countryside, a welcome contrast to the bleak moors of yesterday. My boots were still soaking wet but I was saving my spare pair of dry socks until the boots dried out a bit. I took a public shortcut through the wooded grounds of the Gidleigh Park Hotel, the formal gardens suggesting it had once been a well-endowed estate.

Arriving at the small pretty village of Chagford, I posted off the second parcel of surplus stuff to my daughter Penny. This included a top for sleeping in and a hang-in-a-tree portable shower, unused as I didn't really fancy a cold shower in the middle of nowhere, naked to the elements.

After a few miles I joined the Two Moors Way, a 100-mile trail that crosses Devon from Ivybridge on the southern edge of Dartmoor to Lynmouth on the North Devon coast.

In 1997, I had walked part of the Two Moors Way with my two sons Tim and William, back-packing with a small tent in near freezing conditions. After crossing the south-eastern part of Dartmoor, we reached the hamlet of Holne. On leaving the pub later in the evening, after a good supper and some underage beer, we were stopped dead in our tracks by a truly amazing sight: the Hale-Bopp comet streaking across the star-laden night sky, with its million-mile tail of glowing sodium vapour.

River Teign near Chagford, Devon, Day 15.

Continuing along the Two Moors Way, Castle Drogo is a 1930s mock-Tudor castle that has somehow managed to get listed-building status. It's one exceptional feature is its stunning location with fine views across the wooded Teign Valley. Apparently it was the last castle to be built in England and, as castles go, was state of the art at the time, being fitted with electric lifts powered by a small hydro plant down on the river. I thought it would have made an ideal setting for an Ian Fleming book in which Count Drogo, the evil black-bearded, one-armed nuclear arms dealer, along with his horrid castle, get blown to smithereens.

I was tempted to go through the door to the grounds to seek out the advertised teashop and loo, but settled instead for a healthy drink of water and a pee in a bush before continuing on to Drewsteignton.

The Drew Arms at Drewsteignton is a lovely old place dating back to the Civil War. Popping my head through the door and liking what I saw, I decided to stay the night as fair compensation for the trek across Dartmoor. After a welcome shower I settled down to a gin and tonic followed by a delicious chicken with chorizo dinner, accompanied by a refreshing glass of Chardonnay.

DAY 16: 7 May   Drewsteignton to Morchard Road
Miles this day: **13**   Miles to date: **148**

After a tasty breakfast, I chatted with the pub's owner for a while. He was ex-RAF, having done tours in Bahrain, Afghanistan and other places. I have spent some time in Iran, Yemen and the Emirates, so we found lots to talk about. He explained that Drewsteignton had been a centre for Druids and that the pub had previously been called the Druid Arms but Mr Drogo had pressured them to rename it. He said born-again Druids still visited the pub dressed a bit like members of the Ku Klux Klan, but presumably with different ideas.

On leaving the pub, I stopped to look at a photograph of Britain's longest serving landlady, Mabel Mudge, who had retired at the age of 99 in 1994 after a 75-year tenure. The eyes suggest she would not have been a lady to mess with.

From Drewsteignton my route swung to the north-east towards Exmoor, some 30 miles distant. After a late start I arrived at The Devonshire Dumpling[4] pub at Copplestone at around 7 p.m. after a fairly uneventful day through very ordinary agricultural countryside. At first the landlady said they had no rooms, but when I asked if they might have a cowshed, she offered me the visitor's room that was normally reserved for her son and daughter, with walls adorned with photographs of Peru's spectacular Machu Picchu to make me feel really at home. I dined on extra-garlicky prawns, reliving past adventures in Peru and feeling in good spirits.

DAY 17: 8 May   Morchard Road to Witheridge
Miles this day: **10**   Miles to date: **158**

A bit of a cold miserable morning prompted me to take a coffee break at Morchard Bishop where the young lady in attendance scolded me for putting my rucksack down in the wrong place. My feet were wet after wading through long grass and I decided to reroute on to the quiet lanes, which I planned over a second cup of coffee. It was, it turned out, a very good move.

Later in the day I ducked into the Thelbridge Cross Inn at for an enormous lunch. The miserable weather continued and I didn't fancy camping, so I phoned around to see if I could find

---

4 'Devonshire dumpling' is Devonish for a young lady.

a bed for the night. The Satmap's OS map showed a red square at the Creacombe Parsonage, the symbol normally used for a bunk barn.

With the help of the cafe's Internet I obtained a phone number, and gave them a ring. The lady confirmed they had space and then mentioned it was a naturalist's place, which sounded even nicer. When I mentioned that I was a backpacker, loved birds and animals, and that it would take some time to get there, she paused, and then explained this was a *naturist*, not *naturalist* place, adding, 'But you don't have to take all your clothes off.' I set off in a jolly mood, with images of beautiful bare-footed Grecian creatures helping me off with my huge pack.

Arriving at Witheridge at 6.30 p.m. my painful feet and the miserable weather tempted me to B&B at the Mitre Inn instead. Getting organised in the room I discovered that my Spot satellite messenger was nowhere to be found. Panicking, I phoned through to the Devonshire Dumpling and also tried the fussy girl at the tearoom but with no joy. After a delicious supper I retired and then, rechecking my pack, discovered the wretched Spot hiding in one of the pockets of the waist belt. I went downstairs to send off the nightly satellite 'OK' message and, feeling greatly relieved, took a celebratory nightcap before retiring.

DAY 18: 9 May   **Witherage to Exmoor**
Miles this day: **13**   Miles to date: **171**

Heading off at 9 a.m. I rejoined the Two Moors Way that sensibly now followed the lanes rather than sticky clay fields. Three miles further on, I passed the parsonage, but resisted the temptation to pop in to say hi to the Grecians.

The Two Moors Way leaves the lanes a mile to the south of Knowstone Outer Moor and follows an ancient drove road lined with beech trees with Exmoor just visible in the far distance. The path then cuts through some swampy woodland just before the A361, with duckboard laid on the path to facilitate access to the designated nature reserve. Bobbing along, feeling on top of the world and gazing up into the foliage in search of any wildlife, my feet suddenly shot from under me on the slimy duckboard. Somehow I managed to do a complete somersault, pivoting around my pack in an apparent departure from Newton's Laws of Motion. I was quite surprised to discover that both the rucksack and I had survived without breakages, even though I had broken all of Newton's laws.

I arrived at the Masons Arms in Knowstone just too late for lunch but settled for a cider with a bag of crisps. It was a lovely old pub with a splendid inglenook fireplace that reminded me of our 500-year-old falling-down cottage on the Steyning High Street in West Sussex, which I had propped up with most of my savings to prevent it from bringing tons of Horsham stone flags down on the heads of Bridget and the children. It had amazingly passed a survey that had missed a variety of details: the loose rubble chimney stack, an 18-foot-long oak cantilever beam that didn't quite make it over to the supporting end wall, the rotting

Masons Arms, Knowstone, Day 18.

timber-on-clay footings and Tim's leaking under-stair cubby-hole-cum-bedroom. It hadn't been a wise buy. My hope is that someday the town will put a blue plaque on the outside wall in recognition of me saving this historic building from certain dereliction!

✳ ✳ ✳

Exmoor starts abruptly with a steep south-facing escarpment just beyond Yeo Mill. It is nothing like Dartmoor with its brooding granite tors, for here the countryside is underlain by soft shales that have weathered to produce a much gentler landscape, with upland heaths and deeply incised wooded valleys with hidden streams.

A friendly lady said hello as I passed Badlake Cottage. She was a carer of children with special needs and, with a kind look, gave me two freshly laid eggs in an egg box, offering more had I wanted them. She appeared to have a good eye for people in need I thought, saying goodbye!

I camped that night in dying woodland on Anstey Common with a thick beech hedge sheltering me from the strong south wind. I talked to my middle daughter Amanda who was hoping to meet up with me on the walk for a camping weekend for the spring half-term break, and she suggested we meet at Llanthony Priory on the Welsh Border to coincide with her girls' half term at the end of May.

DAY 19: 10 May   Exmoor to Wimbleball Lake
Miles this day: **12**   Miles to date: **183**

Snuggled down in my sleeping bag with an early morning tea, I caught up with my diary and then thought about how I could make the planned rendezvous with Amanda. Not by festering in my pit, that was for certain. For breakfast I fried up the two eggs in a few drops of precious olive oil, adding a splodge of garlic paste. They were delicious and I wished I had accepted a couple more, even if they are a nightmare for a backpacker to carry.

Saying goodbye to the Two Moors Way, I headed off along the Exe Valley Way to meet the River Barle at Castle Bridge where I crossed into my third county, Somerset. A superb stretch of woodland to Dulverton was followed by a good lunch before I made for Wimbleball Lake. In spite of being spoilt for scenery on this leg of the walk I was today feeling a bit low. My feet were once again wet through, my toes very painful and I was wondering if I was really up to the long road ahead. Trying to shake myself out of this gloomy mood I pushed on.

The dam wall at the western end of Wimbleball Lake was being repaired, and the two security guards kindly supplied me with some bottled water for the night's camping. The guards told me that the newly constructed wall had recently developed cracks – a bit worrying, given the size of the lake. The path along the southern side of the lake was closed off with red tape because of the reparations, so I made my way over the open common, finding a good spot to camp on the northern slopes of Haddon Hill. The temperature dropped overnight and the heavy rain did nothing to improve my flagging spirits.

DAY 20: 11 May   Wimbleball Lake to Gauldon
Miles this day: **12**   Miles to date: **195**

I headed off just after 9 a.m. after a slow start and a couscous breakfast. After about seven miles I made an impromptu stop at the Three Horseshoes in the small hamlet of Langley Marsh and had an excellent rib-eye steak which set me up for the rest of the day, or what was left of it; I did not leave until almost 4 p.m.

At the next hamlet, Brompton Ralph, I spotted a couple with two children enjoying the afternoon sun in their garden. When I asked for water, they kindly invited me to join them in the garden for a welcome cup of tea and a cake. They suggested a nearby camping place next to a small lake used by the Scouts. It sounded just perfect. There is nothing like local knowledge.

The unlocked gate was marked with a polite 'Please Close' notice, and beyond it a track led through the woods to the small lake. On the far side of the lake, two trestle tables had been set out on a flat grassy area, making it the best camping spot of the entire trip. The birds were singing 'Welcome John' and nesting moorhens weaved to and fro, adding reeds to their floating nests. This was paradise.

As I was finalising the perfect pitch, neatly laying out my meagre set of cooking utensils

Otterly Wood in Combe Bottom, near Langley Marsh on Day 18.

on the table, I noticed a chap approaching down the track, out for an evening walk. I waved and said 'Good evening', but he didn't respond.

'What are you doing here?' he demanded, in an unfriendly voice that matched his very unfriendly aspect. I told him about the walk, and that I was on my way up to Scotland, adding that the man at the white cottage up the hill had suggested I could camp here.

'Well, he said, 'You can just pack up yer stuff right now and bugger off.'

I explained that I would be off at 6.00 a.m. the next morning, leaving not a trace, but he wasn't having any of it. I packed up and left with him watching my every move, and he then locked the gate behind me. This was the one and only time I encountered a problem wild camping during the walk, ironically at the only camping spot recommended by a local[5]!

Back on the road I had spotted some woodlands on the map at a small hamlet called Gauldon, only two miles away on my intended route. Halfway there, the Satmap's screen started to blink, warning of a flat battery. As I didn't have far to go, I thought it might last. Then it started to rain fairly heavily and, with the light rapidly fading, the screen suddenly went dead, leaving me map-less. I was in the woods and needed to get my bearings. Digging out my head torch, I managed the battery changeover without mishap whilst squatting in the mud. The Satmap eventually fired, confirming I had made a silly mistake. I got back on to the West Deane Way, camping on a patch of bluebells beneath a large tree at the top of an escarpment.

During the night I was awakened by an unearthly screech. It sounded like a cat that had been nabbed by a fox. The dreadful noise continued for some time and eventually fell silent.

5 It occurred to me later that I should have told him I was leaving now, but would return later in the evening, and leave him waiting for me in the bushes.

Campsite in woods above Gauldon Manor, Day 20.

DAY 21: 12 May   **Gauldon to Fyne Court**
Miles this day: **9**   Miles to date: **204**

After a fairly lazy start to the day with a welcome cup of tea, surrounded by cooing pigeons and clacking pheasants, I stuck my head out of the tent door to discover I was camped in a pretty spot with ancient trees overhanging what looked like an old drove road. After breakfast I had a good look around for bits and pieces of cat, but happily none were to be found. This was the sort of secluded glade where feral cats can hang out, and perhaps the hullabaloo had been two of them having a spring romp – a far better way to spend the night than getting eaten by foxy.

Packed up for the off just after 9.00 a.m., I continued on the West Deane Way towards The Rising Sun Inn in West Bagborough. The pub nestles at the foot of the west-facing escarpment of the Quantock Hills, the last upland area on my route before the Somerset Levels and Britain's first designated Area of Outstanding Natural Beauty, or AONB. Geologically these hills comprise shallow water sediments from the Devonian period that support lovely heathland, oak woodlands and open grassland areas, decked with an abundance of wild flowers.

The escarpment was a good climb up but I was now three weeks into the walk, and getting fitter by the day, and took it in my stride. The view from the top of the Quantocks at Cothelstone Hill was quite spectacular, with the Brendon Hills to the west, Taunton to the south and

Cothelstone Hill on the Quantocks with Bristol Channel in distance, Day 21.

Macmillan Way West on the Quantock Hills, near Ivyton Farm, Day 21.

Macmillan Way West on Quantock Hills, near Ivyton Farm, Day 21.

Bridgwater to the north-east. In the far distance I thought I could just about make out the Welsh hills across the Bristol Channel. The horses nodded and whinnied when I told them I was making good progress.

The lovely countryside coming down off the escarpment reminded me of the Sussex South Downs, with well-maintained land and traditional prosperous-looking farms built of the Quantocks' red sandstone. Approaching the farm at Ivyton, I hurried to catch a car heading towards the farmhouse to ask for water for the night's camp. The mother, a young lad of about 20 and two girls aged about 12 and 14, dressed in neat grey uniforms, were just getting out of the car as I arrived at the gate.

While their mother went to fill up my water bottles, the two girls grilled me about the walk, amazed that someone could walk all the way from Cornwall to Scotland. 'How long did it take to walk from Cornwall?' said one. 'How did you find your way?' asked the other. 'How can you carry food for three months?' 'Don't you get scared camping alone in the woods?' 'Is geology a science? 'What do geologists do?'

I told the girls that geology was a fantastic career, and something they might think about later on if they liked the outdoors, which surely they would, looking around at the inspiring landscape. The young lad was about to leave for Denver, Colorado to work as a football coach. I lived in Denver for six months in the late 1970s so we talked about the Rockies. What a great adventure he would have, I thought.

Fyne Court, about a mile past the farm at Ivyton, had once been a prominent estate

A fine tree at Fyne Court (National Trust), Somerset, Day 21.

belonging to the Crosse family where Andrew Crosse had conducted some of the first scary experiments with electricity in the early 19th century. It now belongs to the National Trust, and a notice by the gate advised that the grounds were open to the public. I liberally took this to be an invitation and entering the grounds I followed the way marked 'Explorer's Trail' through the woodlands, well away from the former estate buildings. This had once been a formal arboretum but it was now wonderfully overgrown, creating a secret garden and the perfect campsite for a secret camper!

It was a lovely sunny spring evening and, after putting up the tent near a wonderful old tree with an unusual corkscrew trunk, I sat quietly listening to the songbirds, warming up for evensong.

DAY 22: 13 May   Fyne Court to Moorlinch
Miles this day: **16**   Miles to date: **220**

The rookery under which I was camped came alive with the first hint of daylight with an unruly cacophony that swamped the songbirds' dawn chorus until the rooks eventually flew off for their sheep-poo breakfast. I had mine in a hurry, just getting away before the Trust's staff arrived. As I headed out of the grounds I heard vehicles approaching, prompting me to duck into the undergrowth and pull off my brightly coloured blue thermal top that made me look like an oversize mallard duck.

King's Sedgemoor Drain on the Somerset Levels, Day 22.

For the next few miles I walked a small section of the Macmillan Way, a 290-mile-long footpath that links Lincolnshire to Dorset. This took me through the splendid Rooks Castle and Kings Cliff woods – the last fading spur of the Quantocks before I entered the flat country of the Somerset Levels. I had just clocked up the first month of the walk, and was feeling in good shape and excellent spirits.

Planning the walk I had struggled to devise a way across the Somerset Levels, a stretch of wetland that is sandwiched between the Quantocks and the Mendips. The main obstacle is the River Parrett that acts as the main drain for the wetlands. But if motorways and railways could cross it then, I thought, so could I.

Now the walk got a bit complicated. It passed under the M5 motorway on the outskirts of the Somerset town of Bridgwater before eventually crossing the River Parrett at the Somerset Railway Bridge, and then following various lanes and footpaths to Westonzoyland.

This was polder[6] country, a former marshland that had been drained by Dutch engineers in the 17th century. A footbridge took me across the Sedgemoor drain, but a second footbridge[7] across the six-foot Sutton Rhyne ditch had been partly swept away by recent floods. The footbridge was closed off and had a warning notice declaring it to be unsafe, with a detour arrow pointing off to somewhere vague. I stood and pondered for a while but in the end I decided to chance it, balancing my way across it on a single girder with outstretched arms and thinking if the worst came to the worst, the pack and I would probably float, at least for a minute or two.

---

6 Low-lying land reclaimed from a body of water and protected by dykes.   **7** ST 3739 3623.

Arriving at the 'dry-land' village of Moorlinch, and feeling a bit done-in after the 16-mile hike I called in for sustenance at the Ring O' Bells pub. They did not do B&B but the landlady telephoned a couple of friends, only getting the answerphone. A couple of locals with a one-year-old child called Ben and a chocolate-coloured Labrador had overheard my conversation with the landlady, and kindly offered me a bed for the night. I joined them for a meal, giving half my dodgy tasting steak to the dog, who woofed it down in one gulp, whacking me with his thick tail in appreciation.

Afterwards, Simon and Jo took me back to their lovely cottage on the western edge of the village. We had a nightcap beer and a sweet Southern Comfort whisky, whilst some of my clothes did a few turns in the washing machine. Explaining the scientific test[8] that my green merino top was undergoing, I held it back from the wash. Jo suggested I contact Macpac who would be most interested in the test-to-destruction that the top and I were undergoing. Simon kindly downloaded all my photos and voice recordings for safekeeping on their computer. My worst nightmare was that I'd fall off some wonky girder and lose hundreds of precious photographs of the trip. Mentioning my plan to camp on top of Glastonbury Tor overlooking the town, Jo warned me that I might have some 'very strange people' for company, and strongly advised against it.

DAY 23: 14 May   Moorlinch to Glastonbury
Miles this day: **9**   Miles to date: **229**

The A39 was very busy so I ducked into Loxley Wood, losing the sound of the traffic in an instant. A well-used semicircular path followed the high barbed wire perimeter fence that I might have tried climbing had it not been for the pack. After going round in a big circle, I eventually I found a way out the wood at the west end (when I should have been heading east) and then followed the quiet tree-lined lanes through the polder country. At one point the trees obligingly stepped to one side allowing me a first beckoning glimpse of Glastonbury Tor.

Entering Glastonbury along Benedict Street in the late afternoon, I was overtaken by an odd-looking man with bloodshot eyes, lank hair, and a glazed look about his unshaven face. Falling into step alongside me, he ranted on about the end of the world. 'I've read the effing book and know all about it, and, let me tell yer, it's effing terrible.'

At first I tried ignoring him but that didn't work and in the end I jabbered back some gibberish like, 'I've read the book, and saw lots of birds in Loxley Wood with rabbits jumping all over the place and deer roaming around and three green wizards … '

He ignored me and the ranting continued unabated so, aiming for a well-timed gap in the traffic, just like they do in the movies, I dodged across the busy street. Glancing back I saw the arms still flailing, and thought Jo's advice not to camp on the Tor was very sound.

---

8 I wore the Macpac merino wool top, day and night, 24/7 from Cape Cornwall to Gargrave, a distance of 594 miles and for 53 days testing and confirming its acclaimed anti-bacterial properties. My daughter Amanda, who darned a couple of small holes on the Welsh Borders, confirmed to her unbelieving sisters that it did not whiff!

Hawthorns Hotel occupies a revamped Georgian townhouse just off Glastonbury's High Street. I thought it a splendid place – especially when Simon the owner did me a special price if I booked for two nights (as I was planning to do anyway.) He said they were having a curry event that evening – the perfect flavours for a long-overdue spaghetti detox, I thought.

DAY 24: 15 May	In Glastonbury
Miles this day: **0**	Miles to date: **229**

The principal reason for my coming to Glastonbury was that it lay on the logical route between South West England and the Severn Bridge. The second reason was to visit the abbey to try to understand better the Dissolution of the Monasteries and the terrible things that had happened here in 1536.

After breakfast I headed to the abbey, enjoying the wonderful floating sensation of walking about without the pack. I asked if there was someone I might talk to about the Reformation, but the ticket lady said the guide was presently busy with a group, and to try again in the afternoon. I wandered round the town taking an espresso in a courtyard with a temple – quite normal for Glastonbury.

The guide was on his lunch break when I returned to the abbey later in the afternoon, but a retired clergyman at the information desk said he would be happy to talk to me about the Reformation.

'Usually all I get asked is "Where is the toilet?" or "Where can I get an ice cream?"' he said, chuckling. We went off to one side for my lesson, and I recorded the following – barely intelligible above the racket of a large crowd of excited school children, laughing and shouting and happily totally out of control.

'Henry VIII's main objective was money,' he began. 'He had frittered away all the money that he had inherited from his father and the crown was almost bankrupt, having spent a lot on these palaces and things. The abbeys themselves didn't much mind if they were under the king of England or under the Pope in Rome. The abbot of Glastonbury, along with lots of others, had already signed the Act of Supremacy acknowledging the king as the supreme head of the English church. They began in 1536 by dissolving the small abbeys, but that, you see, was just a dummy run to test the water. What they were really after were the big rich ones.'

Raising his voice above the hullabaloo of the children he continued. 'Because the abbot knew that the king was after the abbey, he sent one of his stewards to London to hand over the title deeds to the abbey lands. But the crown wanted the abbey itself because, you see, they wanted to destroy the whole structure of monasticism in England. The abbot refused and he was arrested on a charge of high treason and taken to London, followed by a show trial in Wells on trumped-up charges.'

'The abbeys that cooperated with the king's commissioners were treated reasonably and many of the monks were given pensions for life, but they made an example of those that didn't.

Glastonbury Abbey before the Reformation, Day 24.

Glastonbury Abbey after the Reformation, Day 24.

Glastonbury Tor, Day 24.

At Ely, the abbey was turned into a cathedral and the abbot became the first dean.'

'But knowing what was probably in store for him', I asked, 'wouldn't it have been sensible to call it quits and hand over the abbey itself?'

'Well' he said, 'Abbot Richard Whiting was quite an old man, well into his eighties. He had lived out his life, and believed it was his sacred duty to conserve the abbey.'

'It's a sad story', I said.

'Yes, it was tragic, but they wanted to make a dreadful example of what happens when you didn't cooperate with the king's commissioners. This was the second richest abbey after Westminster.' Mr Mudy was now able to hear himself think after the hoard of schoolchildren had run off to rampage elsewhere.

I asked how Westminster Abbey had survived the dissolution.

'Oh, well you see, Westminster was dedicated to Edward the Confessor, and Henry's father was buried there. Also the king needed somewhere to get married! And so the monastery was dissolved but the abbey was converted to a cathedral.' It is terrible to think Westminster's destruction might well have figured in Cromwell's master plan, had it not been for Henry's weakness for weddings.

After looking at the sad remains of the abbey, I climbed up the Tor where on the 15 November, 1539 the aged abbot and two of his companions were dragged on hurdles to be hanged, drawn and quartered, overlooking their beloved abbey.

I like to think that the destruction of the monasteries came back to bite its chief architect, Thomas Cromwell. In 1540 Cromwell's commissioners dissolved Thetford in East Anglia, the last surviving English monastery that housed the tombs of the Howard family. The head of the family, the duke of Norfolk, was a high-ranking powerful conservative Catholic peer and member of the Privy Council at the court of Henry VIII. When Cromwell was arrested in June 1540, later facing execution, Norfolk ripped the Order of the Garter off Cromwell's chest muttering 'This is for Thetford.'

After talking to the retired clergyman I returned to the abbey and sat quietly on the grass, surrounded by ruins of the once-beautiful abbey that had come crashing down on the orders of the king.

DAY 25: 16 May   Glastonbury to St Cuthbert's Swallet
Miles this day: **13**   Miles to date: **242**

I left Glastonbury at 9.30 a.m., dodging around the busy roads by taking an indirect route to Wells. I lunched on a cheese roll sitting on the grass in front of the Cathedral and the Bishop's Palace, home of the Bishops of Bath and Wells for over 800 years. The Great Hall where Richard Whiting's show trial had been conducted fell into ruins shortly after the death of the abbot. The valuable lead was stripped off the roof leaving the hall open to the elements – an efficient and cost-effective way of destroying Britain's monastic heritage.

My route from Wells took me up the steep south-facing limestone escarpment of the

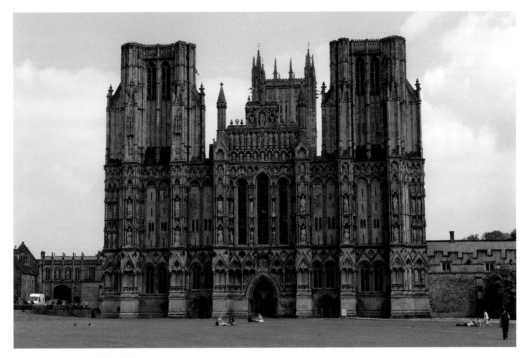

Wells Cathedral on Day 25.

Mendip Hills, with splendid views over to Wells and a distant goodbye wave from Glastonbury Tor. I hurried past Wookey Hole, an interesting cave system that has been turned into a gaudy tourist attraction.

I stopped a short time later at Higher Pitts Farm to ask for water, and chatted to the owner who farms 180 acres for beef cattle. 'It's a way of life, not a living. I couldn't exist without a subsidy. It was OK until about 2000 when all the European rules and regulations came in, so now I do a bit of landscape gardening to make it up.' It's a story you hear from all the upland farmers in the Yorkshire Dales.

I camped that night in ancient, almost magical woodland next to a small stream that is fed by a spring at St Cuthbert's Swallet[9], a mile east of the hamlet of Priddy. A swallet, I later learned, is a Mendip term for a shake hole, the point where a stream disappears underground. A chap came by and told me this was an old lead-mining site, something to look forward to in the morning.

This had been a grand day on the Mendips and I was on top form. After pitching the tent and eating a spaghetti carbonara, I called Amanda to talk about the planned meeting up on the Welsh borders, now just days away. I would have to cover about 85 miles in six days – doable if I didn't dilly-dally.

It was a grand evening, with the setting sun and the birds in full chorus.

DAY 26: 17 May   St Cuthbert's Swallet to Hallatrow
Miles this day: **12**   Miles to date: **254**

The morning was also unbelievably beautiful with a flawless blue summer sky. The path led me through the woods to an area marked 'Priddy Mineries' on my Satmap, heading towards a woodland area at Stockhill. The path and surrounding woodland were littered with small pieces of black glassy slag, a waste product from the smelting of lead ore. Lead ingots found in the area, dated from AD 49, show that the Romans were mining lead in the Mendips within six years of their arrival in Britain, which I find quite amazing. Later, with the help of the Internet, I was able to examine the excellent briefing sheet produced by the British Geological Survey (BGS) that covers the whole of the Mendip lead-mining area.

Crossing the River Chew at Shrew Bridge my route then followed the Limestone Link up a steep sandstone escarpment to Hinton Blewett. Beyond that it curved around to the south of Clutton and on towards the old railway village of Hallatrow where the now disused Camerton and Limpley Stoke railway (the 'Clanker') once joined the disused Bristol to Frome line.

That evening I camped on a grassed-over part of the 'Clanker's' track. I like camping on old railway beds as they are often found well off the beaten track, and abound with wildlife that takes refuge in the now untended embankments. For me, they also stir the imagination with railway ghosts from a bygone age that keep me company until I fall asleep.

---

9 ST 54405, 50702.

There were also a few geological ghosts hanging about in this place, for I was camped less than half a mile from Rugbourne Farm that from 1791 to 1795 had been the home of one of Britain's pre-eminent early geologists, William Smith, the geologist who made the 'The Map That Changed the World' – in Simon Winchester's splendid biography.

Smith had been hired by Lady Elizabeth Jones, a large landowner in the Somerset Coalfield area. Unlike many of Britain's larger coalfields, the coal beds in Somerset occur in rock layers (strata) that were buckled and folded making it difficult for mine owners to follow the coal seams. Smith carefully studied the strata, and in particular the fossil 'markers', and was able to predict the trend of the coal seams.

His first task would have been to understand what was going on at the Mearns Pit, located on Lady Jones' land just a quarter of a mile from his house, and a mile from where I was then camped. By carefully studying the Mearns strata, Smith was able to grasp the fundamentals of stratigraphy (the study of laying in sedimentary rocks), skills he later applied to mapping the geology of the rest of the country, making the world's first country-scale geological map, indeed 'The Map That Changed the World'.

Being of humble background Smith did not move easily in the often well-to-do aristocratic scientific community and his work was largely ignored until he was well into his sixties. He lived long enough, however, to receive the first award of the Geological Society of London's prestigious Murchison Medal in late recognition of his contribution to the new science of geology.

Smith's splendid and very beautiful geological map hangs above a marble stairway at the Society's Burlington House in Piccadilly, protected from the light by a thick velvet curtain. In the early days of our London-based gold exploration company, Mariana Resources Ltd, I would sometimes stay in Piccadilly and wander over to the Geological Society to marvel at the amazingly beautiful map (see overleaf).

Mearns Pit was to geology what the Galápagos Islands were to evolution. It is a great shame that this famous site has been bulldozed into oblivion, and that Smith's commemorative plaque was placed on the wrong house!

Mining of coal at Mearns ceased in 1824 and the last Somerset coal mine shut in in 1973. The canals and railways that they spawned have now almost disappeared without a trace, destroyed or buried under dreadful housing estates.

DAY 27: 18 May   Hallatrow to Bath
Miles this day: **12**   Miles to date: **266**

Another splendid morning saw me up, packed and off by 9.00 a.m. heading off at top speed along the Limestone Link towards Bath. From Hallatrow the trail follows the Cam Valley alongside the remnants of the 18th century Somerset Canal now marked by just a few shallow ditches.

A railway bridge on the disused 'Clanker' railway line, near Radford, Somerset. Day 27.

Continuing towards Bath, I stopped for a while to watch an amazing aerial skirmish between a circling buzzard and two rooks. The rooks would first climb above the buzzard and dive-bomb it in perfect unison. The buzzard with eyes that can look in all directions would deftly sidestep at the last moment and the rooks would then climb back up for another go. This Battle of Britain show lasted a full ten minutes until the rooks eventually threw in the feather and flew off. I imagined they were two males on buzzard-watch duty with their spouses sitting on eggs or chicks in a nearby colony. The buzzard carried on circling on the thermal updraft.

Arriving at the Bath Youth Hostel about 6.30 p.m. I called Kenny, a friend of my eldest son Tim from his Marlborough days. He collected me that evening and took me to his Japanese restaurant that he had set up after studying catering. It was good to see the venture had been a success and we had a good evening. After weeks of pastas I found the endless conveyor belt loaded with fine Sushi just too tempting.

OPPOSITE: William Smith's beautiful 1815 geological map of England, Wales and part of Scotland. *This map is reproduced courtesy of the Geological Society of London.*

DAY 28: 19 May   Bath to Golden Valley, Wick

Miles this day: **13**   Miles to date: **279**

After the hostel's splendid cooked breakfast, I headed across the meadows to Bath, enjoying yet another splendid sunny morning. I had decided to limit my tourism to a visit to Bath Abbey and then try to do something about my leaking boots.

My first port of call was a photographic shop next to the abbey where the chap offered to put my photographs on to a pen-drive for £9.99. He said to come back in about three hours so leaving my camera and pack in his care I set off to explore the abbey's precincts.

Just around the corner I was confronted by a Cotswold Outdoor shop, an irresistible prospect that I immediately succumbed to. I found a young chap who knew a bit about boots and told him about the problem of my leaking Salomons, the reason for which was now pretty obvious with the rubber now lifting off the fabric. He recommended a pair of non-Gore-Tex Scarpas that I tried, liked, and bought. He then phoned Salomon, explaining the situation, and after five minutes they phoned back offering a free replacement or refund. I opted for the latter and Cotswold put £130 back on to my credit card. I had no proof of purchase for the Salomons and any guarantee would have long since expired, although the boots had hardly been used prior to this walk. I was pleasantly surprised at this generous treatment by Cotswold.

I then explained to the young man the problem I was having with my Osprey 58-litre rucksack that I had (unfortunately) bought in the USA. Under the weight of the 50-pound pack the waist belt buckle would slip dropping the pack's full weight on to my shoulders, causing sharp pains after a few hours. Collecting the pack from the camera shop just round the corner the young man exclaimed, 'Well, it's the same problem, lightweight gear that's not up to backpacking with a heavy load.' Perhaps he was also thinking, neither was I!

He showed me an Osprey Aether 70 pack that I took an immediate liking to on account of the broad shoulder straps and the wide waist belt. I bought this and posted off the now redundant Osprey 58 in another parcel to my daughter Penny who was by now assembling a nice set of free kit. I now had some first-rate gear with which to tackle the rest of the walk. Feeling very chuffed I headed out of the city at top speed in the general direction of Wales.

I followed the River Avon Trail making good progress, encouraged by the birds in full voice. I tried to cross the River Avon at Swineford Lock and found myself on an island with a dangerous looking weir connecting it with the far bank. Later on I recorded 'It's 8.30 in the evening and I'm still walking but am feeling in great shape, and reckon I could walk all night'. The new rucksack was proving itself to be a first-rate bit of kit, with a fair bit of the pack's weight now taken off my shoulders. My feet were also happy, enjoying the Gore-Tex-free linings of my splendid new leather boots.

There was a sprinkling of big raindrops that came to nothing and then about 9.30 p.m. I reached to the Golden Valley Nature Reserve that I had spotted on the map. The stiff iron gate squeaked a protest but let me pass. I pitched the tent by torchlight finding a nice flat area, but when I tried to peg out the guy ropes it turned out to be an old road hidden below half an inch of moss.

DAY 29: 20 May   Golden Valley, Wick to Alveston Common
Miles this day: **15**   Miles to date: **294**

The morning was grey, damp and cold. An elderly chap came by as I was packing up and we chatted for a while. He said he had been a keen walker and seeing my obviously new boots he said he fancied buying a pair himself. I love outdoor kit and can imagine buying a nice pair of leather boots long after I needed or could afford them.

He told me this had once been a large ochre quarry.[10] He gave me directions on how to get out of the nature reserve but I found some difficulty with the paths trying to pull me round in circles. To escape I had to climb a high perimeter fence by a dilapidated old barn, a bit of a challenge with the pack. Coils of heavy-gauge rusting steel cable lay around in the undergrowth, suggesting this had once been a quarry cableway for hauling rock. The nettles were hiding what had once been a very active industrial site.

Once out of the woods, the countryside passed through flat and rather boring enclosed agricultural land and to avoid the roads I followed Monarch's Way and Burbarrow Lane to Westerleigh. On the way I noticed that the rubber seal covering the toggle on the Satmap device was starting to split, a potential problem that could let in moisture. As I carried no paper maps the Satmap was vital and now required urgent attention and I cursed myself for posting off the spare device to Penny to save a few ounces. Whilst thinking what was to be done I tucked into a delicious omelette at the New Inn in Westerleigh which offered a two course meal for £6. A large group of smartly dressed people turned out to be a funeral party. The landlord explained, almost apologetically, that funerals were what now kept the pub going. It was a dependable trade, I thought, and one that presumably didn't die off in the long winter months like tourism.

Thinking again about the Satmap, I thought I might be able to temporarily fix it with a carefully applied touch of superglue, but I had finished mine repairing the water bottle. I would have to head into the town of Yate that lay just off my planned route. On the way into the centre I stopped to ask directions from a chap in his eighties who was tinkering with a huge shiny black motorbike. He invited me into his house and gave me the glue to fix the GPS. The town centre was fairly close so I carried on to pick up a few supplies, fighting off the temptation to buy more stuff I didn't need and couldn't possibly carry, although my new rucksack still had some tempting spare space.

The shopping expedition was followed by a nerve-wracking walk along the busy B4059 that was overloaded with speeding traffic, with Yate having grown from a small village to become a large Bristol overflow town. Just about everyone seemed to be in a mad rush, ignoring

---

10 Ochre is red sandstone impregnated with oxidised iron, once used as a colour pigment.

the 30 and 40 mph speed limits. The road was narrow with no pavement and the cars and vans came at me round the blind corners meeting me head-on, with my life depending on a last-minute swerve. After a few serious scares I took to holding one of my walking poles out horizontally into the road, dangling coloured string off the end of the tungsten-tip, a bit like a passed-his-prime Spanish bullfighter. I would later reflect that this had been the most dangerous part of the entire walk!

Once off the nightmare road I called into a dreadful chain pub for water. It had very smelly drains. I then climbed up on to Alveston Common and I camped by a kissing stone. Excitement was now building; tomorrow I would be crossing into Wales!

DAY 30: 21 May   **Alveston Common to Severn Bridge – a part day**
Miles this day: **7**   Miles to date: **301**

As I was having my morning brew a lovely half-crazy black Springer-cross called Mieke came by, and, perhaps under the influence of the kissing stone (or the garlic in my beard) rewarded me with a couple of sloppy licks. Piet, her owner, was from Holland but now lived in the area and we talked for a good while about the walk, dogs, William Smith the geologist, my time spent working in Holland, and all sorts of things. He suggested an alternative route for me to take to the Severn Bridge.

The first port of call on Piet's route was the Crusty Loaf bread shop in Olveston that was run by a friendly lady called Jenny. It transpired she was just a year older than me and when I said I might have chased after her in another life, it made her roar with laughter. I had a PG Tips cup of tea and a Danish pastry that set me up for the morning, and chatted to a French-Canadian guy called Pierre who was in his third year of walking round the world with a three-wheeler buggy, decked out with a Canadian flag. Perhaps I should nick a supermarket trolley, stick on a Yorkshire white rose flag and just keep going after Cape Wrath!

My last stop before the bridge was at the lovely Boars Head in Aust, hidden away in a time warp cul-de-sac, cut off from civilisation by the access ramp of the Severn Bridge. I had a splendid roast lamb meal washed down with Thatcher's cider – one of the best meals of the trip so far. ●

OPPOSITE: Approaching the Severn Bridge, Day 30.

Tintern Abbey revisited – a view to the south-west over the Wye Valley, Day 31.

3

THE WELSH BORDERS

I cross the Severn Road Bridge into Wales and follow the Wye Valley and the Offa's Dyke Path northwards along the beautiful Welsh Borders, passing Tintern Abbey and on to Monmouth. Turning to the north-west, I then discover the stunning Black Hills and visit Llanthony Priory. From there I continue along Offa's Dyke to Knighton and on to the delightful Shropshire village of Clun.

DAY 30: 21 May   Severn Bridge to Wye Valley – a part day
Miles this day: **13**   Miles to date: **307**

There has been a ferry passage into Wales from Aust since the time the Romans first crossed the Severn Estuary to quell the Silurian and Ordovician tribes that occupied the lands of present-day Monmouthshire and Powys. It seems the Roman's main interest in taking this godless country was to get their hands on the rich deposits of lead, silver and gold.

Aust's 40-foot tides are amongst the highest in the world, creating treacherous currents for crossing the mile-wide estuary. The old sailing ferries were superseded by a steam-driven service in 1827, but in 1839 one of these sank in bad weather with the loss of all hands. A second steam ferry sank five years after that, again with the loss of all hands, including the master who was the son of the master lost in the first disaster. Modern ferries operated until the day before the first Severn Road Bridge was completed in 1966.

Few people seem to cross on foot but pedestrians from Aust are given the choice of crossing the bridge on the upstream or downstream side. My map was unclear as to which was the best side for Chepstow so I sought clarification at the maintenance depot, but no one seemed to know.

Once I adjusted to the roar of the speeding traffic and the shaking and trembling of the bridge, I stepped out enjoying the two-mile skywalk over the estuary into Wales. The stiff breeze pushed the cotton-wool clouds across a sea of deep indigo welcoming me to the Welsh Border. I was feeling in top form after the splendid roast lamb lunch in Aust, but beginning to regret the accompanying pint and a half of Thatcher's cider, my new South West England discovery on the walk. About half way across, I was obliged to make an emergency de-cidering stop turning my back to the traffic and coping as best as I could with the stiff breeze, adding momentarily to the tidal surge of Britain's largest river.

After briefly making landfall on a narrow spur of Gloucestershire, the final section of the bridge crosses the River Wye into Wales. At the estimated midpoint of the Wye, I let out a blood-curdling 'Yeaaaaaaaah' with poles raised, to celebrate not only crossing into Wales, but because I knew, as I left England after 300 miles that I would never give up on the walk. I had passed the point of no return. The Welsh Border, the Pennines and the Scottish Highlands were now waiting!

I navigated through the confusing border town of Chepstow using the Norman castle for orientation, stopping for a sit on a bench near the Old Wye Bridge to dress my feet. The blisters had disappeared but the nails on the underpinned little toes were digging in and causing bleeding.

After my shortest country visit ever I crossed back into England on the Old Wye Bridge, a splendid Victorian wrought-iron marvel. A short snicket led me up to Tutshill, the small Gloucestershire town where J.K. Rowling spent her early youth, hoarding some of the characters from her local school to use in her later adventures. Here I joined the cross-borders Offa's Dyke Path, which runs along the English side of the border from the Wye Bridge to Monmouth.

Evening was fast approaching and it was time to look out for the night's camping spot. My planned water refuelling stop, The Rising Sun in Woodcroft, had sadly sunk below the horizon and was boarded up, obliging me to temporarily abandon the Offa's Dyke Path in the search for water. I imagined that Offa's men must have done the same at times for there seemed to be few decent streams along this southern section of Offa's Dyke.

The Severn Bridge into Wales, and the first 300 miles! Day 30.

I cut through the lanes in the hope of finding someone still knocking about but the countryside was deadly quiet. Clouds were starting to close in, threatening rain, and feeling a bit beat, I took a breather in a wooden bus shelter with a bench – just about wide enough to sleep on, I noted. With a well-timed stroke of luck a chap came down a nearby drive wheeling his rubbish bin ready for next day's collection and I ran after him. Satisfied I wasn't a backpacking mugger with a stick, and after explaining my dilemma, he invited me into his house to fill up with water.

Once again my feet were grinding me to a painful halt and I was dying to bathe them in an icy cold stream. The first patch of half-flat ground I came across was going to have to do for the night. The Offa's Dyke Path enters the woods by Dennel Hill Farm, and after 200 yards I found a decent camping spot next to Offa's Dyke. I pitched the tent just as the sun was disappearing into the trees, keeping a sharp eye open for roaming Silurian[1] tribesmen out to nab a wandering walker. For supper, I heated a piece of Jenny's well-matured pizza bread on a saucepan lid that I covered with crinkled aluminium foil to prevent scorching. It was my new hotplate invention.

My last thoughts before falling asleep were that – thanks to the long day – I had just 28 miles to cover in two days to reach Llanthony Priory.

---

1 The Silures were a warlike Celtic tribe that occupied the Welsh Borders area. The third geological period in the Palaeozoic Era, the Silurian, was named after them.

Sunset on Offa's Dyke, Wye Valley, Day 30

DAY 31: 22 May   Wye Valley to Grace Dieu Abbey
Miles this day: **18**   Miles to date: **325**

I slept like a log and was up making a cup of tea before 6.00 a.m., keen to get going. It had rained during the night and the ground was squelchy underfoot.

I found Offa's Dyke rather disappointing, even in daylight, being little more than an over-grown runner-bean trench running along the top of a steep limestone escarpment high above the River Wye. The path was very slippery and I had to use my poles to avoid a sticky backside. A local chap out with a dog that looked like a rolled up bit of muddy carpet said I would be better off following the public footpaths rather than literally sticking to Offa's Dyke. As I was here to explore the Welsh Border, not follow in Offa's footsteps, this turned out to be very sound advice, for I now realised that the thick tree cover was going to block out the views and any chance of getting a decent look at Tintern Abbey – now just a mile further on.

Looking for alternatives on the map I spotted the track of the old Wye Valley Railway that ran along the bottom of the escarpment. The sinuous meanders of the river might add a few extra miles but I would make that up with faster progress once off the muddy dyke. I said goodbye to Offa just below the Boatyard Plantation and headed down a lovely forestry track through the woods and then slithered down a steep muddy slope, hanging on to saplings to land on the old railway track. It was a good move for the track had been revamped to make a splendid path for cyclists and walkers, none of whom were about on this cold, damp morning.

Sunrise on Offa's Dyke, Wye Valley, Day 31.

Kicking into top gear to make up for lost time, I came unexpectedly to a spot where a large tree had been uprooted by a recent storm, creating a convenient window in the burgeoning spring foliage. In front of me, just across the river through the trees, stood Tintern Abbey. We 'did' Wordsworth for our English Literature O-Level, which I narrowly failed in the summer of 1961. I have never been much into poetry, but I recall liking these lines written by Wordsworth after revisiting the Wye Valley in July 1798. Amazingly though, Wordsworth says nothing about the splendour of the abbey ruins!

> … and again I hear
> These waters, rolling from their mountain-springs
> With soft inland murmur. – Once again
> Do I behold these steep and lofty cliffs,
> That on a wild secluded scene impress
> Thoughts of more deep seclusion; and connect
> The landscape with the quiet of the sky.

The words are certainly inspirational, but looking around I couldn't actually see any 'murmuring mountain springs' that would have been most welcome in order to fill my water bottle and wash my feet. Also, the thick tree cover blocked out any views of the 'lofty cliffs'. Peggy, our stern headmistress who took us for English literature, might have raised a wry

Redbrook – a heaving town during the Industrial Revolution, then the world's largest tinplate producer, Day 31.

smile if she ever herself reached immortality with special online access to read this book! But enough thought experiments, I needed to get a move on as another priory and a pair of eager grandchildren would be waiting for me in just two days' time!

Just after Tintern, the Wye doubles back on itself in a tight loop around a spur of sandstone through which the railway disappears into a short tunnel. In a stunning display of tunnel vision, this had been sealed off obliging the walker to climb a steep cobbled path leading over the ridge, perhaps an ancient monk's way. This would be a skimpy climb for a young buck monk, his stomach full of Welsh rarebit and homebrew, but it was quite an effort for an old fart lugging a young fart's backpack.

The next hamlet I came to, Brockweir, was the head of the Wye's tidal navigation for 70-tonne steam packets during the Victorian era. Beyond here, goods were transhipped by special flat-bottomed barges that could cope with the shallow non-tidal part of the river, until these were eventually replaced by the Wye Valley railway that opened in 1876.

From Brockweir I rejoined the Offa's Dyke Path (or rather Offa's Path joined my path) that follows the banks of the Wye to Bigsweir before disappearing into ancient oak woodland that I imagined is an outlier of the Forest of Dean. The walk through these lovely woods was accompanied by a cracking thunderstorm, the sound of which I recorded. I have always enjoyed a good thunderstorm and this one with darkened sky was accompanied by a splendid display of lightning, with jagged streaks of bluish-purple momentarily lighting up the gloomy countryside.

Thankfully unstruck, I emerged from the woods just as the storm was passing. A short while later I came to Lower Redbrook, a small riverside village of 300 or so inhabitants with one run-down-looking pub and a village store-cum-post office. It looks a fairly sleepy place today, but it had been a thriving engineering hub during the Industrial Revolution right through to the 20th century.

The first clue to this is the name of the town, for 'red brooks' usually means the red coloration of a stream by a metal ore of some sort, usually iron. This was extracted near here from the iron deposits mined in the Forest of Dean from about 1300 onwards. The second clue is the huge amount of black glassy material called 'slag', the waste product from the melting of metal ores in furnaces. It was all over the place, on the paths, down the riverbank and even built into some of the walls.

Copper smelting started here when local resident John Coster experimented using coal for the winning of copper from its ores rather than the charcoal that had been used in the first rustic processes. The English Copper Company established a works here in 1692, and by 1725 an incredible 42 copper furnaces were operating in the town. I can imagine, having lived fairly close to a big one at Mufulira in Zambia, that the air would have been laced with sulphurous fumes. The copper smelting business then moved to South Wales, and another entrepreneur stepped in and bought the Redbrook site in 1790, where he produced the world's first tinplate. The tinning business grew after the railway arrived in 1876 and Redbrook tinplate was exported all around the world. The town was then booming and at one time it boasted three breweries and 13 inns. The US imposed levies on imported tinplate in 1891 after which the industry went into decline and the pubs started to close, leaving just one.

The last passenger trains to run on the Wye Valley line were withdrawn in 1959 with the last tinplate works closing two years later. All was not completely lost though, for villagers can still use the old railway bridge to cross over to the Welsh side for a decent foreign pint at the Boat Inn. But I needed to move on; the day was advancing and I was aiming to clear another ten miles before nightfall.

From Redbrook my route followed the riverside Wye Valley Walk. I stopped for a brief sit down at an anglers hut to watching a group of swans cruising about in the river with effortless ease, occasionally rummaging on the bed of the swiftly flowing river, a comical sight with just their wiggling bums visible.

Approaching Monmouth, I stopped by the sad remains of the Duke of Beaufort viaduct that had been partly dismantled by British Railways when the Wye Valley line closed. With a little bit of gumption by rural planners, the old railway track could have been turned into a stunning heritage trail, bringing tourists from around the world and helping to stem the steady economic decline of the Borders, but the overweight railway controller's Reformation axe continued to slash and hack – almost within sight of Tintern Abbey.

On a happier note, a noticeboard by the remnants of the bridge tells how, in April 1937, a certain Francis Gratorex caught a 49lb 4oz cock salmon fishing here using an artificial prawn.

The giant fish shown in the reproduced old photograph was almost as big as the angler. He would have taken memories of that mighty battle with him to the grave.

Crossing the bridge into the town of Monmouth and back into Wales, I followed a trail of enticing smells that led me to the Seven Seas fish and chip cafe run by a friendly Asian chap and where I tucked into a splendid sit-down feed. After getting my headlight organised and putting on my waterproofs I set off into the rain at about 8.30 p.m. I remember passing a large area of woodland to the west of the town that should have offered a good camping spot but I foolishly carried on, in the hope of reaching the site of the Grace Dieu Abbey. Monks chose their monastic sites very carefully, settling for nothing less than a Turneresque landscape that would have gone down well with my morning cuppa. However darkness descended and the light rain turned into a steady downpour and the night turned quite dia-bolical, made worse by the trudge through the clarty clay fields.

With my spectacles dripping with rain, I struggled to follow the Satmap. I think I got fairly close to the site of the privately owned abbey ruins but found the access barred by barbed wire. I carried on, settling for a muddy field in the middle of nowhere some time past midnight and a short while later I was tucked up in my sleeping bag with a hot brew, listening to the rain beating down on the flysheet. It had been a tough night walk and I was feeling tired and very fed up after walking almost non-stop for about 15 hours.

DAY 32: 23 May   Grace Dieu Abbey to Llangattock Lingoed
Miles this day: **10**   Miles to date: **335**

Sticking my head out the tent door I saw that I had camped in front of a large tractor shed. It was a really horrid campsite, possibly the worst of the entire trip, with sticky red clay soil making packing up a slow process. Rain was spitting when I slipped away, turning into a steady downpour as morning progressed. It was the first really wet morning in over a month so I shouldn't really complain.

After crossing three sticky fields where the public path had been wantonly (and illegally) ploughed up, I decided to say stuff it to Offa's Muddy Dyke Path and follow the lanes for a while. The countryside had suddenly turned very 'Welsh' with names like Llanvihangel-Ystern-Llewern and Pen Pwll Y Cach, and a sprinkling of Victorian 'parsonages'. The parsons might not have earned a three-figure stipend but they certainly did themselves proud on the house, which they were expected to fill with lots and lots of God-fearing children. Passing a parsonage, I grinned to myself at the thought of my recent close call with the Grecians.

After a non-stop slog in the rain, I came to Llangattock Lingoed, a pretty hamlet with a name almost longer than the place. It was mid-afternoon and I took shelter in a church porch, feeling cold, wet and a bit miserable. Church porches were fast becoming prized rain refuges and the proliferation of Victorian churches in this rainy border countryside was now beginning to make a lot of sense.

The hamlet also sported a pub called The Hunters Moon Inn, a name that reminded me of my boyhood duck shooting forays in the Ribble Valley, so I thought I had better pop inside to check it out. My curiosity was rewarded with an enormous fire and an all-day menu that I tested with sausage, egg and chips before falling asleep on the sofa. When I came to I studied the Satmap, looking for a solid argument for staying the night in this lovely pub, one of the nicest on the trip so far. Llanthony Priory, where I would meet up with my daughter Amanda and family was still ten miles away, but if I got off to an early start in the morning I figured could be there by early afternoon, which would give them time to get camped. Anyway, I reasoned, if I were to carry on in this foul weather, I would surly miss the views from the top of Brecons that promised to be a highlight of the Borders walk. The remainers finally won the argument and, with a bit of prompting, the landlord reduced the room rate from £60 to £40 – an offer that was now quite impossible to refuse. My only concern was that the mid-afternoon meal might take the edge off the rib-eye steak that I had spotted on the supper menu. I needn't have worried, for come 9.00 p.m., after a fireside gin and tonic and periodically checking on the progress of the steady downpour, I was ready to devour half a cow.

DAY 33: 24 May   Llangattock Lingoed to Llanthony Priory
Miles this day: **8**   Miles to date: **343**

One of the nice things about overnighting in a pub is the sit-down breakfast you are obliged to eat the following morning. Today this comprised scrambled eggs, bacon and tomatoes cooked by the red-haired South African girl who was the wife of one of the two brothers that owned the place.

Heading north across the fields on the Muddy Dyke Path, I crossed the Afon Honddu river on a footbridge near Pandy and headed up into the Black Hills in the Brecon Beacons National Park. Here the river does something strange, taking a major change in direction from north-west to the north-east. It looks like the original route of the river has been blocked by moraine dumped by a glacier pushing its way southwards, which would possibly explain the glutinous sticky glacial clay clinging to my boots.

After a short distance, the Offa's Dyke Path merged with the Beacons Way to climb up an easterly spur of the Black Hills, formed from tough red sandstones and conglomerates of the Devonian Old Red Sandstone formation. The good news was that with the change in geology, the clarty clays were now left behind, hopefully for good.

The weather remained foul with low cloud and strong wind bringing heavy rain and I ended up getting soaked, chilling me to the core. The path climbed steadily to the summit of Hatterrall Hill, 531 metres, and the highest point on the walk so far. The low cloud suddenly lifted just as I reached the col on the Hatterrall ridge, opening spectacular views across the Vale of Ewyas to the west, and the rolling English countryside of Hereford to the east. I stopped for a few minutes to soak up the panorama and the rain.

Llanthony Priory in a stunning setting in the Black Mountains, Welsh Borders, Day 33.

From there it was a downhill dash on the Beacons Way to Llanthony Priory. Walking around the perimeter wall, looking for a way in, I heard a shout of 'Daaaad!' My middle daughter Amanda had spotted a bobbing hat and taken a guess at its owner.

Later that evening I went to the campsite pub located in a steamy monastery cellar for drinks and a supper with my daughter, son in law Pete and their two girls, Fi and Sukie. Getting stuck into the beer, I noticed a chap near the bar who looked vaguely familiar, an echo from the distant past. Every now and then I caught the strain of a Sussex accent above the pub clatter, and then I heard the word 'Coombs' that kicked it all into place. Coombs was a 1,000-acre farm on the South Downs on the outskirts of Steyning where the family had lived until we moved to Holland in 1980, and the voice belonged to Colin Parsemore who had been at university with Bridget's younger brother, Ron. Some years back he had come here to this lovely spot on the Welsh borders and bought the priory and adjoining farmland. He said he had been out with one of the three Stillwell sisters in the 1960s but couldn't remember which one! With a bit of luck, Bridget might have ended up a wealthy land-owning prioress instead of the wife of an itinerant geologist. I had not seen him for over 50 years, and was amazed by the memory-jog.

OPPOSITE: Amanda and family above Llanthony Priory, where the Frog Pond Project was born! Day 35. PHOTOGRAPH BY: *Pete Waldren*.

DAY 34: 25 May   At Llanthony Priory
Miles this day: **0**   Miles to date: **343**

My first rest day in over 100 miles got off to a good start with bacon and tomato baps cooked by Pete, followed by a look around the Augustinian Priory. Norman invader Walter de Lacy founded the priory around the year 1100. Unlike their Benedictine and Cistercian brothers, the Augustinian canons did not lead a cloistered life and shared their ministry and music with visitors. In the evening I could feel their presence, hands together and heads bared, their chants keeping the evil spirits and bats at bay.

Lunch was my treat, a roast Sunday lunch back at the Hunters Moon. After that it was the grandchildren's treat, playing in one of the world's best hide and seek venues as darkness fell, the bats flitting around and joining in the game. Pete cooked up some of Colin's sausages for supper after which we all went spook hunting with torches, keeping very quiet.

DAY 35: 26 May   Llanthony Priory to Bettws Dingle
Miles this day: **14**   Miles to date: **357**

Dawn came all too soon, and soon it was time for me to get going, packing up my gear whilst Pete toasted a deli ham and tomato bap. We all set off about 9.30 a.m. with Pete 'volunteering' to carry my pack to the top of the ridge. Heading north along the ridge I noticed a small peaty pond crowded with tadpoles and scooped up a cupped handful.

This spawned the Frog Pond Project that a year later would hatch frogs in Amanda's back garden in Cardiff. Three years later they are still there!

We walked together along the ridge for a few miles enjoying the sunshine and splendid views before the family headed back to Llanthony, waving like mad as they slowly disappeared over the crown of the ridge.

Alone once again on the hills, I put up a good pace along the border path taking in the views of the Vale of Ewyas to the west and the Golden Valley to the east before dropping down to Hay-on-Wye, a busy border town where a bank holiday book festival was in full swing. I liked the place and allowed myself to be ripped off: £12 for mid-afternoon fish and chips, before heading off across the Wye road bridge back into Wales, or was it back into England?

A short muddy riverside walk along the Wye Valley led me to a wooded dell with the splendid name of Bettws Dingle, a pretty spot administered by the Woodland Trust. This had been a five-star day with fantastic views over both sides of the border, and more was promised for tomorrow.

DAY 36: 27 May   Bettws Dingle to Kington
Miles this day: **12**   Miles to date: **369**

After a night of heavy rain, the morning was fine and fresh with a lovely woodland smell. I was packed and ready for the off around 9.30 a.m.

The day's walk started with a section of low rolling hills, before dropping down to the hamlet of Newchurch on the River Arrow. A sign outside the church advertised refreshments so I popped in for a self-service coffee and biscuit, and talked to some other walkers. I walked on with two of them as far as Gladestry, stopping at The Royal Oak Inn for a plate of chips and a beer.

Leaving the couple to enjoy their lunch I headed up the steep grassy path on to the beautiful Hergest Ridge, 423 metres with splendid views over to the Welsh Borders with a last glimpse of the distant Brecons. Looking around, the irregular terrain suggested a history of geological chaos, with steep fault-controlled escarpments and fault-aligned valleys. The ridge itself seemed to be mostly composed of soft mudstone with a scattering of glacial erratics[2], including dark gabbro and quartzite, possibly ancient rocks from the Precambrian era.

I was feeling in good shape and, for the first time since Dartmoor my feet seemed to be on the mend thanks to a long spell of being dry. After passing a strange Victorian-age hilltop racecourse, the path dropped down into Kington, a pretty unspoiled Herefordshire village. It was early in the day but I decided to overnight and checked into a B&B called The Bench Mark run by an interesting man called Adam who spun wool and wove cloth on a handloom. His front parlour was a wonderful higgledy-piggledy collection of looms, skeins of wool, giant bobbins and hand-knitted garments with an interesting sheepy smell.

That evening, after a lousy meal, I dropped in for a nightcap at The Royal Oak, and chatted to a cyclist. This is where I should have eaten, I thought.

---

2 Rocks transported by glaciers.

DAY 37: 28 May   Kington to Hengwm Hill
Miles this day: **11**   Miles to date: **380**

After a very lazy start talking to Adam and two ladies who were attending the Hay-on-Wye book festival, I left the B&B mid-morning. The steep pull up the south-facing slopes of Bradnor Hill kicked me back into gear, but my logbook records that by 3.40 p.m. I had covered a distance of just three miles! It was here I discovered that I had lost my medical pack with stuff for my feet and a cherished plastic mug – vital for teas and soups.

My path intersected a better-preserved east-west section of Offa's Dyke Path between Rushock Hill and Herrock Hill. The Dyke seemed more impressive when crossing open countryside than in the wooded Wye Valley at the southern end.

I camped that night in the drizzling rain on the northern shoulder of Hawthorn Hill[3], a site recommended by another Offa's Dyke walker who had camped there 20 years ago. Unpacking, I was relieved to find my medical kit, just leaving the mug to worry about. I dined on spaghetti with tomato sauce and then read for a while.

DAY 38: 29 May   Hengwm Hill to Clun
Miles this day: **12**   Miles to date: **392**

The day started quite miserably with low cloud and heavy drizzle. I packed up inside the tent and headed off in the rain, with the day eventually brightening and an early summer feeling to the morning. Unseen skylarks beckoned me to get a move on with their shrill, breathless Morse code streaming down from high in the sky. Shortly after setting off I spotted a small deer. I was starting to enjoy myself again.

The path ran along the north-south ridge of the hill called Ffridd before dropping down to Knighton, a small pretty town that straddles the Welsh border, where I bought a horrid enamel replacement mug that burnt my lips. The name, I learned, has nothing to do with knights of old, but comes from an Old English word that means servant. Knighton is the mid-point on the 177-mile-long Offa's Dyke Path and has an information centre for walkers.

Just beyond Knighton, the Offa's Dyke Path climbs up a steep track leading to the summit of Panpunton Hill, 375 metres, and then runs along the top of a steep escarpment overlooking the broad alluvial valley of the River Teme. However, thick low cloud blocked any chance of the fine views promised by the map. Following a north-westerly heading, the path runs next to well-preserved sections of the dyke, and is later joined by the Jack Mytton Way. Here at Llanfair Hill[4] I said a final goodbye to Offa's Dyke to head eastwards on the Jack Mytton Way.

I had followed Offa's Dyke Path, on and off, for eight days and although the path itself is not anything special, other than marking the historical boundary between two warring nations, it passes through some superb countryside. I was glad to have incorporated it in the walk, and one day I will go back to explore this lovely border country.

3 SO 284 687.

Shropshire hills and Knill Wood near Knighton, Day 37.

Shortly after turning towards the east in the late afternoon I heard my first curlew of the trip, a clear sign I must be getting somewhere! Just before 7.00 p.m. I crossed the 14th century bridge into Clun, a pretty redbrick Shropshire village that retains both the vestiges of a Norman grid layout and its medieval charm. The youth hostel, located at the eastern side of

4 SO 251 800.

the village set in beautifully kept grounds, is a magnificent mill conversion incorporating much of the original mill machinery.

Although small as youth hostels go, it was full of very interesting people as often happens in tucked-away places like this. The volunteer warden Leonard Roach first took me on a conducted tour of the mill. Later I talked to a walker aged over 70, who had climbed 200 winter Munros until the onset of arthritis left the rest of his challenge unclimbed, as well as three nice girls from London, one of whom was a recent graduate geologist. Happily I also found an email from Adam saying he had found my mug and offered to post it off to Yorkshire. It rejoined me later on, halfway up the Pennine Way.

After a jolly good shower I stepped into the garden ready to head off to the village but was stopped dead in my tracks by the splendid evensong from the massed choir of the Shropshire songbirds that I recorded with my digital device. I listened to this recording again just before writing this section of the book in Manabi, Ecuador.

The Sun Inn was fully booked for supper but there was a space at The White Horse where I found myself sitting next to the village brewer, Matt Williams, who had made the beer I was drinking. By coincidence he was going to camp in Llanthony Priory the following weekend so I filled him in on Colin, the millionaire-farming abbot who cleans the public toilet on the campsite. Supper was a plate of lamb chops, the first of the season for me, making a fitting conclusion to the beautiful Welsh Border section of the walk.

I would rank the part from Llanthony Priory to Clun as having some of the finest scenery of the entire walk. ●

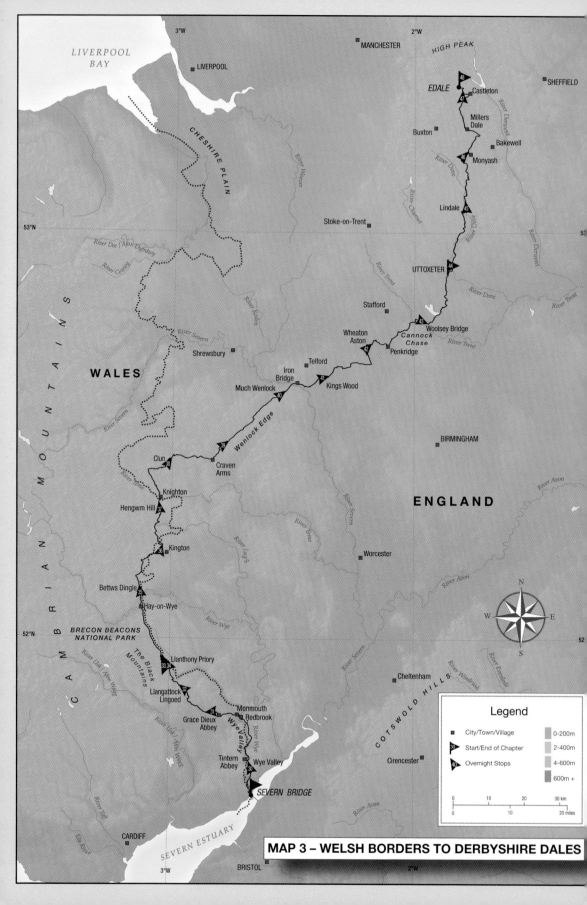

MAP 3 – WELSH BORDERS TO DERBYSHIRE DALES

4

THE MIDLANDS

*From Clun I walk along Wenlock Edge and cross the River Severn at Ironbridge.
Following the Monarch's Way to Wheaton on the Shropshire Union Canal,
I then join the Staffordshire Way to Cannock Chase and Uttoxeter –
the gateway to the Derbyshire Dales.*

DAY 39: 30 May   Clun to Alcaston (Wenlock Edge)
Miles this day: **14**   Miles to date: **407**

Leonard, the volunteer warden, shared some of his cereal with me and afterwards we sat around the fire spinning yarns and talking with the other guests, enjoying a short time together before our mutual departures. One chap picked up the youth hostel's copy of

A.E. Housman's *A Shropshire Lad*, published at the turn of the last century, and read aloud some of the poems.

> When I was one-and-twenty
> I heard a wise man say,
> 'Give crowns and pounds and guineas
> But not your heart away.'

Very good advice, I thought, having given away several. The retired Munro walker then asked to try out my pack and headed off around the hostel grounds, returning 15 minutes later slightly out of breath and red-faced but visibly excited. I think the feel of the pack and the adventures it could carry might have inspired him to have another go at walking. I sincerely hope so for I could tell he was missing the hills, as I know I will one day.

After agreeably frittering away most of the morning I headed out of Clun along the Shropshire Way to climb up a steep escarpment to Sunnyhill, 393 metres. The ground on the top of the hill had a disturbed look about it, leaving me wondering if it was perhaps an ancient mining site, something I keep an eye open for as a geologist. Then I spotted an information board that explained that I was standing on the edge of an Iron Age fort known as the Bury Ditches, dated at about 500 BC. The Forestry Commission had obligingly cleared some of the trees to open up fine views of the surrounding Shropshire countryside, as well as exposing the fort's impressive oval arrangement of four earthen ditch and rampart defences that extend over an area of about 350 by 250 yards. Leaving my pack in the custody of the noticeboard, I wandered around hoping to spot a discarded Bronze Age gold brooch lost in some violent Ordovici pillaging foray. The short search revealed no gold but I did bump into the three girls from the youth hostel.

With wild thoughts (of the fort) running through my head I set out eastwards through the glorious Shropshire heath country, passing the hamlets of Kempton and Hopesay, named after 'Hope de Say', a Norman baron from Clun Castle. It was gone 6.00 p.m. when I dropped down off the hills to Craven Arms, a small 'transit town' built on the River Onny at the south-western extremity of Wenlock Edge, where the busy A49, two railways and the Roman Watling Street all vie for space on the narrow flood plain of the river.

The evening was advancing rapidly so I called in at a pub for the night's water and a bite to eat. Chatting to the landlord, I learned he was originally from Iran, something I had suspected from his aquiline nose and dark features. I said to him in Farsi, '*Man chahar sal tu Iran buddam*[1]', at which he nearly fell over, replying with a fast string of Farsi that I struggled to follow after more than 40 years of disuse and memory attrition.

I told the landlord how, in the spring of 1970, I had headed out to Iran to join a team of young geologists who had been hired by a UK mining company to explore for copper in Kerman Province of South-East Iran. After a while, Bridget and the three girls came out to

---

1 Meaning 'I spent four years in Iran'.

join me, and we lived in a small noisy medieval alleyway called Kutche Aberdini that was just wide enough for a string of camels with panniers to trundle through. The girls attended a small Anglican missionary school where biscuits were offered around with a 'Have a biscuit, God is love.' Once in a while the girls had a special treat when a snake charmer would pitch up in the alleyway just in front of our kitchen window with a sack full of wriggling cobras, the girls jumping up and down with glee from the safety of the kitchen sink.

After that I moved to Teheran to start a two-year country-wide reconnaissance programme, organising mule expeditions to Iranian Azerbaijan close to the Araxes river bordering the former USSR, exploring the wild and dangerous Baluchistan frontier country bordering Pakistan, and the remote north-eastern Afghan border area. It was one of the most interesting periods of my career as a geologist.

✳✳✳

I headed off up the steep escarpment of Wenlock Edge at about 7.30 p.m. enjoying the beautiful evening, and stopping to record the songbirds' evening chorus. On the lookout for a campsite I entered the woods at about 8.00 p.m. The thick tree cover now blocked out most of the remaining daylight as I made my way around scattered tree trunks and fallen branches that lay rotting, imparting a dank toady smell to the marshy ground. With nightfall closing in I found a slightly less soggy spot to camp next to an ancient coppice[2], and then settled down in my sleeping bag with a hot drink. This was the best part of the day, a time to plan and reflect and enjoy my little cosy world, drifting in and out of this and that, recalling the noisy alleyway with baggy-trousered snake charmers and camel trains, and the wonderful smell of baking Persian bread from the bakery next door that wafted in through the slatted kitchen windows.

DAY 40: 31 May	Alcaston to Much Wenlock
Miles this day: **14**	Miles to date: **421**

After an early morning tea I was keen to get going to check out the 20-mile-long Wenlock Edge. This steep north-easterly trending escarpment is revered by geologists for its ancient reefs that date from the Silurian Period, some 425 million years ago – a time in the Earth's history when this area lay close to the equator. My path continued on the Jack Mytton Way, also called the Shropshire Way, through a delightful series of coppiced deciduous woodlands; starting with Alcaston Coppice where I had spent the night, followed by Long Coppice, Burwood Coppice, Flat Coppice, Eaton Coppice and finally Stars Coppice.

About halfway along the escarpment, I came to a small cottage about half a mile beyond Wilderhope Manor and saw a lady tending her cottage garden. I stopped to ask for water,

---

2 Woodland in which the trees or shrubs are periodically cut back to ground level to stimulate growth and provide firewood or timber. A good example of a coppiced tree is shown on Day 68.

and after chatting the friendly lady, Brenda, invited me in to her delightful higgledy-piggledy cottage for a cup of tea. There were cats everywhere, ten in total I believe. Her friend from next door then came in with two smooth-haired Jack Russells. Most interesting for me, however, was a giant fossil turtle that she pulled from under a chair that, she said, had been dug out from under the roots of a tree by a friend. My guess is that would have been at least 100-million years old (plus or minus 50 million years) from the late Jurassic to middle Cretaceous period.

With its narrow streets and timber-framed buildings, I very much liked the look of Much Wenlock and decided on to overnight there. I found a bed at the Old Washroom B&B, not cheap at £50, but beautifully set up as a self-contained flat.

DAY 41: 1 June   **Much Wenlock to King Charles' Wood**
Miles this day: **11**   Miles to date: **431**

The new month was blessed with an absolutely perfect morning, with not a cloud to be seen. Before leaving town I visited the 12th century priory; a worthwhile visit with the sad relicts contrasting against the beautifully manicured lawns that left me feeling a bit morose. Following the stripping of the abbey's lead roof, a great deal of the valuable dressed stone had been carted off, but mercifully enough walls and haunting archways had been left – like a partially completed jigsaw puzzle – to bring the place alive. The ruins, I reflected, had outlived all of the 20 or so kings and queens that had ruled our lands since Henry VIII's assault on monasticism.

Just before Ironbridge, the Shropshire Way enters more splendid ancient woodland before dropping down a steep escarpment towards the river. I crossed over into the town on the famous Iron Bridge at about 2.00 p.m. – my fourth and final bridge crossing of the River Severn on the walk.

The town was busy with an upbeat summer holiday atmosphere but I noticed that most of the Sunday visitors seemed more interested in ice creams and trinket shops than the world's first iron-arch bridge. For some reason I didn't feel very comfortable with the noisy crowds, perhaps I had just spent too much time on my own in recent weeks.

Retreating from the busy streets I ordered a late Sunday lunch at The Malthouse pub. It turned out to be belly pork, very tasty but with soggy crackling. I asked a friendly waitress if there was any chance of a bit of real crackling and she did me proud, bringing me a giant piece. Getting into the swing of things, and enjoying the feast I went off to the bar to get a glass of wine. When I got back my plate had gone and when I complained to a frightful fifty-something waitress with waxed hair, she said, 'We always take away the plate when the food is left.' Pointing to my rucksack almost sitting at the table I said that it hadn't been left, I had just gone to the bar. She got all stroppy and said she was just trying to do her job as a waitress, to which I replied I was just trying to get something to eat. I suppressed my rising

Much Wenlock Abbey, Day 41.

Ironbridge: the world's first iron-arch bridge, Day 41.

The Hay Inclined Plane was used to transfer boat cargos between the River Severn and an upper canal. Day 41.

hackles and the temptation to give her a blast of North Yorkshire that I had learned from my sheep farming brother-in-law, which could make sheep scatter in panic over into Lancashire. I finished the meal on a better note with a huge plate of strawberries with ice cream, served by a pleasant wax-free waitress.

I had intended to overnight in the town but the stolen crackling, the milling crowds and the pressure of the miles ahead urged me to move on. Heading out of town I stopped briefly to take a quick look at the Hay Inclined Plane. Completed in 1792, this marvellous bit of canal engineering was used to tranship industrial goods, mainly coal, iron ore and engineering goods between the Shropshire Canal and the River Severn waterway that is located 200 feet vertically below, cleverly avoiding a long and costly flight of locks. Goods were shipped in specially designed 20-foot-long 'tub boats' that were loaded into submerged cradles. These were then hauled up or down the plane carried on dual, steeply inclined railway tracks in a counterpoise arrangement, a heavy load coming down pulling the empty tub going up, with a steam engine providing the extra pull for any shortfall. A short section of the Shropshire Canal that leads off from the top of the ramp still survives, but most has been filled in to make way for housing estates, parks and duck ponds – but I must not be too hard on the town planners!

After climbing up the steep flight of steps next to the tracks, I headed off into the woods on the Monarch's Way, struggling to follow the path with head-high brambles and chest-high nettles that had gone ballistic with the advent of summer, stinging and tearing at my arms and bare legs.

Managing to escape their grasp and clear of the woods the path wound through flat fields to Kemberton where I called in at The Masons Arms for water with the now customary half pint of cider for payment in lieu. A small group of locals enjoying a quiet Sunday afternoon drink around the bar asked me what I was up to. Giving them a quick rundown, one chap kindly offered a barn for me to sleep in and another offered me a bed, but I said I was heading for the King Charles wood a mile or so further. They couldn't understand why I would prefer a tent in a wood with the creatures of the night, to a soft bed. It's not an easy point to get over!

The narrow strip of woodland that I was making for lies just off the Monarch's Way. I set up camp under a lovely old beech tree overlooking an overgrown millpond, a perfect campsite apart from the absence of a crystal clear stream to bath my feet in. Through the trees I spotted a stern-looking swan on the millpond, silently patrolling to and fro. It was one of those special evenings, with the setting sun disappearing slowly into the foliage as I listened to a duet from a hidden thrush and blackbird settling down for the night.

'Well I'm in my nest now and its really cosy' said one. 'But my nest is higher up than yours and made with straw and lined with horse's hair', replied the other. 'Well, I'm closer to the ground and can spot the beetles and marching caterpillars', replied the first. Other birds joined in, but one by one they all signed off until all was quiet apart from a distant barn owl on the hunt for a mousy morsel.

Snuggled in my sleeping bag with a hot drink, I thought about King Charles's connection with these woods. When I had planned the walk in 2012–2013, I had tried to incorporate a section of the Monarch's Way in my trek across South West England. The 625-mile-long footpath, one of Britain's longest, traces Charles II's daring escape after the Royalists' Civil War defeat at the Battle of Worcester on September 3 1651. The king, now with a price on his head, spent six weeks on the run disguised as a woodsman, living by his wits with the help of loyal Catholic families who risked the dreadful traitor's death if caught. It was easy to cross part of his escape route because the poor man fled from pillar to post in ever increasing circles around southern England and the West Country to avoid capture. A few months later, after lots of narrow escapes, the king sailed from Shoreham to France, just a few hours before Cromwell's men came to arrest him to face an ugly trial and a certain public execution.

Wondering if he had slept nearby, a late fly-past of honking geese told me it was now time for me to get off to sleep.

DAY 42: 2 June   **King Charles' Wood to Wheaton Aston**
Miles this day: **14**   Miles to date: **446**

Another lovely morning followed a great night's sleep. Whilst packing up the gear with head down and my mind on the job, a woman popped out from the undergrowth walking her dog, scaring the living daylights out of me, and I her. After recovering we chatted for a while and I headed back on to Monarch's Way, crossing under the M54 and A41 and passing close to a hamlet called Tong. My poor old dad was always talking about one of his Norton motorbiking bachelor friends, Frank Sugden, who had once lived there.

Just a mile or so to the east of Tong are the remains of White Ladies Priory where Charles II is said to have hidden after the Worcester defeat. White Ladies was a small Augustinian nunnery that at the time of the Civil War was owned by the Catholic Gifford family who had risked their lives helping the king during his escape.

At Brewood I joined the Shropshire Union Canal and followed it for three miles into Wheaton Aston, where I chatted to some local lads at The Hartley Arms, joining them for a beer or two and then ordering some greasy fish and chips.

Heading up the towpath in search of a campsite I passed an interesting notice attached to a canal bridge stating that 'This bridge cannot carry loads heavier than is normal for the district'.

I found a place to camp in a field just off the canal some 200 yards above the bridge. It started to rain just as I was putting up the tent at about 9.30 p.m. It didn't bother me; I supposed this was *normal for the district*.

DAY 43: 3 June   **Wheaton Aston to Wolseley Bridge**
Miles this day: **16**   Miles to date: **462**

I wasn't entirely happy with the high visibility of my campsite so close to civilisation, so I was up at 5.30 a.m. and off less than two hours later – another record early morning start.

After just over a mile I joined the Staffordshire Way to Penkridge trailing through long grass over wet muddy fields and getting progressively wetter legs and feet. After a good fried breakfast and a sock change in Penkridge, I continued on a short section of the Staffordshire and Worcestershire Canal to Park Gate Lock, and then on to Bednall and Cannock Chase.

Cannock Chase was one of the really lovely surprises of the walk. It has an area of about 26 square miles (66 square kilometres) with a mix of natural deciduous woodland, planted forests and open heathland, and is designated as an AONB (Area of Outstanding Natural Beauty). Much of the area is additionally classified as a Site of Special Scientific Interest, being the home to a number of endangered species of plants and butterflies and a 600-strong herd of fallow deer. For me, coupled with Wenlock Edge, it presented an ideal way to cross the Midlands so close to Britain's – sometimes grim – former industrial heartland. It is beautiful walking country, surrounded by large towns and cities and yet strangely there was not a soul about.

There aren't too many single boulders marked on OS maps but I had spotted this one marked on the map[3] when planning the walk in Miraflores, Lima, two years before. I thought the 'Glacial Boulder' might be a good reference point to aim for in an area criss-crossed with paths in all directions. And there it now stood right in front of me, just where it had been dropped by a glacier perhaps 10,000 years earlier. What a coincidence, I had travelled

---

3 SJ 981, 182.

The landmark decorated glacial boulder at Cannock Chase, Day 43.

over 6,000 miles to meet a boulder that had been pushed perhaps 1,000 miles, some 10,000 years before. I wanted to climb on top of it but saw that, almost sacrilegiously, it had been decorated with confetti and condoms after some goodness-knows-what ceremony. I didn't hang about, a bit afraid of what might jump out of the bushes.

The heathland area of Cannock Chase is underlain by relatively hard Triassic bunter sandstones and conglomerates, accounting for the raised elevation of the heath and the firm sandy footpaths. Several crystal clear streams cross the heath offering excellent possibilities for an overnight camp, but it was too early in the day – and uncomfortably close to the 'decorated' boulder.

Crossing Weetman's Bridge over the River Trent to Little Haywood, I followed the towpath of the Trent and Mersey Canal for just over a mile to the Wolseley Bridge and found a good camping spot next to the canal. As a courtesy I asked the lady in the nearby narrow boat if she minded if I camped there, and she said it was fine.

DAY 44: 4 June   Wolseley Bridge to Uttoxeter
Miles this day: **14**   Miles to date: **475**

The lady from the narrow boat dropped by early with her huge Alsatian. He couldn't figure out what an earth a tent was doing right here on *his* bit of the canal. He had a good sniff round and with a bit of encouragement he almost ventured inside the tent but his nerves

Early morning on the Trent and Mersey Canal, Day 44.

and crouching legs started to shiver and shake at the last minute. In a very kind gesture, the lady then brought me a mug of tea and two rolls in a cellophane bag to see me on my way.

It was almost 10.00 a.m. when I headed off in drizzle. The towpath was lovely, more like a country footpath with overhanging trees, making me wonder if I should have incorporated

more canals in my walk. The canal ran next to the River Trent but was built some 10 foot above it, adding some water engineering to the general interest.

Studying my map, I reckoned that I might just make it to the River Dove by nightfall, my gateway to the Derbyshire Dales. I had knocked off some miles and was now getting near to 'Up North' country and starting to get excited at the prospect of getting on to the Pennine Way. But first I had to explore the unknown treats of Derbyshire, for me some new territory.

The euphoria was short-lived as my route left the towpath to head over muddy fields, following farm tracks or skirting around ploughed field edges with lots of wasted mileage, like the knight's 'two forward and one to the side' moves on a chessboard.

After a long slog in the rain I finally reached Uttoxeter (a name derived from 'Wuttuc's homestead on the heath') in the early evening, and decided to stay the night in town as I needed gas and other supplies. Local advice directed me to the Bank House Hotel on Church Street where I negotiated a £40 deal for a £60 room. Their specialty was Vietnamese food, and that sounded interesting.

A group of friendly chaps, including the hotel's owner, were watching an Ecuador–England friendly football game in the bar. I'm not much into football but this game was very different, for every time a goal was scored I called or texted an old friend Vanessa in Ecuador who was, not surprisingly, also watching the game. Happily it concluded with a 2–2 draw. The friendly atmosphere, the excitement of the game, and Vanessa's long distance presence, rounded off with a delicious meal cooked by the Vietnamese chef, all made for a most splendid evening to celebrate my walk across the Midlands and tomorrow's start on the Derbyshire Dales. ●

5

THE DERBYSHIRE DALES

*From Uttoxeter, I cross into Derbyshire and then head northwards into limestone country.
A delightful succession of half hidden limestone dales and pathways takes me to
Castleton where I meet up with my youngest daughter Beth and family
before dropping down to Edale for the start of the Pennine Way.*

DAY 45: 5 June   Uttoxeter to Lin Dale (near Ilam)
Miles this day: **16**   Miles to date: **492**

Getting out of Uttoxeter proved to be a bit of a nightmare with frightening morning traffic
hurtling straight at me from all directions around a series of scary roundabouts. Fortunately
the chaotic A50 bypass has left the 15th century Old Dove Bridge splendidly isolated from
the chaos, to enjoy a well-earned retirement under the protection of a grade II listing.

River Dove at Uttoxeter, and so into Derbyshire, Day 45.

Looking down at the six-arch sandstone bridge from the bypass, I was surprised by the size and vigour of the River Dove, not some murky East Midland's sluggish drain but a vibrant river born in the hills and caves of limestone country. I love rivers, and this one was a most welcome sight, beckoning me on towards its source as all rivers do if you let them.

For much of its 70-mile length, the River Dove forms the county boundary between Staffordshire to the east and Derbyshire to the west. I should now be heading up the Derbyshire side, if only I could figure how to get down to it from this wretched bypass. I later realised that whilst running the gauntlet with the lunatic traffic I had missed the pedestrian underpass that allows safe passage for the Staffordshire Way user. There was no way I was going back and through a series of unconventional and unlawful manoeuvres, complicated by the awkward pack, I managed to climb off the edge of the bridge, drop on to a steep grassy bank and slither down to the footpath below, instantly cutting off the roar of the bypass traffic.

The Dove Dale gorge still lay some 10 miles away and for now I had to be content with the broad floodplain of the mature River Dove and its steep eastern glacial escarpment. The Staffordshire Way runs along the top of this for a short distance and then cuts diagonally down to the level of the flood plain, through pretty deciduous woodland on overgrown paths that I found difficult to follow. In the distance I started to hear the sound of gunshot, not the double-barrel discharges fired at the backsides of fleeing pigeons, but a steady fusillade that could only mean I was approaching a shooting range. (I find it very strange that the Ordnance

St Bertram's Bridge, Ilam, on the Staffordshire–Derbyshire border, Youth Hostel beyond, Day 45.

Survey do not show such deadly features on their maps, given that most people who use them are walkers.) With overgrown paths leading off in all directions, I came across another unhelpful notice warning me 'Stay on the Authorised Path' with absolutely no indication of which one was authorised!

Emerging from the woods near Eaton Hall Farm, I found myself in the middle of an array of clay pigeon ranges. Feeling a bit like a sitting duck, I fell in step behind a couple of shooters, believing they surely wouldn't take pot shots at a fellow member. Heading towards the club hut, I noticed that all the guns were aimed at clay traps over toward the river, and not towards the woods from which I had just emerged unscathed. I took advantage of the club's après-shoot cafe for a mid-morning cup of tea and a welcome sit down, minutes before heading off towards the Roman town of Rocester.

On the way there I stopped at Lower Ellastone to talk to a chap who was monitoring a bike race. I was again struggling with my feet, having tried in desperation taping two bleeding toes together to reduce friction, with disastrous results that I won't describe. He mentioned that there was a medic on call in nearby Upper Ellastone for the race, but I found no sign of him.

After Ellastone the Staffordshire Way changes its name to the Limestone Way and climbs up an escarpment. I had spotted an alternative route through Gold's Wood. On the map, it looked a bit more interesting for a semi-retired gold explorer, and I decided to give it a try. The path through the woods was soggy and overgrown with the way occasionally blocked by fallen trees. But it was lovely strip of 'wild wood', jam-packed with huge luxuriant ferns that perhaps could easily hide a raptor on the run from Jurassic Park, stalking a brace of song-birds with which the place teemed.

At Ordley Bank, just east of the village of Stanton, I climbed back up on to the official path and was rewarded with a distant view of the white limestone escarpment at the entrance to Dove Dale gorge. This was my gateway to the Derbyshire Dales, and aching shoulders and painful toes were soon forgotten. Dropping down off the escarpment towards the River Manifold I spotted an imposing mansion that was marked on the OS map as a youth hostel. I needed Internet access for some work stuff and, judging by the size of the place, I imagined it would have a large refectory and perhaps a cosy oak-panelled bar. Since many youth hostels allow camping on their grounds, I figured I could camp out and nip back inside the next morning for a spot of cooked breakfast before heading off.

Encouraged by these thoughts, I approached the grounds of the Ilam[1] Hall hostel from the southern side, to be confronted by an ancient stone-built stile of unusual design. It was a narrow slot some twelve inches wide and about six feet high and allowed me, but not my pack, just enough room to squeeze through. Forgetting the challenge of the stile, I climbed over a locked gate and crossed the river on medieval St Bertram's Bridge and into the hostel grounds.

My spirits sank when the young lady in reception told me the entire hostel had been booked for a large group of school children and was unfortunately closed to all, even YHA members. Seeing my disappointment, she then asked if I had had supper, explaining that the children had just been fed and there were some spare seconds if I would like some. She then very kindly brought me an enormous plateful of fish and chips, asking somewhat awkwardly if I could please eat them in the foyer area, as the rest of the hostel was off-bounds. I sat in the splendid entrance hall and ate the meal on my knees whilst reading some of the information about the place.

The original Elizabethan Hall had been built on the confiscated lands of Burton Abbey and for the next 250 years had been the home of the Port family, until it was sold in 1809. The new owner commissioned the present building and it must have been quite magnificent, but their family fortune had apparently waned and the house fell into disrepair, and then in the 1930s it was sold for demolition. Demolition was in actually in progress when Sir Robert McDougal, the flour miller of fame and fortune, stepped in and bought the hall for the nation. He then gave it to the National Trust, who then leased it to the YHA who now use it mainly for conventions and school visits, as well as feeding the occasional vagrant backpacker on their way up to Cape Wrath, but who aren't allowed stay there in case there are any 'youths' also using the hostel! After narrowly escaping complete destruction, the house it is now protected from further architectural vandalism by a grade II listing.

Aware that I was about to enter the world-famous sacred dry fly waters of the River Dove, I cautiously asked the young lady where I might find a quiet spot off the beaten track to put up my tent. She seemed to have local knowledge and directed me to Lin Dale, adding, with a grin, 'That's where we go when we want to get away.'

---

1 Ilam – pronounced 'Eye-lam'.

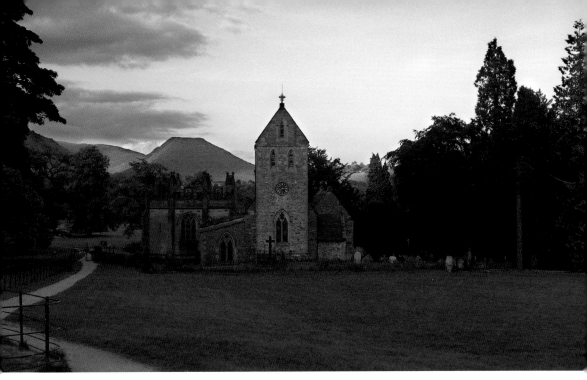

Church of the Holy Cross, Ilam, Day 45.

It was getting on for 10 p.m. when I headed off carrying the night's water supply, but with the Summer Solstice now just three weeks away there was still plenty of light. Skirting around the limestone scar to the east of Ilam Hall I passed the Izaak Walton Hotel, named after the legendary 17th century father of the art of angling who had fished the Dove with his friend James Cotton.

Just past the hotel, I left the open country and entered the lower reaches of the Dove Dale gorge. Lin Dale, where I was heading for the night's camp is a small side spur that branches off the main gorge. I would have loved to carry on exploring the main gorge, but Dove Dale is one of the most visited beauty spots in the UK and might be teeming with people early in the morning. Also it would be best left to enjoy in daylight.

Lin Dale is a good example of what is termed a 'dry valley' with the stream that had once formed it now taking a hidden underground route. I felt very much at home here camping on the same Carboniferous limestone that I grew up with as a lad. With the tent up and sipping a fruit tea I watched the rabbits having their last chase around of the day and soon dropped off to sleep, excited at the prospects of tomorrow.

DAY 46: 6 June   **Lin Dale to Sparklow**
Miles this day: **13**   Miles to date: **504**

I was up and about early with a brew and then headed off to explore Dove Dale. The early morning sun had just started to filter down through the thick foliage of the ash trees to bounce off the white porcelaneous limestone blocks and boulders that decorate the gorge.

Fossil crinoids, Dove Dale, Day 46.

Everywhere I looked I could see limestone karst[2] features, ranging from dog holes to the dark rift-like openings of cave passages that begged for exploration had I not been in a hurry. Underfoot, zillions of walkers had polished the limestone to expose a wealth of fossil remains. These were mostly crinoids, primitive creatures that anchored themselves to the seabed, and with branching plant-like arms. They relied on drifting currents to put food on their table rather than chasing after it like later, more 'advanced' creatures are obliged to do. I sat down on a block of ancient seabed to heal my bare feet in the rushing waters, letting the mind-stretching images and sounds of this magical place flow over me for a while.

Dawdling my way up the dale, savouring every nook and cranny, I reached the small hamlet of Milldale just as the tiny village store was opening, just in time for me to stock up with fruit gums and Kit-Kats. I also savoured a delicious Walls Carte D'Or mixed berry extravagance – the backpacker's perfect mid-morning snack. After a couple of teas to wash down the ice cream it was time to move on.

I soon fell in step with another lady walker who had taken to long distance walking to help get over a recent bereavement. Last year she had walked the Camino de Santiago in northern Spain, and she advised me that if I ever did it to remember to take a large bed sheet to keep the bedbugs at bay. After a couple of miles my planned route climbed out of the River Dove gorge up into the Biggin Dale dry valley so we went our separate ways. The ash tree groves and limestone gorges gave way to the green fields and limestone walls of Hartington, where

2 Karst is a landscape formed from the dissolution of soluble rocks such as limestone.

Limestone arch, Dove Dale, Day 46.

sheep have been reared since the Cistercian monks first established a monastic settlement here in the 13th century. I was making for the Tissington Trail, a bridleway that follows the old track bed of the Ashbourne to Buxton Railway that closed in 1963. I followed this along the effortless sweeping contours for the next six miles to Sparklow and camped next to the old rail tack, conveniently located just a few hundred yards from The Royal Oak hostelry.

DAY 47: 7 June   Sparklow to Castleton
Miles this day: **15**   Miles to date: **520**

I had arranged to meet up with my youngest daughter Beth and family at Castleton the next day so an early start was needed to get me close to the town before evening. After a brew and a simple Kit-Kat breakfast, I was packed up and off before 7.00 a.m. From Sparklow I headed over the fields for two miles to Monyash, a quiet, pretty village that had once been a prosperous centre for lead mining in the 19th century when it had boasted five pubs, a blacksmith's shop, a wheelwright, a joinery, several shops, cobblers, butchers, shoemakers and dressmakers, with a population several times that of today's. As the Quaker London Lead Company acquired and developed mines in Derbyshire, Monyash became an important Quaker centre and this is preserved in the architecture and layout of the village.

   As a geologist, I have always been fascinated with the Quaker involvement in the mining industry, especially in the great lead mining areas of the North Pennines, and not forgetting

The Monsal Trail goes underground in Millers Dale, Day 47.

some of their other enterprises, including the establishment of Barclays and Lloyds banks, Clarks the shoemakers, and the great chocolatiers, Frys, Rowntrees and Cadbury, as well as some noteworthy overseas enterprises such as the State of Pennsylvania.

As I made my way northwards across the fields towards Deep Dale, I watched as ominous black clouds started to gather on the horizon and then speed towards me, as if spurred on by wraiths. Daylight dwindled and the birds fell silent and I scrambled to dig out my waterproofs just as giant raindrops began to splat on the top of my head. Covered up, I took shelter under some trees to await the expected splendid show of lightning as the backdrop to the mother of all storms. Disappointingly the downpour fizzled out after just a few minutes and the lightning show was cancelled, perhaps due to poor attendance. The daylight was switched back on and the birds resumed their summer singing.

Deep Dale starts as a shallow grassy valley that quickly develops into a gorge dropping some 600 feet in just over a mile. The old miners' track took me past some mining relicts with grassed-over spoil heaps and twisted ironwork poking out of the ground by the filled-in remains of ancient mine shafts. A track named Wheal Lane testifies to a Cornish influence in the shaping of this fascinating mining landscape.

After a mile or so, Deep Dale joins the much larger Monsal Dale where a short section of the old Midland Railway track has been turned into a high-level cycle and footpath called the Monsal Trail, incorporating – I later realised – several old railway tunnels. Construction of this railway, clinging as it did to the side of the Monsal Gorge high above the River Wye,

A Miller's Dale mill, Day 47.

was a worthy feat of Victorian engineering that was forced on the railway company by the Duke of Devonshire's insistence that the railway did not pass too close to his estates at Chatsworth and Rowsley. Similarly, the 1,058-yard-long Haddon tunnel was made at the insistence of the Duke of Rutland, with the shallow 'filled-in trench' tunnel construction designed to keep the railway hidden from sight of his residence at Haddon Hall. Part of the deal he cut included the construction of his very own railway station (but well out of sight of his stately home) that still bears his coat of arms.

The Monsal Trail was easy walking but I had several near misses with speeding cyclists who came up behind me without warning and I quickly realised that thick tree cover was going to rob me of the views of the impressive gorge below. A clearing in the trees opposite the Ravenstor Youth Hostel gave me a rare glimpse of the river and the sheer limestone wall beyond that was being tackled by a number of intrepid young rock climbers. Leaving the Monsal Trail I scrambled down the side of the gorge and crossed the River Wye on a conveniently sited footbridge. It turned out to be a good move. I left the walkers and cyclists duelling up in the trees and had a quiet lane next to the beautiful river Wye all to myself. But it got even better, for just around the next corner I came to a splendid pub called the Anglers Rest where I tucked into a simple, old fashioned roast chicken lunch with all the trimmings, including a surprise Yorkshire pudding, which I took as an omen that I was at last heading in the right direction.

After fighting the urge to fall asleep at the table, I headed off with the intention of following Monk's Dale northwards but switched to an alternative route that took me up the steep valley side to join the Pennine Bridleway. This turned out to be good move, with the old high-level railway track sweeping me on through open countryside on gravity-free contours past a cluster of interesting old lead mines to the north of the hamlet of Wheston. Some bore names such as Hazard Mine, Clear-the-Way Mine, Starvehouse Mine. From the look of it this would have been a metal mining district of some importance until the mid-19th century, when cheap imported metal rendered the working of most of Britain's lead mines uneconomical.

The lead mines of Derbyshire and the North Pennine Orefield of Yorkshire, Durham and former Westmoreland are based on narrow veins of lead and zinc-bearing minerals that cut through Carboniferous strata. Limestone predominates in the lower part of this sequence to form the White Peak District of Derbyshire and the fells of the Yorkshire Dales, whilst gritty sandstones occupy the higher ground of the Dark Peak in Derbyshire and the North Pennines to host the endless miles of upland moor and peat bogs. The lead veins generally formed along fault lines that allowed the hot metal-rich fluids to rise and deposit the metal ores. Unlike the tin and copper bearing veins of Cornwall and Devon, granites played no part in their formation, with these deep fractures being formed during the gentle folding of the rock strata in the Pennine mountain-building process.

Starting the steep descent down the limestone escarpment to Castleton, I was very careful to avoid a slip or a trip that could have sent me into a headfirst somersault on rocky terrain – a real possibility with tired legs and a heavy pack. I made my way down Cave Dale under Peveril Castle, entering the town from the south.

The town was very busy with lots of people milling around: some, I later concluded, were themselves looking for a bed for the night. I headed towards the red YHA triangle marked on the map, but couldn't find the hostel. Three lads then convinced me it was about a mile out of town on the Hope road, and on the way I checked a number of B&Bs but everywhere was full. I then met another couple who insisted the Youth Hostel was back in town, 'Turn right, turn left at the church', and so forth: so after dithering for a while, I decided to head back and give the town centre another try, for after all this was what the map showed. This turned out to be another up-a-gum-tree search and half an hour later I was back, heading east on the Hope road. I met the three lads again and prodded them for specific directions. This time they said, 'We are actually staying there, and it's about a mile that way', pointing convincingly in the general direction of Hope.

The road seemed endless and it was getting late. I was hungry but finding a bed was now a priority. Eventually I spotted a green triangular 'YHA' sign taking shape in the distance. The hostel was set in huge grounds, which might have added a touch of grandeur to the former stately home, but for me it meant a trudge across the fields to get to the hostel.

As I half expected it was full, and no, the not very helpful girl said, 'We don't allow camping in the grounds' and, 'Yes, I know some do, but we don't.'

Heading back into town I vowed to cancel my YHA membership[3] after decades of support whilst living overseas. I kept an eye open for campsites on the way back into town but these fields were overlooked by adjoining farms and houses, with no woodland patches to hide an itinerant backpacker. I tried a few more B&Bs with the same result and so, with nightfall approaching, I decided to cut my losses and head back into the open fell country south of the town that I had passed through earlier that day. It was a very uninviting prospect, involving a steep climb back up the scar with daylight now descending quickly. Putting on my headlight and some warmer clothing, I decided to avoid Cave Dale, with its stony track, and climbed back up the steep pathless grassy escarpment, made even more treacherous by a heavy dewfall.

With all the trailing about I had missed out the chance of a late supper in Castleton, but had managed to fill up with water at the George Inn. I made a quick spaghetti and soup nosh before crashing into my pit close to midnight. With all the add-ons I had covered over 25 miles and was feeling a bit done in.

---

3 Which I did on completion of the walk.

DAY 48: 8 June   Castleton to Edale
Miles this day: **5**   Miles to date: **524**

After an early start I headed back to Castleton by the same route as the previous evening, giving the tricky Cave Dale ravine a miss. I passed close to Peak Cavern, one of several popular show caves in the area. I remembered the tragic caving accident that had filled the national newspapers and our local *Craven Herald* and *Yorkshire Post* in the spring of 1959. Neil Moss, an Oxford undergraduate, had got himself wedged in a narrow rift about 1,000 foot in from the cave entrance somewhere below where I was now walking. Several attempts were made to pull him up the rift but the ropes kept parting, and eventually he lost consciousness. His father requested that no further lives were to be put at risk by attempting to recover his body, and the rift was then sealed off with a concrete plug and a commemorative plaque. Participating in the rescue was the intrepid Yorkshire caver Bob Leakey who discovered the tortuous and hazardous six-mile long Mossdale Caverns, a Yorkshire system which was itself the scene of Britain's worst caving disaster in the summer of 1967.

Mossdale is considered one of the most arduous and challenging caves in Britain on account of its long lengths of flat low-level passages, known as 'bedding plane crawls' that in places are just ten inches high. At about 2 p.m. on 24 June 1967 a group of ten cavers entered the cave. Four of the party returned to the surface at about 5 p.m. with the other party of six pressing on to reach the end of the explored system. That evening a thunderstorm struck, transforming the cave entrance area into a small lake. A girl in the first party, the fiancée of one of the party of six, returned to the cave entrance that evening and, alarmed at seeing the state of the river, ran across the moors in darkness to raise the alarm. A dam wall was hastily built and fire engine pumps tried to contain the flood, but the six were overtaken by a deluge of water as the cave system flooded to roof level, and all were drowned. A commemorative visit was made to Mossdale by relatives and friends of the cavers who lost their lives on the 50th anniversary of the terrible tragedy.

✳✳✳

I had arranged to meet my youngest daughter Beth and her family in Castleton and whilst waiting for them to arrive I treated myself to a cooked breakfast. I was enjoying several catch-up cups of coffee and some quiet relaxation when eight-year-old granddaughter Charlotte burst in on the scene. After lunch at The George Inn we all walked up to Hollins Cross via Little Mam Tor, with son-in-law Greg carrying my pack and young Charlotte proudly taking charge of my walking poles.

Hollins Cross is located on the watershed ridge that separates the vale of Castleton from the Edale valley and lies on an old coffin route that once connected the two towns. It is a

Daughter Beth and family, Castleton, Day 48. **PHOTOGRAPH BY:** *Greg Adams.*

splendid vantage point with fine views over to Edale, the start of the Pennine Way, and above that to Kinder Scout and other gritstone tabletop summits.

It was soon late afternoon and time to say goodbye after an enjoyable family day during which I had covered a record four miles. After goodbye hugs, Beth and her family headed off back to Rugby and I continued the leisurely two-mile walk to Edale, enjoying the evening sunshine.

Arriving at the village I called in at Ye Olde Nags Head, the official start of the Pennine Way, I met a chap called Ben who recommended a nearby campsite. It was the perfect spot with a clear mountain stream flowing through the grounds and surrounded by woodland. After pitching the tent, we went back to the Nag for a beer or two, followed by a good supper and a pre-Pennine Way whisky to set me in good stead for the next leg of the walk.

I was feeling chuffed having completed my 132-mile link from Clun on the Welsh Border, crossing the West Midlands and a first visit to the Derbyshire dales. Ahead of me now lay 250 miles of Pennine and Cheviot upland country on the grandfather of Britain's long-distance paths. I would cross a few roads but hopefully see more curlews than people. I couldn't wait to get cracking! •

Signpost, Castleton, Day 48.

Beth and family, Castleton, Day 48. **PHOTOGRAPH BY:** *Greg Adams.*

Looking back to Crowden, with Kinder in the distance, Day 50.

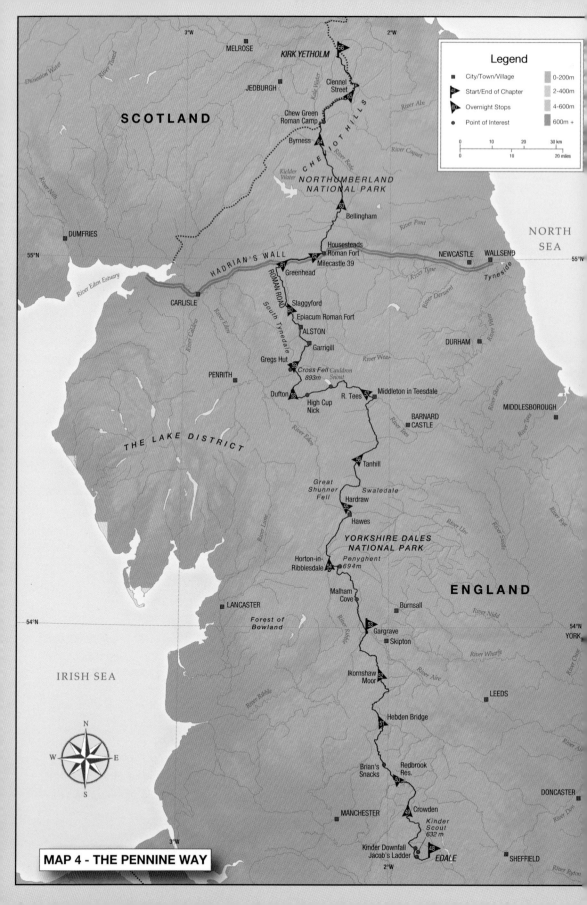

MAP 4 - THE PENNINE WAY

6

THE SOUTH PENNINES

When it first opened in April 1965, after 30 years of drawn-out negotiations with land owners, the Pennine Way was Britain's first long-distance footpath. This chapter covers the 70-mile section from Edale in Derbyshire to the village of Gargrave at the start of the Yorkshire Dales. From Edale the Way climbs up through the Dark Peak's gritstone country to Kinder Scout and Kinder Downfall that give way to high moorland, fringed by dark towns with their now-silent mills. Approaching the Aire Gap, I get a distant glimpse of the limestone fell country of the North Pennines, and get the feeling that I am making progress.

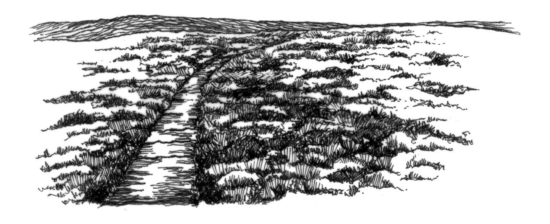

DAY 49: 9 June   Edale to Crowden
Miles this day: **16**   Miles to date: **541**

After a few overnight showers, the morning got off to a bright start. Ben shared some of his scrambled eggs with me for breakfast and I was ready for the off just after 9 a.m. The infamous peaty clough[1] of Grindsbrook that runs due north from the Nags Head is now officially closed, and walkers are now directed to Upper Booth Farm where a stiff 1,200-foot climb on to the Kinder plateau awaits them.

---

1 A clough is a water-worn ravine cutting through the peat, sometimes slippery and difficult to cross.

Looking over to Edale and the start of the Pennine Way, Day 49.

Jacob's Ladder on the Pennine Way, Day 49.

Kinder Low in the High Peak, Day 49.

Upper Booth is a National Trust farm dedicated to 'classical' farming methods and offers camping and farm visits in a lovely setting where Crowden Beck spills out from the Dark Peak plateau. A noticeboard said refreshments were served in the farmyard but there was no one around to make me the longed-for cup of tea. From the farm the Way heads north-west for about one level mile to a narrow rustic bridge of ancient aspect, before climbing on to the Kinder plateau via Jacob's Ladder, a steep path that the National Trust has relaid with flagstones to limit erosion – and provide a direct *Stairway to Heaven* for any walker who might keel over during the very first challenge.

The Kinder plateau is a strange, eerie sort of place. It comprises a peaty high-level plateau some eight square kilometres in extent, roughly triangular in shape and bounded on all sides by steep escarpments. Several indistinct summits rise above the general level of the plateau including Kinder Scout, 636 metres. The otherwise featureless plateau is dissected by a network of deeply incised drainage channels called groughs (pronounced 'gruffs') or hags (pronounced 'hags') that combine to form the headwaters of River Kinder to the west and Crowden Beck to the south. In his book *On the Pennine Way*, Alfred Wainwright[2] commented 'One wonders how this flat tableland came to earn its name as The Peak. Nothing less like a peak can be imagined.'

The wind was now getting up and with it came a sudden stinging blast of icy rain that grew in force as I slowly made my way over the escarpment towards the Kinder Downfall where the young Kinder River crashes over a gritstone lip. With an unfavourable wind direction,

2 Published in June 1985, Alfred Wainwright's book *On the Pennine Way* remains a classic book on the walk.

as was the case today, a considerable part of the stream's flow is thrown back as icy spray into the face of the walker, like an inverted shower. Here I met several people heading towards Edale but we were unable to shout above the howling wind and rain. I started to laugh at the absurdity of the weather and they joined in, hanging on to their half-drowned crouching dog lest it took off in the mighty wind. This was the first 'laughing conversation' I think I have experienced, and we ended the attempted conversation with a grasping handshake and waving cheerios.

The worst of the bad weather was left behind as I dropped off Sandy Heys, and then a silly lapse of concentration left me shooting off in the general direction of Manchester, having missed a fork in the path. When the Pennine Way first opened, this next section would have been especially grim until the National Parks people paved the path with heavy flagstones rescued from the floors of old mill sites, forming a snaking trail that weaves its way across the desolate moors. It's a feature that will doubtless be visible from outer space for aeons to come, if there's anyone out there watching. Future archaeologists visiting from distant galaxies will debate what on Earth this winding ribbon of flagstones means, apparently linking nowhere to nowhere. Was the snaking trail some sort of Stone Age coded message beamed to the far side of the galaxy?

A section of particularly infamous bogs on Featherbed Moss has now been tamed by these paving stones, for some to applaud, and others, perhaps, to regret. The splendid moorland isolation is then rudely interrupted by the A57 that drives a black winding ribbon through the aptly named Snake Pass, an ancient thoroughfare used by the Romans linking the forts of Melandra near Glossop and Navio near Bradwell. As I approached the road was not initially visible due to a slight crown of the hill, and after a day of isolation it was disconcerting to watch an endless line of trucks driving effortlessly across the peat – a sort of boggy mirage! Expunging the image of the invasive motorway, I then watched oxen carts hauling precious Roman lead ingots destined for urgent plumbing work at *Aqua Arnemetia* (Buxton), a favourite Roman watering hole in this heathen, squelchy country that was definitely not suitable for Roman sandals. By the Gods, how they must have hated the peaty Pennines!

The noise of the traffic was thankfully blown away by the wind once I crossed the snaking motorway, with the Way then heading north-easterly through a seemingly endless succession of peat ravines before reaching the slightly less soggy Bleaklow Ridge. Here the National Park must thankfully have run out of paving stones and one is able to savour the slippery heather-clutching peat hags that so characterised the old Pennine Way. Here some care is needed to avoid disappearing from sight in the mire.

So far on my traverse from Edale I had enjoyed good visibility apart from brief periods when I had to stow my spectacles whilst crossing the Kinder plateau. Providing the walker's GPS does not play up in the wet weather, there is no real possibility of getting lost on the Pennine Way, and the modern backpacker can come to no real harm in this squelchy terrain. This was not the case some 50 years ago when the Way first opened and walkers came back

Dropping Down to Crowden, Day 49

with tales of getting lost on the moors and losing their boots in thigh-deep bog. I take my hat off to these early veterans, battling along with leaking dubbin-soaked Hawkins boots, trying to fend off the driving rain in barely shower-proof Egyptian cotton anoraks with just a misted-up glass-fronted compass and a disintegrating map to guide them.

Once over the watershed, the Way drops down to the Longdendale valley and at the top of an escarpment, the Torside Reservoir comes into view, followed by Reaps Farm, the first habitation since leaving Upper Booth. The Longdendale Valley was once home to the River Etherow until it disappeared under five back-to-back Victorian reservoirs that now occupy a five-mile section of what must have once been a splendid valley. The dams were built to supply water to Manchester and the surrounding wool and cotton boomtowns. The Way makes use of the Torside Reservoir to cross the flooded valley, but first you are directed on to a short section of bridleway, the Trans Pennine Trail. This part follows the track of the Victorian-built Woodhead railway line, which opened in 1845 to link Sheffield and Manchester. A key engineering feat of the line was the construction of three parallel tunnels, each three miles long, hewn through the hard Pennine millstone grit. When it opened Woodhead No. 1 was amongst the longest railway tunnels in the world. Perhaps forgetting the blood and sweat that went into the construction of this amazing feat of Victorian engineering, the line was controversially closed in January 1970, but there are still occasional distant rumblings about a possible re-opening.

But it was time to move on and cross the dam wall over to Crowden. After the rough weather on the High Peak, the storm clouds had cleared and the sun lit up the heather and heathland of the Longendale valley, turning this into a beautiful afternoon. I thought I might try to camp in the grounds of the Crowden Youth Hostel. I had just nibbled some nuts along the way and was ready for a good feast. Again I looked in vain for the once-familiar green triangular YHA sign, which was nowhere to be seen. I called in at a Caravan Club campsite to ask for directions. The site manager, who was just getting ready to lock up his office, said, 'Ah! You are just two months too late; the hostel has now shut. But you are welcome to use the campsite here.' It looked pleasant enough, with just a few campers in amongst the trees, and he did me a special £5 grey-beard knackered-looking backpacker rate. I bought a few goodies a the site shop, tinned potatoes, chilli con carne, plus some eggs for breakfast – all prohibited items for the weight-conscious backpacker.

I had spent a lot of time planning for the midges that plague the Scottish Highlands but, this far south, I was totally unprepared for the voracious attacks that assailed me when I tried to set up camp. Possibly the shelter of the Longdendale valley with the higher humidity levels shedding off from five miles of back-to-back reservoirs had made Crowden a southern stronghold for midges. I went back to talk to the friendly site manager who seemed to be half expecting me. He showed me his arsenal of midge deterrents and I bought a bottle of Avon's *Skin so Soft*, a skincare concoction that the midges seem to dislike, unless they get really obsessed.

Sitting back in the tent, smelling like a girl with soft skin, and enjoying the good 'all-in' teenage nosh with tinned potatoes, I thought about the closure of the Crowden Youth Hostel. For many walkers setting out on the Pennine Way, Crowden would have been an almost obligatory stopover after the fairly arduous 17-mile hike over from Edale on the first day. Surrounded as it is by high moors, there didn't seem to be anywhere else that might offer beds in this area. This would mean a walker in search of a bed being met by one of the hikers' bag-carrying services to whisk you off the Pennines to one of the surrounding mill villages. This is not really an option for the younger walker on a tight budget, and for me being whipped off by a waiting taxi to a surrounding town after a day on the moors infringes on the remoteness of the Way. The half-paved Pennine Way is not what it once was.

DAY 50: 10 June   Crowden to Redbrook Reservoir
Miles this day: **11**   Miles to date: **552**

I allowed myself a bit of a morning lie in and then got stuck into a real breakfast treat with a porridge starter, followed by garlic-fried potatoes and two garlicky fried eggs. Afterwards, I went back to the campsite shop to talk more about midges, for here, hidden away in North Derbyshire, I seemed to have stumbled across a real expert. Over a cup of coffee, he strongly recommended citronella sticks for the Highlands – very valuable advice as it turned out.

I treated myself to a breakfast dessert of a Walls Magnum ice cream and, enjoying the good coffee and sugar high, then set off in a northerly direction, climbing up the western side of the deeply incised valley of Crowden Beck. I lost the path somewhere in the heather so, when I spotted a bobbing head making good speed, I set off in hot pursuit. However, a GPS check later confirmed I was heading off course, and so I gave up following the bobbing head, getting back on track by plodding through knee-high heather towards Laddow Rocks. An hour or so later, the bobbing head caught up with me, presumably having realised his navigational skills were somewhat wanting.

I found this moorland section a bit monotonous, especially the long drag up the Black Hill – one of those 'receding horizons' that you never seem to reach. The bobbing head told me he was doing all the highest hills in each of the historic English counties, with Black Hill, 582 metres, being the highest one in Cheshire and the most northerly of the Peak District's gritstone peaks. I stopped for a snack and a chat before he finally bobbed off leaving me once again alone on the moors.

I watched ominous black clouds gathering on the horizon as I approached Wessenden Lodge, and managed to get my waterproofs on just in time to beat an icy cold downpour that wasn't far off landing as hail. It was over in no time and then the sun came out again. This is a pretty area, one where rhododendrons have taken a serious hold on the countryside. A long way from their native Nepal, these colourful immigrants make a welcome change to the sometimes-dreary native moorland.

Just beyond two small dams, the Pennine Way joins forces with the Standedge Trail near the indistinct summit of Warcock. Here, the walker is rewarded with a splendid panoramic view of Redbrook Reservoir, a possible camping spot with a supply of quality drinking water that could serve me for a billion years.

I left the Pennine Way to head down to the western shore of the reservoir, and followed this round to The Great Western pub (named after the Victorian railway company). After checking whether they would be open later in the evening for food, I found a place to camp near the reservoir, settling for the grassy track that runs along the top of the dam wall to get above the marshy ground surrounding the reservoir.

Happy to have a plan, I made my way back to the pub where I was made very welcome and settled in for a lovely evening. I ordered homemade pate, followed by chicken done in a black bean sauce, rounded off with a splendid trifle. The highlight of the evening was learning from a chap called Gary that I was now a few hundred yards inside my native Yorkshire! With dusk descending, I made my way back to the dam wall to pitch the tent.

DAY 51: 11 June   Redbrook Reservoir to Hebden Bridge
Miles this day: **15**   Miles to date: **567**

Missing my accustomed blue sky start to the day, I headed off around the southern edge of the dam to rejoin the Pennine Way at the point where I had left it the previous evening.

Once across the A62 at Standedge, the route briefly joins Oldham Way and makes its way into gritstone country at Millstone Edge, the sandy paths making a welcome change to yesterday's endless peaty miles. Here, the Pennine moorlands are now reduced to a five-mile-wide strip, with built-up areas of former mill towns encroaching on both the eastern and western flanks of the Pennines. Although the sense of remoteness had all but disappeared, I found this section enjoyable, especially after catching a glimpse of the distant Pendle Hill. Pendle is a landmark that looks down on to the Craven district of North Yorkshire where I was brought up, and spotting it gave me a boost for the morning.

Despite its proximity to the historic Yorkshire border, Pendle Hill is a true Lancashire peak, surrounded by natives who speak with a different northern accent, drink different beers and eat different cheeses to those of nearby Yorkshire. And, if you believe in folklore and the historical findings of the Lancaster courts, there are other deeply-rooted differences: the Pendle district was once the haunt of witches!

On 18–19 August 1612, seven women and two men were found guilty of causing death by witchcraft at the Lancaster Assizes following an investigation by Roger Nowell, King James' chief witch hunter, and were hanged on Gallows Hill the following day. These were uneasy times, just seven years after the discovery of the Catholic Gunpowder Plot, and many Pendle people were, and still are, followers of the 'Old Religion'. The great abbey at Whalley, that had looked after the well-being of the local community for hundreds of years, had been destroyed some 75 years earlier during the Reformation and the people in this large isolated rural parish had been largely left to their own devices. At that time, witches played an accepted role in village life, scratching a meagre living by selling lotions, potions and spells to cure the sick. Being a witch was no longer considered a felony, but courts that had tried them believed these witches had caused death by casting lethal spells.

My sister Barbara was for many years a teacher at Bowland High School, located about four miles to the north-west of Pendle Hill, and had taught one of the descedents of one of those executed. At her trial Alice Nutter, the wife of a well-off Yeoman farmer, refused to testify other than entering a not guilty plea. The evidence presented at the witch trials was based largely on hearsay, but in 1998 the then Home Secretary, Jack Straw, refused a petition to pardon those executed. Does this mean he also believed in witchcraft?

Another trunk road, the Huddersfield Road, snips off yet another strip of moorland and then a number of radio masts come into view just as you approach the M62. But then another feature caught my attention: an orange flag flying high on a mast that belonged to Brian's Snacks, strategically located just off the A672, about half a mile to the south-west of Junction 22 on the M62. The incongruous but welcome smell of frying bacon that came wafting across the moors confirmed it was open for business.

Over a delicious egg and bacon roll, Brian explained that he had been serving food and drink there for 36 years. Most of his regulars came off the motorway, after spotting the flag that is flown during his 4.00 a.m. to midday, seven days a week opening hours. In winter,

The Pennine Way over the M62, Day 51.

he replaces the flag with an orange light. He said that most of the Pennine Way walkers drop in to his wayside cafe, which is advertised in some of the guidebooks. He said that in summer the numbers of walkers could reach 30 to 90 per day, with a lot of people opting for a September walk because the weather could be more settled at the back end of the season.

He was just about to pack up his stuff when another truck pulled in. The driver was trying to make up his mind what to order and I strongly recommended the egg and bacon roll. Sheepishly, he confessed he was without his bottom teeth, having set them down somewhere and forgotten where, but I reckoned it must have been after a wild night out. My sales pitch earned me a free mug of tea, giving me the bright idea of wearing a billboard for Brian's cafe all the way to the top of Scotland, at which we all had a good laugh. Come to think of it, a well-ventilated sandwich board might work better than some of the freaky Gore-Tex wonders that float around in the hills these days.

Leaving Brian to pack up his stuff, I headed off over the arched footbridge that spans the cutting over the motorway, presumably a requirement as the Pennine Way was a right of way that predated the motorway. I stopped in the middle of this splendid bridge to digitally record the roar of the traffic, to make a subtle change from the hours of plaintive curlew calls that by now must have filled a fair bit of the recorder's memory. Crossing over the bridge, I was surprised how quickly the roar of the traffic was left behind and once again I was alone on the moors except for the breathless Morse-code chortle of the skylarks. Recording their song, my hope was that skylarks will survive and eventually outlive the motorways, but it seems touch and go.

A mile or so further on, the Pennine Way drops down off Blackstone Edge to intercept an old packhorse road at an ancient waymarker called the Aiggin Stone. It follows an earlier Roman road and it seems this once remote Blackstone pass had been an ancient thorough-fare of some importance. Once again I conjured up an endless line of people before me: helmeted soldiers in squelching sandals carrying shields and 50-pound packs of weapons and vitals; then some slow moving reddlemen[3] with bags of precious ochres strapped to their ponies, to be rudely pushed aside by a careering stagecoach that drenched them with slushy black bog-water as it swept past.

Perhaps swayed by some ancient lure from another age, I drifted off the Pennine Way and started following the Roman road, heading north-east and almost reaching the A58 before realising my silly mistake. I backtracked a mile or so across the moors to get back on to the Way, but it was a worthwhile detour in order to walk with the Romans for a short while.

One consequence of the detour was that I missed the opening hours of the White House pub where I had fancied a lunch stop but arrived just five minutes after their cast-in-stone last orders deadline. Back in the days of the stagecoach they would, I am sure, have rustled up some food and grog at any hour of the day or night, or risked a cocked flintlock …

After Blackstone, the Way skirts around a number of reservoirs, which, although manmade, I found of interest as part of the tapestry left behind by the Industrial Revolution. Then, in the distance, the massive obelisk of Stoodley Pike came into view, a memorial to celebrate the Peace of Ghent and the abdication of Napoleon in 1814. The views from here are command-ing, looking out over the Calder valley. This is the start of the steep climb down to Hebden Bridge, the final part of which follows a pretty lane through the Callis Wood before spilling out into a tangle of communications where the Rochdale Canal, the A646 and the Leeds to Manchester Trans-Pennine railway are all squeezed into the narrow Calder valley.

Being almost out of food, I made for the town and stopped to talk to a chap carrying a bundle of children's clothes. Aware that I was uncomfortably close to a large town, I asked him whether or not it was wise to camp on the towpath. The clothes were destined for the son of a lady who lived on a narrowboat and he said to follow him there. They made me a brew, showed me a place to camp on the towpath near the narrowboat, and then suggested I could try the Stubbing Wharf pub for some supper.

I really liked Hebden Bridge with its lively 'alternative' atmosphere that reminded me of Glastonbury. The town has grown from a medieval packhorse bridge across a swampy gorge into an important Victorian textile-weaving centre due in part to the district's relatively recent glacial history. First, the glaciers of successive ice ages carved broad valleys through the hard millstone grits, and then alternating periods of thawing released torrents of meltwater that gouged through the glacial U-shaped profile to form the steep-sided valleys seen today, with their vast potential for waterpower.

A boom followed the opening of the Rochdale Canal in 1794 and then the railway arrived and replaced it in 1840. The Victorian period saw the construction of large numbers of

---

3 In times gone by, tinkers who travelled the countryside sold reddle, an orange ochre, to farmers for marking their sheep.

Hebden Bridge with Victorian high-rise workers' housing, Day 51.

cotton mills in the Calder and tributary valleys. Space for the growing population was a problem, partly solved by the proliferation of tall, Victorian 'high-rise' terrace houses that today populate the hillsides overlooking the town's centre.

As the mills started to close in the mid-20th century, the town somehow managed to avoid the post-industrial gloom and decay that hangs over many former mill towns in the north of England, and Hebden Bridge grew into a funky arts-minded community. Thankfully, the Victorian terraces were preserved through pioneering conservationist work, and today give the town its special character.

I was puzzled as to why the Pennine Way had been routed to cross the Calder valley at a sewerage works, a mile to the west of the town, leaving Hebden Bridge off the route. Like me, the average walker would have depleted their supplies on their two-day walk from Edale, and the town has lots of resonably priced accommodation.

The canal-side Stubbing Wharf pub, recommended by my new canal friends, was a lively spot. The place was packed but I managed to find a space for both the pack and myself, and enjoyed a very pleasant evening. It was getting dark when I made my way back along the towpath to pitch the tent and crawl into my sleeping bag, excited at the thought that I was sleeping in Yorkshire, just a two-day walk from home.

Locks on the Rochdale Canal, Day 51.

DAY 52: 12 June   Hebden Bridge to Ickornshaw Moor
Miles this day: **14**   Miles to date: **581**

I enjoyed a fairly lazy start to the day with Sophie from the canal boat offering me a brew. The steep climb out of Hebden Bridge on to Pry Hill reminded me of the grinding power of glaciers, with part of the altitude painfully gained then blown, by dropping down into the Colden Valley before climbing up again on to Heptonstall Moor.

Here, another very obvious rerouting of the Pennine Way is called for! From Stoodley Pike the proposed diversion would head down to Hebden Bridge by Pinnacle Lane. After revictualling, and possibly overnighting, the Way-walker could then head up the lovely wooded National Trust valley of Hebden Water past the NT's splendid renovated Gibson Mill and the landmark beauty spot of Hardcastle Crags. He could then rejoin the Pennine Way just after an early lunch stop at the Pack Horse[4]. This is about a million times nicer than the Way's present routing past stinky sewerage works. I suspect that when the Pennine Way was originally devised 75 years ago, there may have been no public access past Gibson Mill, and the sewerage works was perhaps less stinky. But times and stinks change – and so should the Pennine Way!

OPPOSITE: Ancient bridge, Colden Water, north of Hebden Bridge, Day 52.

4 The Pack Horse Inn was under new management in 2017, and is much improved!

The Pennine Way climbs up a 'snicket' out of Hebden Bridge on Day 52.

Rhododendrons at Black Clough hill, Walshaw Dean Lower Reservoir (drained) on Day 52.

I made a detour to the Pack Horse Inn located on the moors in the upper part of Hebden Water, but arrived seven minutes after the lunch deadline and settled for a bag of crisps and a cider. Whilst I crunched away at the lunch, the landlord took great pleasure in showing me the largest collection of whisky I have ever seen, although I wished he had rather spent the time rustling up a sandwich.

From the 'Whisky galore but nowt t'eat' pub, the Pennine Way climbs past the three end-to-end Walshaw Dean reservoirs, located in a pretty moorland valley that is a mass of the vivid green and purple of rhododendron and heather in full bloom. A mile further, on the Way enters Brontë country on Withens Height, followed soon by the ruined farmhouse of Top Withens. Helpful signposts, with Japanese translations explain: 'This farmhouse has been associated with Wuthering Heights, the Earnshaw home in Emily Brontë's novel. The buildings, even when complete, bore no resemblance to the house she described, but the situation may have been in her mind when she wrote of the moorland settings of the Heights.' On the walk, I saw many ruined farmhouses that had given up the battle to stay habitable, and, like Top Withens, now cast a melancholic shadow on this fragile interface of moor and impoverished farmland.

The Pennine Way goes tantalisingly close to Haworth, but once again passes some two miles to the west, perhaps to keep you firmly bogged in on the moors rather than to let you succumb to the temptation of the town's many fine hostelries and supply shops. Grimacing and muttering about rerouting, I carried on.

Shooters' Hut, Ickornshaw Moor, Day 52.

After Ponden Hall – by repute the Thrushcross Grange of *Wuthering Heights* – the Way climbs up on to Ickornshaw Moor, a delightful stretch of moorland that sits just to the south of Cowling. I found a place to camp next to a shooting hut at the north end of the moor, surrounded by very noisy curlews, unsettled because I had encroached their nesting grounds without permission.

DAY 53: 13 June	Ickornshaw Moor to Gargrave
Miles this day: **13**	Miles to date: **594**

Awakened early by the early call of curlews, I headed off just after 8.00 a.m., skirting around the northern edge of Stott Hill Moor to the pretty hamlet of Lothersdale. After that the Way heads up on to Carleton Moor, the last mile of moorland before crossing the Aire Gap. From its highest point, Pinhaw Beacon, I spotted the limestone escarpments just beyond Malham and picked out the faint outline of Pen-y-Ghent, up which I would soon be hauling my pack, hopefully with now-repaired feet.

The Way then crosses the green hilly drumlin[5] country of South Craven to join the Leeds to Liverpool canal at East Marton. The double-arched bridge over the canal was originally a packhorse bridge that was later raised for the new A59.

Instead of continuing along the delightful towpath all the way to Gargrave past The Anchor pub, the Pennine Way inexplicably leaves the canal at East Marton to head across some boring

---

5 A drumlin is a small rounded hill or hummock, usually clay, that was left behind by a retreating glacier.

Ruined dales farm above Cowling, Day 53.

hillocky fields to Gargrave. Here I would break my journey for a week and head over to my cottage in Burnsall, but first I paid a visit to my mum who is in a care home in the village. She was now just a month away from her 100th birthday, which we would be celebrating just after I reached Fort William. I had now clocked up about 600 miles and was almost half way into the walk – a satisfying thought.

A neighbour collected me in the village and took me to my home some 10 miles away. I fished the key to my cottage out of the pack, put the kettle on and fired up the water for a jolly good shower. It was good to be home.

It was good to think the pack would be off my shoulders for a week, but my first priority was a long overdue medical appointment to sort out my feet. My then neighbour from the

Two-decker bridge on Leeds–Liverpool Canal at East Marton on Day 53.

end cottage, a retired GP, kindly had a good look at my feet (after the extended shower) and educated me all about trench foot, which had been the scourge of World War I trench warfare. He confirmed I had an infection and that it didn't look good, warning that unchecked trench foot could result in amputation, which would make the walk even more challenging! This news sent me scuttling off to the local health centre at Grassington early the next morning for my awaited appointment where I was prescribed a course of antibiotics. After that my feet were more or less OK until I switched to my fourth pair of boots – an uncomfortable pair of La Sportiva Trangos – at Fort William, but that's a story for later! ●

7

THE NORTH PENNINES AND CHEVIOTS

*Continuing on from Gargrave in the Yorkshire Dales, the Pennine Way climbs up over
Fountains Fell and Pen-y-Ghent to Britain's highest pub at Tan Hill. Leaving Yorkshire behind,
the Pennine Way then cuts over the moors to Teesdale before crossing over the
Pennines to Dufton past a succession of nature's amazing landmarks.
Cross Fell, the highest peak in the Pennines is followed by the River South Tyne.
I then walk along Hadrian's Wall – one of the highlights of the walk – and then head up
on to the Cheviots and over the border to Kirk Yetholm.*

DAY 54: 22 June   Gargrave to Horton
Miles this day: **21**   Miles to date: **615**

After enjoying home comforts for a week back at my cottage in Burnsall, I was ready to get
back on the trail.

From Gargrave, the Pennine Way crosses a small bridge over the Leeds and Liverpool
Canal and then heads across hilly drumlin country to Malham. This small but quite lovely

A Viking terraced field system, Malham, (2017 photo) Day 54.

village used to be a quiet peaceful spot until the BBC discovered the Yorkshire Dales with *All Creatures Great and Small* in the late 1970s. These days it can get so busy with visitors that it is not worth being one, but in my boyhood days it was a quiet backwater. We lived just six miles away and, as a young lad at primary school, we would often come here with the dog on a sunny summer evening after Mum had shut up the village shop. I would stand and crane my neck, gazing up at the 300-foot-high cliff of Malham Cove until I got that slightly dizzy, unsafe feeling and had to look away. The River Aire bubbles out from the foot of the cove, a mysterious phenomenon for a lad of seven or eight to get his head around.

Years later I would begin to understand. Malham Cove stands close to the line of the Craven Fault, the most important geological structure in the North Pennines. The fault comprises three principal planar fractures, or splays, that run for roughly 30 miles in a west-north-west direction, with Malham standing on the South Craven splay. The rock masses across each of the faults have been displaced vertically with the combined vertical movement – or 'throw' – exceeding an impressive 2,000 metres in places.

Before leaving the village I stopped at the Buck Inn for a sandwich and a cider. I stayed here with Vanessa my Ecuadorian friend back in 2007 after she had jumped out of nowhere in the dark days following my unexpected divorce. After attending the gym for several months to get in shape with painful crouched duck-walk exercises, I brought her to England to shock my mother and daughters, and to walk part of the Pennine Way from Malham to Hadrian's Wall. I would feel her watchful presence for the next 10 days.

Malham Cove, a 300-foot-high limestone cliff on the South Craven Geological Fault (2017 photo), Day 54.

After leaving Malham the Way heads up the dale, passing the ancient[1] terraced field system or lynchet field and a stone clapper bridge to the foot of the cove. A steep climb up the fault escarpment on the west side then takes you on to the limestone pavement, a natural karst landform found on weathered limestone outcrops. After more than 60 years, Malham Cove never fails to impress me, and for the Pennine Way walker, it marks the start of the best part.

After the steep climb up the side of the Cove, I took a breather to take a last look back to Malham Dale with its patchwork of emerald green fields and stone walls, and the dazzling white limestone bluffs. I let my mind drift back to earlier days – my dad with a wartime khaki knapsack, and then flashbacks of Bridget and our three girls, Penny, Amanda and Beth, walking very carefully across the limestone pavements, having been warned by dad of the dire consequence of slipping down a crack (something they still laugh about). I watch my two young sons Tim and Wills, weighed down with climbing gear and setting off to tackle some of the shorter pitches to the west of the main cove. Good days, but sadly now a long way off.

✳✳✳

From the top of the cove the Way follows the splendid dry valley that was formed by the stream that once drained the Fountains Fell catchment. The river still exists but takes a devious underground route, disappearing down a prominent water sink just below Malham Tarn, to emerge partly from the low flooded cave at the foot of the cove as the nascent

---

1 Believed to date back to the Iron Age and later developed by the Vikings.

River Aire, but mostly from the Aire Head Spring[2]. An entrance into this hidden cave system has been sought by many cave diggers and divers and was for many years the Holy Grail of the Craven Pothole Club. The CPC's legendary Malham Dig was finally abandoned in 1952 after excavating tonnes of loose rock that filled the once active stream passage. The dig started to look unsafe and, after years of getting nowhere, was finally aborted, no doubt with a frank Yorkshire assessment of 'Bugger this for a lark!'

Towards the head of the dry valley, the Way climbs up the rocky east side to an area marked Combs Hill on the OS map, where the walker is rewarded with a splendid panoramic view looking back down on the dry valley. A pleasant walk along the east shore of Malham Tarn follows before the Way enters the grounds of the Malham Tarn House Field Centre, set at the foot of a limestone scar and surrounded by woodland frequented by friendly chaffinches, tits and robins. The ancient oaks give the place a magical character; it is a Rivendell[3]-like safe haven beyond which endless peat bogs and other challenges lie in wait for the weary Pennine Way walker.

Clear of the woods, I had to stop to tend to my feet, a very disappointing development as I had just completed a course of antibiotics during my eight-day stopover in Burnsall.

They had looked in better shape but after six hours of walking on very straightforward ground they were again bleeding and looking tatty. Would they ever get better, I wondered? I tried out the Omnifix surgical dressing tape that was recommended by my retired GP neighbour back in Burnsall, and it seemed to help.

By 4 p.m. I had cleared Tennant Gill and reached the summit of Fountains Fell, 668 metres. I had been up here many times to fossick around the shallow coal pit shafts, but this time there was no time to lose with Pen-y-Ghent, one of the top-ten highest mountains in the Yorkshire Dales, awaiting me on the horizon.

2 According to dye-testing.   **3** The Elven realm in Tolkein's *Lord of the Rings*.

First though, I had to fritter away hard-earned altitude by dropping down to Rainscar Farm before taking the track past Dale Head and starting the steep ascent of Pen-y-Ghent, 694 metres. It was 7.45 p.m. by the time I summited, making the 9 p.m. supper deadline in Horton in Ribblesdale now looking doubtful.

ABOVE: Pen-y-Ghent, 694 metres, racing to beat the food deadline, Horton in Ribblesdale, Day 54.

Taking extra care not to trip head first, with aching legs and a heavy pack, I began the steep descent off the mountain. On past the impressive 100-metre-long chasm of Hull Pot, I hurried on down the rough track and got to The Crown at Horton at 10 minutes after the 9 p.m. kitchen deadline.

Being a Sunday evening the pub was almost empty, and, not surprisingly, I was told they had stopped serving food. Trying not to panic, I put on a cheerful face and explained to the tall chap behind the bar that I had just walked here from Cornwall and was running 10 minutes behind schedule. I also told them I was about to keel over from lack of nourishment, adding, in case it helped, that I was a member of the Craven Pothole Club that owned the cottage next door. The barman started to cave, and offered, 'I might be able to fry you up a few chips if you give me a few minutes.' I managed to weasel in a suggestion he might throw in a couple of fried eggs, and he agreed.

Before heading off to the kitchen, he served me a pint of Tetley's (the beer not the tea) and an interim packet of crisps. I was well and truly knackered after the trek over the hills and both beer and crisps disappeared long before the barman re-appeared with an award-winning plateful of egg and chips.

When I later analysed the day's walk with my RouteBuddy software, I saw I had covered 21.1 miles with a total ascent of 1,013 metres, which is a fair hike for an old bloke with a big pack. Allowing for the quick lunch snack in Malham and a couple of photo stops, I reckoned I had been walking for about eleven hours, making it one of the toughest days of the walk so far.

At least tonight there would be no scrabbling around in the twilight hours looking for a place to camp, for somewhere in my pack I had a member's key to next door's cottage. Tomorrow was another longish day so, after washing down the supper with a nightcap beer, I made my way next door to sleep on the luxury of a real bunk bed.

I first joined the Craven Pothole Club as a 16-year-old lad in the summer of 1961 whilst working on a school holiday job at Keighley Laboratories, where my supervisor, Mr Hardy, was an active CPC member. In the three years before heading down to London to study geology, I attended meets to most of the major cave systems in Yorkshire. In those days, the club owned one of the cottages above the Helwith Bridge Quarry, where I got a job as a labourer for the latter part of my 'gap year'. The gap year was my reward for failing O-Level French – in those days a general matriculation requirement for most universities except the London ones. Most weekends would find me in the Foredale cottage, or down in the pub at Helwith Bridge, then run by a retired bank manager who set his own licensing hours in the then wonderfully unpoliced Yorkshire Dales.

DAY 55: 23 June   Horton to Hardraw, near Hawes
Miles this day: **16**   Miles to date: **630**

From Horton the Pennine Way heads northwards past Sell Gill Holes, one of the early pot-holes I explored with the CPC in about 1961. I still remember the stinky decaying sheep at the bottom of the first wet ladder pitch. Sheep are stupid but sure-footed; most likely the dead sheep had been chucked down the pot by the farmer to save the effort of a more sanitary burial.

I passed a ruined barn and reflected on the similarities between the fates of the Yorkshire barns and the monasteries. First the roof goes, either through unchecked decay, or in the case of the abbeys when the lead was filched by the king's agents to help replenish his wilting coffers, perhaps to build more palaces or wage war on the Scots and the French. In the 20th century, a barn's prized roofing flags were often carted off by the local farmer as an easy one-time 'cash crop'. The abbey and barn walls were then removed, bit by bit, for recycling until all that was left was a broken molar-like remnant.

At midday I paused at Ling Gill, a lovely tree and boulder-filled gorge that swallows a siza-ble beck at its top end, surely a major collapsed cave system. Beyond that, at Cam End, the Pennine Way crosses a Roman road and the Dales Way to then head up on to Dodd Fell, where I got a last glimpse of Pen-y-Ghent before making for the market town of Hawes in Wensleydale. After replenishing supplies, I crossed the broad glacially shaped valley of the

Pennine Way above Horton in Ribblesdale on Day 55.

Dry Lathe barn on the Pennine Way, Old Ing, Day 55.

Above Hardraw looking over to slate mines on Abbotside Common, Day 56.

River Ure to the delightful hamlet of Hardraw, the home of The Green Dragon Inn, where I rested with a pint. This is a relatively rare survivor of the unspoilt Yorkshire Dales pub, cosy inside when the fires burn in winter, but this evening I sat at an outside table to enjoy the late sunshine, listening to the end-of-day chatter of the birds.

With the evening advancing, I headed up the rough lane behind the pub and found a good spot to camp next to a small patch of woodland just over the wall from the track. I settled down to try out my new Trangia meths stove with some Tesco five-minute spaghetti embellished with a deli Crossman's sauce.

DAY 56: 24 June   Hardraw to Tan Hill
Miles this day: **14**   Miles to date: **645**

I was in the final stages of packing up when a grey-bearded head appeared over the wall. After a brief exchange, he said, 'You must be John Sutcliffe.' The beard, it transpired, belonged to a geologist called Chris, a good friend of another Yorkshire geologist mutual friend called Andrew, whom I worked with in Venezuela in the late 1980s. Andrew had followed the preparations for my Cape to Cape walk and told Chris 'to keep an eye open for me' in the summer. By one of life's strange coincidences, he had been in The Green Dragon when I had ordered my pint! We hatched a vague plan to meet up at the Tan Hill that evening.

From Hardraw, the Way climbed steadily over a splendid expanse of moorland, dotted with cairns and primitive coal shafts, to head towards Great Shunner Fell, 716 metres. This splendid vantage point, the haunt of curlews and skylarks, justifies the five-mile steady climb. Looking back, I could make out the recently climbed Pen-y-Ghent that Great Shunner pips by a measly 22 metres, although few would dispute that the former is the much finer mountain. I would have loved to dawdle but if I was going to meet up with Chris later on I had better get a move on.

The final part of the four-mile descent to the hamlet of Thwaite followed a walled track strewn with wobbly cobbles, some the size of a dales teapot, which made for slow and painful progress for a near-knackered walker with a big pack. Grateful not to have tripped up, a dangerous move with a heavy pack, I reached the hamlet of Thwaite in the early afternoon and made an impromptu stop at the Kearton Coffee House for a splendid mid-afternoon bacon and egg breakfast. The cafe is named after the naturalist and wildlife photographers, the Kearton brothers, who were born here in the 1870s.

The next section of the Pennine Way takes the walker through some of the grandest scenery in Yorkshire. The path first bears north-east, climbing up to the 400 metre contour, which then heads northwards along the steep bank of Kisdon Side through woodland and bracken. From the path you can take in the splendid views across the River Swale to the Crackpot Hall, a ruined hunting lodge that dates back to Norman times.

Yorkshire writers Ella Pontefract and Marie Hartley write of Crackpot in the 1930s with 'barefooted children, clambering like animals over the loose stone walls' and of a four-year-old child named Alice 'with the madness of the moors about her, marching along the rough lane followed by two white cats'.

They wrote then of the Hall's slipping foundations and how 'the bedroom floors tilt like the rolling deck of a ship'. The slippage continued and the hall slowly fell into ruins, but the Gunnerside estate that now owns it has more recently taken steps to conserve the remaining ruin, with help from the EU[4], bless them.

Large spoil heaps of mining waste extracted from the Beldi Hill and Swinner Gill lead mines covered the hill slopes next to Crackpot Hall. The rich veins of lead-bearing minerals found throughout Swaledale are part of the North Pennine Orefield that produced lead from Roman times through to the mid-Victorian era. As a young lad, I would often come here with my dad to explore Swaledale's old mining districts like the Gunnerside, Old Gang, and Surrender mines located on the south facing slopes of the dale. It sowed a seed that would ultimately lure me into a career as a geologist, taking me to distant lands, leaving behind my beloved Yorkshire Dales for the next 50 years. By the time I came back my dad was long dead.

It was time to get going, leave behind the green meadows and memories, and climb back on to the gritstone grouse moors and peat hags for the last challenging part of the day: the climb up to Tan Hill, Britain's highest pub. To get there, the Way first crosses the footbridge at Keld and follows a narrowing strip of former meadowland for about two miles until the moors finally close in after passing the last farmstead at Frith. By now, walkers from Hawes

---

4 But with the money apparently now spent the tilting continues, as judged during a recent visit of mine.

or Hardraw will feel their aching legs on the last two-mile drag over peaty moorland with its tantalising ever-receding horizon, until finally the distant speck of Tan Hill comes into view. When I first did this walk with Vanny from Ecuador in June 2007, she was down to her last ounce of energy, and when the inn failed to appear as promised on successive horizons, rebellion had threatened!

The Tan Hill Inn lies on the watershed between the Richmondshire district of North Yorkshire and the bordering counties of Durham and Cumbria. Four packhorse tracks converge on the building that dates back some 600 years, the inn prospering during the 17th and 18th centuries when coal mines operated almost directly under the pub. The poor-quality coal was used to power the steam engines of Swaledale's lead mines. The last coal mines closed in the 1930s and some of the inn's walls are adorned with splendid black and white photographs of mining in the early 19th century.

The pub has lots of character and keeps a fire burning all through the year: at an elevation of 528 metres, the fire is welcome on most days, even in summer. I had thought of camping here but Tracy, the landlady, offered me a bunk bed for £15 with access to a shower – an offer I couldn't refuse. I was already feeling cosy just looking at the fire. After a shower, I pulled off a loose toenail that had been troubling me, and then headed down to the bar. Here I met two other walkers, Dave and Nigel from over Manchester way. I joined them for supper and we had a companionable evening.

DAY 57: 25 June	Tan Hill to Middleton-in-Teesdale
Miles this day: **18**	Miles to date: **663**

Almost recovered from the late night, I headed off across Sleightholme Moor, struggling to keep pace with Dave and Nigel for about five minutes until I let them push on ahead. They were hoping to make their Middleton hotel in time to catch a key football game, and carrying next to nothing they were 'fast and light'.

The Way's routing across the moor to Sleightholme Farm follows the Frumming Beck, which meanders through mile after mile of mucky mire. It is poorly way-marked and care is needed to avoid a mishap. Even so, I found this wild waterlogged land of gills and gutters frequented by snipe and lapwing very appealing – a place not to rush, and to savour on your own.

A mile beyond the farm, the Way splits with a more easterly alternative taking in the historic village of Bowes. I had already decided in advance to follow the more direct route over the natural limestone arch of God's Bridge and then head across Cotherstone Moor to Blackton Reservoir, the site of yet another closed youth hostel. Another section of moorland took me

OPPOSITE: Crackpot Hall, Keld in Swaledale, a former medieval hunting lodge, photographed in 2017. The P.W. crosses the lower slopes of the fellside opposite, on the right. Day 56.

over Kelton Hill to Lunedale but I needed to push on over one last section of moorland over Crossthwaite Common before beginning the grassy descent down into Teesdale.

Middleton-in-Teesdale is one of my favourite Dales market towns. It used to belong to the historic North Riding of Yorkshire until civil servants re-organised the county boundaries in 1974, the changes appropriately taking effect on April Fool's Day of that year. The accents are, however, still solidly Yorkshire, with not a hint of distant Durham to which it now belongs.

The London Lead Company moved its headquarters to Middleton in the early 18th century, bringing a Quaker influence to bear on the town's architecture. They improved the town, adding public baths, a library, chapels, and a school. For their workers, they built solid traditional cottages, and, perhaps to ensure punctuality, a clock tower.

I headed up the market place to the Teesdale Hotel, a fine 18th century coaching inn where I had stayed with Vanny in June 2007. I was a bit disappointed to find that the splendid mural on the arched stagecoach passage leading to the old courtyard, had now been painted over.

I joined Dave and Nigel in the bar for a swift half before heading off just after 8 p.m. to look for a camping spot. It was a grand evening and I enjoyed the walk through the meadows alongside the River Tees. After a few miles, I found a good spot to camp near Park End Wood, at getting on for 10 p.m. I had found the day quite tiring and silently congratulated Vanny for her sterling effort of seven years earlier.

DAY 58: 26 June   Middleton-in-Teesdale to Dufton
Miles this day: **18**   Miles to date: **681**

I was up and away by 7.30 a.m. hoping to get a head start on the two lads who I knew would be delayed by their obligatory full English breakfast served on a crisp white tablecloth in the Teesdale's elegant dining room. I had the advantage because I knew that the masses of crunchy bacon, grilled field mushrooms and tomatoes, a pair of fried eggs, fried bread, and perhaps a splodge of black pudding wouldn't be served until about 8.30 a.m. – and then there would be several cups of wonderful black coffee to work through! But why should I feel miffed? I'd had my porridge with the curlews!

The day was overcast but the cloud base looked fairly high, crucial for the scenic delights in store for me later in the day. Above me on the fellside I spotted a line of disused quarries, my first sighting of the Whin Sill, a rock formation that is responsible for several striking geomorphological landmarks that I would pass later. Unusually for this part of world, this black rock has a volcanic origin and got here by forcing its way into the layering of the Carboniferous-age sedimentary rocks about 300 million years ago, forming a tabular layer, or sill, up to 70-metres thick that now overlooks the River Tees from the old Yorkshire side.

This section of the walk was quite special, with superb riverside meadows decked out with flowers that gradually gave way to woodland. Even better was in store, for soon the noise of the river was turned up to mid-volume as I approached Low Force, the first waterfall formed

Cronkley Scar, Upper Teesdale, Day 58.

where the Whin Sill interrupts the course of the river. This barely prepares the walker for the full volume thunderous roar of High Force, a mile and a half further on, where the full force of the Tees crashes over the sill in a smoking 70-foot plunge. Approaching with care, you can still make out the roughly hexagonal columnar jointing caused by cooling of the hot igneous rock, identical to that seen at Fingal's Cave on the Scottish island Staffa and the Giants Causeway on Northern Ireland's Antrim coast. But it was almost 10 a.m. and I needed to hurry on, for Manchester lads would be chasing me and I was keen to get up into the High Pennines.

Two miles further along, the river splits with the main tributary heading westwards. Just above, under Cronkley Scar, lies an inlier of older Palaeozoic rocks from which the 'lead' for the graphite core of pencils was once dug for processing in a small water-powered mill. The farm opposite is called Widdy Bank Farm, 'widdy' apparently being a local name for pencil.

The river is then squeezed into a narrow section with progress hindered by the awkward boulders of Whin Sill that shed off from Falcon Clints, requiring some care to negotiate with a pack. The scenery is superb and I was tempted to look upwards, when extra care was needed to avoid a twisted ankle. Around the next corner, the volume is suddenly turned back to full as Cauldron Snout comes into full view with a 180-metre-long cascading torrent that crashed over yet another outcrop of the Whin Sill. Thinking about it, I wonder if the Whin Sill is not the most 'scenic' rock formation in the whole of Britain!

Just above the waterfall, thankfully hidden from view is the two-mile-long Cow Green Reservoir that was completed in 1971 to regulate the flow of the Tees for water abstraction lower down. Despite fierce opposition from botanists, wildlife lovers, scientists and the outdoor

A tributary of the Tees crashes over an outcrop of the Whin Sill at Cauldron Snout, Teesdale, Day 58.

community, and with support from abroad, the construction went ahead. After flooding the valley, the surrounding area was subsequently declared a National Nature Reserve within the North Pennines AONB. As Wainwright pointed out at the time, 'Surely the beautiful Tees, of all northern rivers, was born to run free.' The developers wouldn't have got away with it today … or would they?

Slowly but surely the walker eventually out-walks the Tees as it narrows to a mere trickle above the inflow from Maize Beck. Even though the map warns walkers of what lies ahead, nothing adequately prepares you for the awesome sight of High Cup Nick as you stand on the cliff edge, looking to the west over an almost perfect U-shaped glacial valley. This huge amphitheatre of brilliant greens is rimmed by a line of black cliffs of the Whin Sill basalt. Far below, a meandering newly born stream dawdles its way westwards to eventually join the Eden, a reminder for the walker he has crossed the Pennine watershed.

When I came here seven years ago, a thick mist obliterated this splendid view and it was cold, miserable and potentially perilous. I was very grateful for today's near perfect visibility and, despite the lateness of the hour, I just had to sit down to take it all in. My dad always talked about bringing me here as a youngster but sadly we never made it.

I got down to Dufton just before 8 p.m., checking into the youth hostel overlooking the green. It is a pretty village with the houses now built with the distinctive red sandstone of the Permo-Triassic age, deposited when the present-day Vale of Eden area was a desert terrain, some 200 million years ago.

Glaciated 'U' valley, High Cup Nick, Day 58.

By the time I got over to The Stags Head, I was told they were no longer serving food, so I rushed back to the hostel, only to find they had also stopped serving. However, the manager amiably warmed up the set meal curry, which was really good. Afterwards I went back to The Stag for a couple of beers with Dave and Nigel. They were debating whether to head back to Manchester or carry on to Cross Fell.

DAY 59: 27 June   Dufton to Greg's Hut
Miles this day: **9**   Miles to date: **690**

After a good YHA breakfast, I said cheerio to Dave and Nigel. I had enjoyed their company for two or three days and hope they are still friends. I headed off, stopping after just a few steps to call in at an irresistible cafe right next door to the hostel for an unearned mid-morning coffee. Running out of further excuses I headed out of the village a short while later, following a lovely tree-lined wall path of ancient aspect that passes just to the west of Dufton Pike.

This distinctive conical-shaped hill is one of several prominent hills that are found along the western escarpment of the Northern Pennines. They are the oldest rocks I had seen so far on my walk along the Pennine Way. About 400 million years ago a series of massive volcanic eruptions, centred on the present day Lake District, threw out a kilometre-deep layer of volcanic ash and debris covering a large part of North West England. The volcanic ash

Cross Fell summit, with highest sheep in the Pennines helping to build new shelter, Day 59.

consolidated to form a greenish, finely banded rock known as tuff. The best examples of this rock formation is the Borrowdale Volcanic Group, found closer to the volcanic centre, which make prized ornamental stone that is exported from quarries far and wide. It must make it of one of the world's most widely dispersed volcanic rocks. But I digress, and must now get going on this multi-peak day!

Just after crossing Swindale Beck, the Way passes close to an area of shake holes, then follows a shallow man-made ravine called Knock Hush, a relict from the lead mining era. Hushes were made to prospect for concealed mineral veins, by releasing dammed water down a hillside to expose the rocks below, and hopefully reveal hidden mineral wealth.

Knock Fell provides an 800-metre-high warm up for the day, but the sense of remoteness is suddenly shattered by a section of tarmac and a bristling array of antennae that decorate the summit of Great Dun Fell. Some might justly feel outrage at this blasphemy, but I will never forget a day, seven years earlier, struggling in thick mist without a GPS, trying to find this wretched summit, and remember the feeling of sheer joy when the tops of these man-made trees appeared out of the mist like a Christmas tree miracle.

The next summit of the day, Little Dun Fell, 842 metres, is half a mile further along the ridge. This is followed by the final summit of the day, Cross Fell, 890 metres, the highest point in the Pennines. Here I observed the highest sheep in the Pennines working on the summit's new stone cross-shelter. When completed it will provide a welcome refuge on a wild day when the Pennines turn ugly.

Vanessa by the old Cairn on Cross Fell Summit in 2007 before getting lost in the mist, Day 59 of this walk.

It was on this featureless summit, seven years earlier, that I had an unforgettable day on the hills with my friend Vanny from Ecuador. The morning had got off to a bad start at the B&B, a mile or so out of Dufton. I was replying to a barrage of work emails over several coffees when the owner burst through the door of the detached chalet to clean up.

'Goodness, what are you doing still here at this hour?' she admonished. 'Most people heading over to Garrigill are chomping at the bit to get off at 7 a.m., and here you are still, gone 10.30 a.m.! And anyway this is no fit day to be heading up to Cross Fell!' she said, waving towards the fell. We packed up in a hurry and were on our way by about 11 a.m. The fell was covered in low cloud from about the 300 metre contour but I wasn't unduly worried as we expected to be following a well-trodden path. Anyway, with an itinerary of pre-booked B&Bs, there wasn't a great deal we could do about it – we just had to go.

After a long slog up the fell my phone rang just as we reached the Cross Fell summit at about 5.00 p.m. It was my middle daughter Amanda, worried because she had just received a jumbled phone call from the lady at the next B&B over in Garrigill. This morning's landlady had called her friend in Garrigill, saying she doubted we would ever make it because of the foul weather and our very late start. The Garrigill lady then phoned Amanda, who had made the B&B reservation, scaring the living daylights out of her saying we were lost on the moors in bad weather, and leaving Amanda wondering if she should contact the mountain rescue. I reassured her saying we were quite safe and on target to arrive at the Garrigill B&B in the early evening.

After a quick photograph we looked around for the path leading off from the summit but found lots of random sheep tracks heading off in all directions, but going nowhere. Of course, my map and compass would point us in the right direction but I wanted to get on to the actual path to keep us out of the bogs and ankle-grabbing heather to save time and effort. With the mist getting thicker we started circling around the boulder-strewn plateau looking for the path. Turning round to shout something I discovered that Vanny was no longer behind me. I called out to her but my shouts were drowned by the howling wind. Vanessa had no previous mountain experience and could not be left on her own in this weather on top of the Pennines. With panic setting in, I expanded my search area but she was nowhere to be seen. After walking around in circles in the mist I was getting disorientated and for a while unable to relocate the summit cairn. Imagining an unfolding disaster I eventually caught a faint plaintive shout in a lull of the wind and moving towards it Vanessa stumbled into view, frightened and very upset. We met up with the biggest of hugs. I often think back to the various scenarios that might have unfolded had we not been so lucky. Two whistles and two emergency bivvy bags, weighing and costing next to nothing, will keep you out of harms way in a situation like this when thick mountain mist suddenly envelopes you, but foolishly we carried neither. I remember we got to Garrigill by a complete fluke at one minute past our 7 p.m. ETA.

Seven years later on this beautiful afternoon I easily found the track leading off the summit and left the solitary sheep busy bricklaying as I headed down towards Garrigill. After about 300 metres of vertical descent the track passes in front of Greg's Hut, a former miners' hut that is now a bothy, looked after by the volunteer-run Mountain Bothies Association, or MBA.

Bothies are left open and free for anyone to use. Most are equipped with a wooden sleeping platform so you need a sleeping bag and mat as well as a stove and cooking stuff; in fact, all the backpackers' usual gear apart from the tent. Most bothies have a fireplace but finding wood within a reasonable radius of the bothy is usually a challenge. However, in this treeless terrain, a supply of coal had been thoughtfully provided by the MBA. I didn't need to overnight here but I found the prospect too tempting and made myself comfortable. After lighting the fire, I turned on my ancient tinny radio, recovered from the 'sent home items.' It worked remarkably well up there on top of the Pennines.

According to literature left in the hut, Greg, or John Gregory, after whom the hut had been named, had died in a climbing accident in 1968 whilst attempting a high-level climbing route from Saas-Fee in Switzerland to Argentière, at the head of the Chamonix Valley. His climbing mate had held him on a rope all night but he died before the rescue helicopter arrived the next morning.

I lit the fire, but felt a bit sombre after reading about the tragic Saas-Fee accident, then recalling my own 'lost Vanny' incident here on Cross Fell, and then later losing her for good in Ecuador. Despite having just passed the equinox, I found the hut got cold very quickly when the fire died down and slept in my thermal jacket inside the sleeping bag. Lost on the hills with just summer clothing in bad weather you would really struggle.

Greg's Hut, a bothy on Cross Fell, Day 59.

Leaving Greg's Hut on Cross Fell, Day 60.

DAY 60: 28 June   Greg's Hut to Slaggyford
Miles this day: **15**   Miles to date: **706**

Up at 5.30 a.m., I spent a couple of hours cleaning the bothy and burying a vast accumulation of other people's ashes. After a couscous breakfast, I headed off into the cold mountain mist. I wasn't worried about visibility today as the way followed the old mine track from Greg's Hut all the way down to Garrigill.

The mine workings extend over a distance of about two miles, starting just below the hut. The mine track had been dressed using old mine waste and for several miles you walk over a mineral collection that includes specimens of the zinc ore, sphalerite and galena, the shiny lead ore and, best of all, lots of purple cubic fluorspar. I noticed the track had been well picked over since I walked down here in 2007.

Arriving at Garrigill just before midday I was sorry to see that the George and Dragon Inn had closed, thwarting my lunch plan. I picked up some odds and ends at the tiny village store, washing down a few Jaffa cakes with a hastily made, lukewarm cup of tea from the storeowner. I then dug out a bag of rubbish, mostly other people's tin cans, that I had brought down from Greg's Hut. The tea man took the bag and hurled it into a corner of the shop with great vigour, shouting 'Greg's Hut!' in a quite extraordinary display of either temper or humour.

Just after noon I set off down the lovely South Tyne valley, meeting a three-generation family from Newcastle, somewhere before Alston. They were having an old-fashioned weekend picnic with pop and sandwiches – not something you see much of these days. I stopped

and chatted for a few minutes, and later on sent them an update on the progress of the walk that they much appreciated.

After a quick lunch at The Angel in Alston, I stocked up with supplies at Spar and after faffing around re-organising my kit, headed off shortly after 5 p.m., just as it was starting to spit with rain. I'd had a grand day and had the lovely walk in the Tyne Valley to look forward to later in the evening; a spot of summer rain wasn't going to worry me.

Tunnel vision near Slaggyford on the Pennine Way. Day 60.

At Alston, the Way leaves the river to climb up the western slopes of the South Tyne Valley and on to the little-known Whitley Castle, the modern name for the Roman fort called *Epiacum* built early in the second century, presumably to safeguard the Roman lead mines in the area. The fort comprises an impressive rectangular array of about six concentric banks and ditches and, apparently, has never been excavated.

I found a suitable spot to camp in on the wooded banks of the River South Tyne, a mile before the small village of Slaggyford. The Tyne is a good salmon river and I sat outside the tent hoping to catch a glimpse of an otter until the midges got the better of me.

DAY 61: 29 June   Slaggyford to Greenhead
Miles this day: **11**   Miles to date: **717**

Just beyond the farmstead at Burnstones, the Way climbs up on to the moors and for the next three miles follows the Maiden Way, a Roman road linking *Epiacum* with Hadrian's Wall. It's very easy to lose yourself in time, walking along this ancient thoroughfare. I thought I spotted remnants of ancient cobbles embedded in the turf, perhaps dating from Roman times. From here I caught the first hazy outline of the distant hills of the Scottish Borders. They looked an awfully long way off.

Leaving the Pennines behind me, I then crossed the Tyne Gap and hurried towards the pretty hamlet of Greenhead, located just to the south of Hadrian's Wall. Greenhead's former youth hostel is now a splendid bunk barn owned and run by the Greenhead Hotel, an excellent family-run hostelry.

After a superb meal I dropped off to sleep thinking about the Romans I would encounter on Hadrian's Wall in the morning.

DAY 62: 30 June   Greenhead to Milecastle 39
Miles this day: **8**   Miles to date: **725**

Hadrian's Wall is the greatest and most impressive monument from Roman Britain and, I'm told, the largest structure in the entire Roman world. It marked the northern limit of the Roman Empire, separating the civilised Roman world from the barbarian northlands.

Getting underway, the Pennine Way meets Hadrian's Wall at the attractive hamlet of Holmehead and then runs eastwards, closely following the Wall. The next eight-mile section, running through an AONB, was the scenic highpoint of the entire walk. Here the Wall is built along an outcrop of the same Whin Sill that shaped the landmarks at High Cup Nick, Caldron Snout and High Force, which I had passed four days earlier.

I had forgotten just how much up-and-down legwork is involved following this undulating ridge. Heading downhill, I overtook two young Canadian women who were carefully picking their way on a steep rocky descent. They then overtook me on the next uphill section, my heavy pack now giving them a clear advantage. In this way we leap-frogged along together for the next few miles.

Later that afternoon I stopped off at a farm to ask for water for the night's camp. Two chaps wearing blooded plastic aprons were skinning a calf, strung up by its hind legs. They told me they were going to tie this skin on to another calf that had lost its mother, to help with the 'adoption' process. It seemed a bloody awful way to adopt someone.

In the early evening I talked to an American man with two children who was revisiting Britain after a long absence. Britain, he said, had changed a lot since he was last here, with the bobbies now carrying guns. He opened the conversation, having spotted my green Appalachian Trail neckband that I had bought after I walked a very short section of the 2,200 mile-long trail near Harper's Crossing in Pennsylvania a few years earlier. I told him that I had thought of attempting the full walk but had been put off by tales of the dense view-blocking forests and the hungry bears that over the years have gotten a lot smarter, so that hanging food up in a tree no longer deters them from their free lunch.

The evening was advancing and just about everyone had headed home, apart from a few patrolling curlews and two lads who were out for an evening climb on Windshields Crag. It was a lovely summer evening and I sat down on a grassy bank for a while to watch them climb.

I set up camp at Milecastle 39 on Steel Rigg, one of the 80 fortlets that the Romans built along the 72-mile-long wall. Each milecastle was manned by 20 to 30 non-citizen soldiers drawn mostly from Continental Europe as it was Roman policy not to recruit locals to defend their own territory. With the sun setting over the Solway, I pitched the tent under the watchful eye of a centurion soldier heavily disguised in sheep's clothing and then proceeded

to prepare my evening meal to round off a truly fantastic day.

Bedding down in my sleeping bag, I wondered what life would have been like for the 20 or so auxiliaries who, 18 centuries ago, would have guarded this milecastle. Men who had perhaps joined the Roman army as young trainee recruits from the conquered lands of Gaul and the Mediterranean had once slept where I would soon be sleeping. On a summer's night like this one, it might

Sheep's nest on Hadrian's Wall.
Day 62.

Milecastle 40 on Hadrian's Wall near Crag Lough tarn. Day 62.

A Roman guard in sheep's clothing watches over me at Milecastle 39, Hadrian's Wall, Day 63.

not have been too bad but what about during the bitter northern winters? I saw the night watch warming themselves on the glowing brazier, telling tales of bloody skirmishes and fallen comrades and remembering the taste of seafood and the handsome Thracian girls with long black hair – anything to take their minds off the fierce *Brittunculi* fighting men who still roamed in these woods. They threw more logs on to the brazier, sending dancing cascades of orange sparks high into the night sky, as they peered out over the moonlit clearing to the north of the wall, waiting for the first faint glow in the east that would signal the end of their long watch …

DAY 63: 1 July	Milecastle 39 to Bellingham
Miles this day: **15**	Miles to date: **740**

The reason for my early 5.30 a.m. start was to make a surprise dawn raid on Housesteads Fort before the first contingent of the Housesteads Heritage Guard would arrive. Before leaving the milecastle, I tucked a pound coin into the milecastle's wall by the north-east corner to appease the gods and thank them for their protection, hoping they would not be too scornful of my enfeebled British pound.

A few minutes after leaving the protection of Milecastle 39, I stopped to photograph the tree that grows alone in the Sycamore Gap. This was featured in *Robin Hood, Prince of Thieves* and won the Tree of the Year Award in 2016 after saving an urchin that was being pursued by a hoard of nasty Normans.

Hurrying along the Wall, I entered the Housesteads through the fort's unguarded and easy scalable north gate, just like the *Brittunculi* might have done in the waning days of the Roman Empire. It was lovely to have the entire fort to myself, but for prudence I kept the visit to a short one, to avoid capture and perhaps a painful crucifixion, pinned to the Wall.

I left the fort and crossed over into the barbarian lands, heading north-west for a few hundred yards before rejoining the Pennine Way on Ridley Common. Here the Pennine Way leaves the splendour of Hadrian's Wall and heads across moorland before disappearing into lifeless pine forest to emerge later at Warks Burn, the name promising the approaches to Scotland.

Just after this, I passed Horneystead Farm where the farmer's family had left a selection of biscuits, soft drinks, tea and other items, with an honesty box that I topped up with a £5 note for a welcome snack and a coke. From the visitors book I noticed another walker had recently passed through, also heading to the top of Scotland.

Shitlington Hall, which is next approached, was previously called Shotlyngton and mystery surrounds the name change. This is followed by a lovely expanse of moorland heather on Ealingham Rigg, after which Bellingham, pronounced 'Bellinjam', comes into view – a welcome sight for the weary walker from the wall country. The town sits next to the South Tyne River, famous for its sea trout runs and the otters that feast on them. I looked half-heartedly for

Robin Hood's famous tree at Sycamore Gap, Day 63.

Under-floor heating (for some) at Housesteads Roman fort on the wall, Day 63.

a place to camp but then went on to explore the town. There would be no more supply points until I got to the Kirk Yetholm – still some 40 miles away. I was getting a bit low on supplies, and I decided to overnight there in a very comfortable bunk barn and shop in the morning.

Once organised, I headed to the Cheviot Hotel for a splendid feast starting with a game terrine and followed by a cooked-to-order roast topside and a junkety dessert. I talked to several young army lads from the nearby Otterburn camp, enjoying the apparently unlimited supplies of draught Peroni. They told me umpteen times that they preferred Northumberland to serving in Afghanistan!

DAY 64: 2 July	Bellingham to Byrness
Miles this day: **15**	Miles to date: **755**

Before leaving, I paid a visit to the museum based in the old railway station, one of the nicest small-town museums I have come across in recent years. I learned that the town once boasted a lovely rural railway that ran from Riccarton junction on the Waverly line down to Hexham until the axe fell in 1958, and another possible World Heritage line was ripped up.

Stocked up with fuel and provisions and well breakfasted at the Rocky Road cafe, I headed up on to the moors at mid-morning. The Way passes some old coal mine workings and a derelict farm before climbing up to Whitley Pike, 356 metres.

Further on, I met a deaf walker heading south, who was able to read my lips providing I looked straight to him and spoke clearly and slowly. He would have been about 30 years old and this was his first attempt at backpacking, and I felt humbled by his efforts. He somehow explained he was getting a lot of pain in his shoulders and, remembering the start of my own walk, I gladly passed on the advice that I was given by the young lady at Porthtowan some two months earlier. I helped him adjust his straps and waist belt to get some of the weight of the pack on to his hips. We struck up an immediate long-distance walkers' friendship and vigorously shook hands before heading off in opposite directions. He was the only person I saw that day on the hills.

Just beyond Brownrigg Head, the Way enters the eastern side of the Kielder Forest, the largest man-made woodland in Europe that surrounds the UK's largest artificial reservoir. From my earlier cycling experiences, I'd say it is also home to Europe's largest midge colony.

Arriving at Byrness, which has the aspect of a Canadian logging camp, I discovered that the former youth hostel is now a comfortable and privately owned bunkhouse called the Forest View Inn. For those who might follow, the hostel is located in the middle of the small village and is not very well signposted.

OPPOSITE: The Scottish Border at Clennell Street, on top of the Cheviots on Day 65.

DAY 65: 3 July   Byrness to Cheviots
Miles this day: **14**   Miles to date: **769**

I set off in lovely sunshine, heartily prepared for the climb up on to the Cheviots after my last splendid full English breakfast. The climb up out of the valley first led me up a steep, rocky and recently logged escarpment, before I emerged on to open moorland at the summit of Byrness Hill, 414 metres. This was the start of a splendid three-mile ridge walk over Houx Hill, Ravens Knowe and Ogre Hill, names that fire the imagination.

It was getting hot and I was starting to run short of water. This was remote uninhabited countryside and, following a watershed, lacked surface water – something that should have been readily apparent on the map but which I had carelessly overlooked. Fortunately the Pennine Way leaves the watershed temporarily to take in the large Roman camp at Chew Green where I was able to fill my water bottles from the peaty headwaters of the River Coquet, once, no doubt, the Roman soldiers' watering hole. The Coquet was my last English river of the walk, and one I was very grateful for.

Archaeologists have struggled to unravel the history of this complex site, which includes a large trapezium-shaped Roman fort, two Roman fortlets and two overlapping Roman camps, all apparently built in different periods. To crown the confusion, the site was then partly overlain by a medieval village. The Roman Dere Street, that runs from York to the Antonine Wall, passes close to the camp supporting the idea that this was a marching camp rather than a permanent settlement. This makes sense, for there is no other earthly reason why one would want to build a camp here.

For the next nine miles, the Way closely tracks the Scottish border, which appears to follow a wire fence designed to keep the sheep either in or out of Scotland. This is still the subject of a debate that the sheep will eventually settle by a referendum, if this is allowed by the Head Sheep of both countries. All the sheep are really interested in are mutual cross-border grazing and cross-fertilisation rights.

In times of poor visibility the fence would have been welcomed to guide the early Pennine Way walker across this featureless peaty terrain, but on an evening like this with splendid views over the Scottish Borders it is an entirely different matter; I was on top of the Cheviots with my feet in two countries, and savouring every mile. The wind steadily strengthened during the afternoon, reaching near gale force by the time I took up the challenge of pitching the tent on a grassy patch on the medieval Clennell Street later in the evening. First I secured the tent by anchoring the rear guy line to the rucksack, but once erected, the geodesic design of the Soulo drives the tent into the ground, making it stay put even without the guys. This was very reassuring on such an evening such as this with the wind howling; yet the moors still bathed in bright sunshine.

DAY 66: 4 July	Cheviots to Kirk Yetholm
Miles this day: **11**	Miles to date: **780**

The wind had eased somewhat during the night but then it got up again in the early hours, this time laced with stinging rain, making for a cold, horrid start for my last day on the Pennine Way. I was off early, stopping mid-morning briefly to escape the elements at the Auchope Refuge Hut. I was, however, just putting off the inevitable and I soon left to battle with the elements. From the hut the Way heads unnecessarily up a series of annoying little hills, the last of which is the 601-metre Schil.

Another rerouting of the final part of the Pennine Way is definitely called for: leave the Way at Red Cribs, near a second mountain refuge at NT 877 201, and then follow a bridle path down the lovely College Valley past the Mounthooly Bunkhouse. From here, one could then follow a bridleway down College Burn to Hethpool Mill, now converted to holiday accommodation. Once there, St Cuthbert's Way will then take you to Kirk Yetholme.

Anyway, I didn't do that and instead stuck to the accepted Pennine Way down to the Border Hotel at Kirk Yetholm to take my reward of the finisher's free pint, courtesy of Alfred Wainwright, the first guidebook writer. The dinner menu looked great but I was told all tables were fully booked, which was a disappointment; tonight, above all, called for a celebration. A young lady waiting at the bar overheard this and invited me to join her group for dinner, providing I didn't mind sitting with five ladies. What a thought! I gladly accepted and then set off to look for a bed for the night and found space at the youth hostel. After a quick shower, I smartened myself up as best a man carrying no spare clothes, other than a change of underpants and socks, can do. The ladies were all from Newcastle, colleagues working in the public health sector, and it was a jolly evening. I munched through a steak pie, sharing a bottle or two of celebratory wine with the girls, and rounding off the evening with several Black Bottle[5] whiskies.

The Pennine Way had been on my to-do list since it was officially opened in 1965, but then the years slipped by with the complications of overseas work and five children until, nearing retirement, the crackpot idea of walking the length of Britain had begun to take shape. It wasn't the highlight of the entire walk, that was still to come, but it was a grand experience, passing through some of the magical country where I spent my early years. Having followed in the footsteps of the thousands who had gone before – when the southern section was a legendary quagmire – I take my hat off to those first intrepid Pennine Way walkers. ●

---

5 A blended Scotch whisky with a peaty Islay taste.

… and into Scotland. The Border Hotel at Kirk Yetholm, at the end of the Pennine Way, Day 66.

End-of-the-Pennine-Way celebration at The Border Hotel, Day 66.

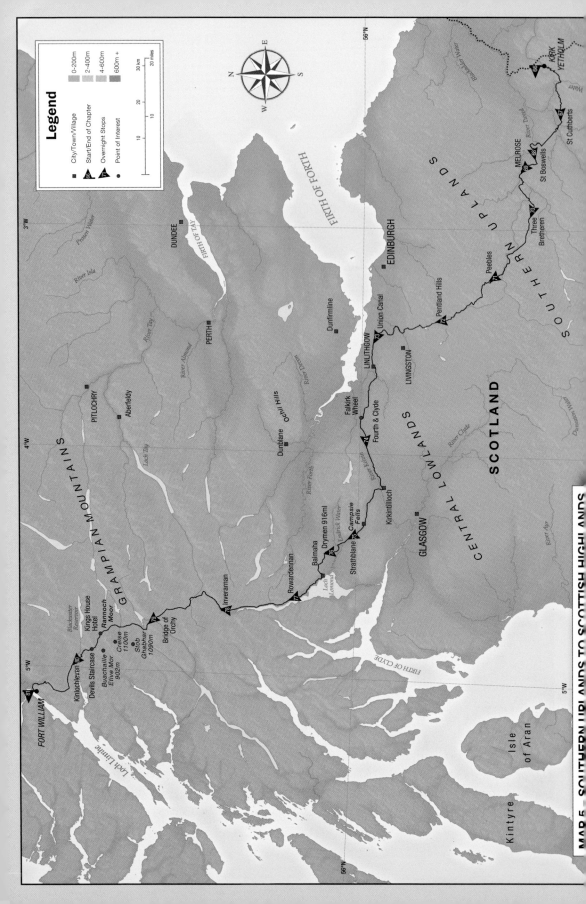

Legend

0-200m
2-400m
4-600m
600m +

City/Town/Village
Start/End of Chapter
Overnight Stops
Point of Interest

30 km
20 miles

56°N

FIRTH OF FORTH

3°W

DUNDEE

River Isla

River Tay

Preen Water

River Almond

PERTH

PITLOCHRY

Aberfeldy

Loch Tay

River Tay

Ochil Hills

Dunblane

River Forth

River Devon

Dunfermline

EDINBURGH

Pentland Hills

LINLITHGOW

Union Canal

Falkirk Wheel

Fourth & Clyde

River Kelvin

LIVINGSTON

LIVINGSTON

SOUTHERN

UPLANDS

KIRK
YETHOLM

St Cuthberts

River Tweed

MELROSE

St Boswells

Three
Bretheren

Peebles

SCOTLAND

Blackshiel Water

Dunnan Water

4°W

GRAMPIAN MOUNTAINS

Blackwater Reservoir

Kings House Hotel

Rannoch Moor

Creise 1100m

Stob Ghabhar 1090m

Buachaille Etive Mor 902m

Kinlochleven

Devils Staircase

FORT WILLIAM

Loch Linnhe

Bridge of Orchy

Inveraman

Rowardennan

Balmaha

Drymen 916ml

Campsie Fells

Strathblane

Endrick Water

Loch Lomond

Kirkintilloch

GLASGOW

CENTRAL LOWLANDS

River Clyde

River Ayr

FIRTH OF CLYDE

5°W

5°W

Isle
of Aran

Kintyre

56°N

MAP 5 - SOUTHERN UPLANDS TO SCOTTISH HIGHLANDS

8

SOUTHERN SCOTLAND

*From Kirk Yetholm on the Scottish Borders I follow St Cuthbert's Way to Melrose
and Peebles on the River Tweed, and then head over the Pentland Hills into
the industrial heartland of Scotland that I cross on the towpaths of the Union Canal
and Forth and Clyde canals to Kirkintilloch. The John Muir Way then takes me
on to Strathblane ready to join the West Highland Way.*

DAY 67: 5 July   Kirk Yetholm to Blindswell Plantation
Miles this day: **13**   Miles to date: **793**

Before heading off, I returned to the Border Hotel for a splendid full Scottish breakfast,
complete with black pudding (blood sausage), and over a coffee I perused some of the
books in the lounge. Opening Wainwright's book *On the Pennine Way* at the Hadrian's
Wall section, he wrote 'The Roman Wall is an obvious climax to a walk along the Pennines,

Waist-deep in breakfast cereal, on St Cuthbert's Way, Day 67.

being situated at the end of the range, and Housesteads would provide a grand finale, the supreme moment of achievement and an objective far worthier of attainment than the village green at Kirk Yetholm. From here on the Pennine Way is a misnomer.' I could not agree more.

Just as I left the hotel late in the morning it started to rain. My head felt like it had been whacked by a Black Bottle, adding to the misery of the morning. For the first half mile, I trudged across wet water meadows but then as I started to climb up on to Crookedshaws Hill on the St Cuthbert's Way I began to realise that this lowland section of the walk was full of surprises.

First I spotted a deer, or rather the head and ears of one just sticking up above the corn. The weather improved steadily and then the sun came out, prompting me to stop at the Temple Hall Inn at Morebattle for a thirst-quenching cider and to fill my water bottles. I passed the nearby Cessford Castle, once the stronghold of the Kerr family. This stocky tower stands forlornly abandoned but serves as a reminder that the Border Reivers once ruled this landscape.

I was enjoying the evening sun and, as atonement for my late start, I kept going until late in the day, taking pleasure in the gentle countryside – a very different landscape from the high moors of recent weeks, but surprisingly kind on the eyes and legs. An hour later I came to a beautiful narrow strip of mixed woodland that looked out over a field of wild flowers touched with gold. The sun was sinking rapidly and I dropped my pack to enjoy the last few minutes of sunset before putting up the tent on a thick carpet of moss beneath an oak tree. A campsite did not get any better than this, I thought.

Campsite on St Cuthbert's Way on Day 67.

DAY 68: 6 July   Blindswell Plantation to St Boswells
Miles this day: **13**   Miles to date: **806**

I slept like a log, awakening to the sound of birds in lovely sunshine and the barky smell of damp woodland. I was keen to get going and after packing up and leaving no mark on this special campsite, I continued along the path, passing through more delightful strips of ancient woodland. St Cuthbert's Way was a lovely surprise for me, weaving through the countryside on a network of ancient footpaths. Two miles further on, the Way joins the Roman Dere Street, last met on top of the Cheviots. After crossing the River Teviot on a suspension bridge, the Way wiggles around Monteviot House before continuing straight as a Roman die, directly towards Melrose.

Approaching Melrose, the Way passes a grave-marker from the 1544 battle of Ancrum Moor, fought during Henry VIII's 'Rough Wooing' campaign. Henry tried to secure an alliance with Scotland, by proposing the marriage of his infant son Edward to the infant Mary Queen of Scots. The Scots would have none of it. Henry's response to this affront was to declare war on Scotland, laying waste to much of the Borders, and torching Edinburgh in 1544. The worst atrocity was committed by Sir Ralph Eure in 1545, when he burnt Brumehouse Tower with the mistress of the house and all her ladies locked up inside. Eventually, the Scots assembled a well-trained force to put a stop to these atrocities, resoundingly defeating the English army of 5,000 men at Ancrum Moor, scattering the survivors into the surrounding hostile countryside.

Coppiced trees on St Cuthbert's Way, Day 68.

Eildon Hills approaching Melrose on Day 68.

A plaque to Maiden Lilliard, Day 68.

The grave bears this inscription dedicated to the memory of Mistress Lilliard who was traditionally believed to have fought at the battle after the death of her lover at the hands of the English:

> 'Fair maiden Lilliard
> lies under this stane
> little was her stature
> but muckle was her fame;
> upon the English loons she laid monie thumps
> and when her legs were cuttit off
> she fought them on her stumps.'

The glorious River Tweed, Day 68.

A kindly gesture from the landlord of The Buccleuch Arms, Saint Boswells, Day 68.

At 7.00 p.m. I got my first view of the River Tweed that once powered a succession of Tweed mills built along its banks. It is one of my favourite British rivers, flowing timelessly through this tranquil land of abbeys, watched over by the Southern Uplands. Back in Peru, I had planned my route to keep it company for a few special miles.

As I approached Melrose I kept an eye open for campsites, but the footpath now ran through populated country with no hidden dell, and I was getting a bit hungry. Walking through the small riverside town of St Boswells, where the Tweed takes a sweeping meander around Dryburgh Abbey, I passed the Buccleuch Arms. Straying inside this very traditional Scottish 'town hotel', built of red sandstone, I took just a few seconds to decide on a meal stop.

The hotel staff was incredibly friendly. Over a beer in the bar, I ordered fried calamari and an Angus braised steak, one of the best meals on the whole trip and a splendid, if rather late, Sunday lunch. I fancied staying the night but the rooms were quite expensive. Then the manager, Nicu, who had listened with interest to the story of my walk, made me a very kind offer: he said I could put my tent in the hotel's garden, and he'd leave a side door to the hotel unlocked so I could use the 'facilities', adding that I was invited to a complimentary breakfast in the morning. With the campsite settled, I relaxed, enjoying the rare treat.

DAY 69: 7 July   St Boswells to Melrose
Miles this day: **6**   Miles to date: **812**

After a splendid Scottish borders breakfast I headed back to the River Tweed. Dryburgh Abbey, another casualty of the rough wooing, had been destroyed by Henry's troops in 1544. I regretted not having the time to cross on the suspension footbridge to look around, but Melrose and the Highlands beckoned.

A sad morning at Melrose Abbey, which bore the wrath of Henry VIII's 'rough wooing'. Day 70.

After a short stretch of riverbank, St Cuthbert's Way turns to head south-west away from the river, following an insignificant burn to climb up the triple-peaked Eildon Hills that overlook Melrose. This intentional detour was designed to take the walker up to a splendid vantage point. A cloudburst turned the path into a slippery challenge just as I started the climb, but the view was well worth it.

I wanted to look around the abbey but decided to first look for a B&B and leave the abbey until the morning. This turned out to be a mistake. The town was quite dead but I had a nice meal in the Burts Hotel.

DAY 70: 8 July   Melrose to Three Brethren
Miles this day: **11**   Miles to date: **824**

The weather had deteriorated overnight, and by morning it was cold and wet as I made my way to the Melrose Abbey for what was to be my third visit. The first time I came to look on these ruins, some 15 years earlier, was during a Scottish Borders cycle trip up from Yorkshire. I had just reread H.V. Morton's *In Search of Scotland*, written in 1929, describing his first tour of Scotland in an aging motorcar, and was keen to visit the Borders.

He wrote, 'So these abbeys, Kelso, Jedburgh, Dryburgh and Melrose, as close together as the abbeys in Yorkshire, preached the gospel of love in a land of hate. They were situated gallantly in the front line like four padres, helpless to stem the tide of war, nevertheless a comfort to friend and foe. When you see them one after another in a day, as I did, you appreciate the horror that must have swept through the lowlands when men ran panting with the news: "Melrose is burning! Jedburgh's afire! Kelso's no more!" It must have seemed the ultimate blasphemy even to a land brought up on curses.'

Three Brethren cairns on the Southern Upland Way, which marked the joining of three great estates, Day 70.

Ayee, a wee drap on the Southern Upland Way, Day 70.

Perhaps revisiting the abbey was a mistake, for the dismal morning drew out the sorrow that lingered in the cracks and crannies of the 800-year-old sandstone ruin, and recalling Morton's words almost brought me to tears.

After stocking up on supplies I left the town at midday, continuing along the Southern Upland Way on the riverbank. A couple of miles further on I stopped just above the old railway bridge to eat a sandwich in the rain, surrounded by annoying midges. Just behind me three anglers were also taking a break, one having just landed a 4lb sea trout. The Tweed ranks as one of the world's most revered salmon rivers, and watching fish rising to the fly helped raise my spirits.

The Way leaves the Tweed to skirt around the base of Gala Hill before rejoining the river briefly at Yair Bridge. From here it heads up through superb woodlands where I filled my water bottles for the night's camp from a crystal-clear stream that drains Muckle Crib[1]. Shortly afterwards, the Way leaves the woods and goes into beautiful open moorland to follow an old drove road past the Three Brethren, a trio of 10-foot-high cairns said to date from the 16th century.

Surrounded by these magnificent moors I was once again feeling back on top of the world, and about 7.30 p.m. I stopped and put up the tent next to the grassy track. For two days now I had done poor mileage and was beginning to wonder if I would make it to Fort William in time for a train back to Yorkshire for Mum's 100th birthday on 22 July. It would be a close call but with the abbeys behind me, I could now put my foot down.

DAY 71: 9 July   **Three Brethren to Peebles**
Miles this day: **16**   Miles to date: **839**

I awoke to brilliant sunshine, thinking that it doesn't get any better than this; if this was a sampler for the Southern Upland Way, then it was a walk I should think seriously about for the future. Setting off towards Hare Law, I could have sworn I saw one, which would have made it the only hare I saw on the entire walk. Walking in the Yorkshire Dales as a lad I would be unlucky not to see at least half a dozen on a good hare day.

The Way follows the old drove road along an undulating east-west ridge of rounded hills, the bright green ferns contrasting with the purple heather and the dark patches of spruce. Geologically, the Southern Uplands are composed of Silurian-age deep-water sediments, pushed up from the seabed about 400 million years ago. These rocks weather evenly to produce fertile rounded hills that are easy on the eye and on the backpacker's legs. Best of all, these lovely hills seem to be off the radar screens of most walkers and I only saw two along the Southern Upland Way.

Taking a breather I was surprised to be overtaken by a lone young lady carrying a fair-sized pack. We struck up a conversation and walked together for a while. Emily was also walking from Cornwall to the top of Scotland, mostly camping but not in the wilds on her own. She looked

1 NT 442 317.

Hare Law, Southern Upland Way, Day 70.

very fit, ran marathons, and played and taught music. She was changing jobs and her new employer had agreed to a late starting date to allow her to complete her end-to-end walk.

Walking along, we noticed a chap approaching us from the south, from the general direction of Yarrowford, to intercept us near Brown Knowe hill. He wore a floppy felt hat that had become a mobile home to an orbiting swarm of horse flies. It resembled a slick Brian Cox demonstration of a well-populated planetary system, or at the subatomic end of the scale, a diffuse cloud of whirling electrons held in orbit by some fiendish force emanating from beneath the floppy hat, perhaps a brain wave! He began his conversation whilst well out of earshot, and after closing in we were obliged to listen to a potted discourse on Scottish history in which the English got repeatedly thrashed. I stepped back to escape the horse flies' orbits but he wasn't having it, and kept stepping forward bringing my nose back into range. Having disgorged the potted saga of Scotland, the felt-hatted man wandered off, thankfully taking the Airborne Border Regiment of Horsefly with him as he carried on yattering until his voice was lost in wind.

After a brief stop at Minchmoor bothy[2] to fix my painful feet, we continued to Traquair, said to be Scotland's oldest inhabited house. The ticket lady wanted us to pay the entrance fee for the house and was incredulous, even offended, when we said we just wanted to visit the tearoom and weren't going to visit the house. After a welcome sit down and an afternoon tea, we parted company – Emily went to a campsite at Innerleithen while I continued to Peebles.

2 Thought to have since been pulled down.

I opted for the easy route to Peebles following the quiet B7062, but later regretted not having taken the longer high-level route following the Cross Borders Drove Road over Kirkhope Law.

Peebles was an important wool town until the mills closed in the 1960s but the town has retained a pleasant aspect, with none of the usual post-industrial mill-town malaise. The main road was very quiet for a mid-summer evening and I wondered if I might have left it a bit late to find an open restaurant. I really fancied a good feed and, persisting, came across Franco's Italian restaurant that overlooks the Tweed by the town's magnificent medieval bridge – Peebles' feeble answer to the Florentine Ponte Vecchio.

Eyebrows rose slightly when this strange weather-beaten man trundled into the smart restaurant hugging a ginormous rucksack, but after the initial shock, I was made most welcome by the staff. It was to be one of the very special meals of the whole walk – a seafood salad starter followed by pez espada (swordfish) with lashings of garlic and a glass of wine, or was it two, rounded off with a tiramisu, a coffee and a courtesy slug of grappa. I felt very much at home with the friendly Italian staff who served every plate with a smile, laughing and chattering away simultaneously in Italian and gesticulating wildly as they worked.

After filling up my water bottles and bidding them all goodnight, I headed off to find somewhere to sleep. It was getting late as I headed off on the Cross Borders Drove Road towards Hamilton Hill, and, with daylight fading, settled for a small grassed-over stone quarry overrun with scampering rabbits. A lovely sunny summer evening ended this perfect day in which I had clocked up 16 miles. After several lazy days I was getting back on target.

DAY 72: 10 July   Peebles to Pentland Hills
Miles this day: **15**   Miles to date: **854**

Setting off in lovely sunshine, I continued on the drove road along the west side of the Eddleston valley and then entered the lifeless Harehope pine plantation. Once clear of the woods, the drove road passes through the small village of West Linton where I had some very ordinary fish and chips and bought a few supplies.

Leaving the village, the drove road climbs up on to lovely open moorland and past Baddinsgill Reservoir and into the heart of the Pentland Hills. My old dad was always on about 'rattling around in the Pentlands' and I wonder if he ventured up to these parts on his old Norton before he donated it to the war effort, a few years before I was born.

I had no water for the night camp and so I kept a sharp eye open for a decent stream. Ravendean Burn looked eminently drinkable and, out of curiosity, I followed an ancient boggy track downstream to see where it would take me. The hunch paid off for after half a mile I came to a rickety wooden hut[3]. Not having to put the tent up would save valuable time for an early getaway, and I decided to overnight here. Rows of wooden pegs fixed to the outside wall suggested the hut might have once been used by shooting parties, but it was now apparently used exclusively by wild birds and animals. I hadn't seen a single grouse crossing the moors

3 For thirsty followers, at NT 1207 5741.

The drove road crosses the Pentland Hills, Day 73.

on the way there, which could explain the change of usage. The floors and table were covered in dust and generations of dead creepy-crawlies that I did my best to sweep up without a brush, but then decided to sleep on the table for fear of puncturing my inflatable sleeping mat on the floor. The table would keep me well clear of any pattering late night visitors, which left just the possibility birds and bats in the rafters as the only potential threat to the promised slumber. As a precaution, I positioned some rickety chairs next to the table to break my fall in case I rolled off in the night.

I had a very comfortable evening, dining on spaghetti with mushroom soup for sauce, with a nip or two of malt whisky from a small hip flask that I had bought in Melrose. Doing the tally for the day I saw that I had completed 15 miles and was satisfied being more or less back on schedule.

DAY 73: 11 July   Pentland Hills to Union Canal
Miles this day: **17**   Miles to date: **871**

The drove road climbs steadily for a further mile to a low pass called the Cauldstane Slap, marked by a cast iron plaque erected in the 1880s by the Edinburgh Rights of Way Society. Another notice explains that the drove road was used for taking cattle from the trysts (markets) at Falkirk and Stenhousemuir to Peebles. Apparently, there are still people in West Linton whose grandparents remember the cattle droves in the early 1900s.

Sunset just off the Union Canal on Day 73.

Ancient thoroughfares are magical to walk on and this one, winding over the moors, was a bit special, making it hard to believe that I was barely a dozen miles from Edinburgh. Once over the watershed, I sped down off the Pentland Hills and headed into the Lowlands, cheered up by the thought that the next set of decent hills I walked over would be the Highlands!

The route I followed from here led down to Little Vantage, a former coaching Inn. Skirting around the large town of Livingston, I then headed over to the deeply incised wooded glen of the River Almond, a veritable oasis in this barren former industrial landscape. Following the glen downstream for a couple of miles, I arrived at Lin's Mill where an impressive aqueduct carries the Union Canal across the narrow glen. The canal's engineer, Hugh Baird, built this canny tribute to Scottish engineering in 1821, helped by another canny Scott, Thomas Telford. Five magnificent stone arches carry the canal in a cast-iron trough 23 metres above the river. The Union Canal was built as a 'contour canal' to avoid the construction of locks, that were not only a drain on the canal's precious water but also on the canny Scottish investor's pocket. This was a calculated trade-off, with the more circuitous route following the sweeping contours through the countryside. The canal was initially a financial success but, like other canals, went into decline with the arrival of the railways. It was finally closed to commercial traffic in 1933. Few footpaths cross the former industrial heartland of the Central Lowlands but in planning the walk I had counted on the canal towpaths to offer tranquillity and hopefully safer places to camp.

I left the canal briefly at Broxburn to pick up some supplies and grab some nasty fish and chips. It was a pretty grim town. Rather than live in a place like this, I thought, I'd prefer the life of a travelling vagrant, and then I reflected I almost was one!

Once past Winchburgh, the scenery started to improve with trees now bordering the canal. I started to relax and look around for a place to camp but the towpath was hemmed in between the steep bank leading down to the canal and a wide ditch filled with black toady water. A bridge carrying a farm track offered a chance to find a drier campsite and, after crossing a railway line, led me into open countryside. I found a decent spot to hide my tent in undergrowth at the edge of a cornfield.

Thanks to a bit of towpath fast-tracking, the tally showed I had covered a respectable 17 miles for the day, and was now 10 miles west of Edinburgh[4] and just two miles south of the Firth of Forth.

DAY 74: 12 July   Union Canal to Forth and Clyde
Miles this day: **21**   Miles to date: **892**

A lady on a horse passed in front of my tent and waved to me, laughing, as I was drinking an early morning cup of tea, still in my cosy sleeping bag with the door unzipped to let in the cornfield. I waved back and bid her good morning. If I'd carried a spare mug, I might have invited her in for tea and treated the horse to some imported porridge oats.

Since joining the Union Canal at Lin's Mill I had been walking across the Midlothian coal field, part of the Carboniferous age coal basin that extends over a large part of the Midland Valley of Scotland that had once helped fuel Britain's Industrial Revolution. Cheap imports, industrial turmoil and Margaret Thatcher's policies had resulted in the closure of all the deep coal pits in the Midlothian field, throwing tens of thousands of workers on to the dole heap and bringing post-industrial gloom to many of the formerly prosperous coal-mining towns. Open pit mining, employing fewer workers, continues in a few localities with some scarring of the landscape.

Clearly visible from the towpath were numerous elongated waste dumps called 'bings' with a distinctive pinkish-brown coloured waste, not the blackish tips normally seen near old coal mines. Later, I discovered that these were actually waste dumps from an embryonic oil shale industry of the mid-19th century, when near-surface oil-bearing shales were dug and heated to drive off paraffin for oil lamps. Oil shales are now being studied around the world as the next generation replacement for hydrocarbons, but the canny Scots beat them to it by almost two centuries.

In Santiago de Chile I worked with a canny Scot from Linlithgow who eventually married my beautiful secretary. I used to tease him about coming from a grim coal-mining town. As I walked into the town along the towpath I could now understand his indignation, for it looked a pleasant place, and a befitting birthplace for Mary Queen of Scots, born here at Linlithgow Palace in 1542. I regretted not taking some time off to explore the town but my

---

4 I had been following a circumferential route around the city for some time.

On the Union Canal, Day 74.

The 2,000-foot long Falkirk Tunnel, Day 74.

99-year-old mother took precedence over the Scottish queen.

The next section was most interesting for I was now approaching Falkirk and its famous millennium wheel. First I had to negotiate the 2,000-foot-long Falkirk Tunnel, a challenging piece of early 18th century tunnel engineering, poorly lit with dripping water turning to a shower-bath in places. Further in there was no guide rail between the towpath and the black waters of the canal.

Emerging into dazzling daylight, the canal then takes a sharp left turn passing close to the barely discernible temporary Roman camp at Tamfourhill, with the main Roman fort at Rough Castle located a mile to the west. These were part of the defences of the Antonine Wall that ran for 37 miles between the Forth and the Clyde. The wall was built by

The Falkirk Wheel – a millenium splash resembling an inverted tin opener. Day 74.

Hadrian's successor, Antoninus Pius, between AD 142 and 144. I suspect it might have been a case of the 'new broom' or the new Hispanic sword, for it was abandoned after just 20 years when the Romans retrenched back to Hadrian's earlier defences.

The millennium-inspired restoration of the Union Canal had called for a great deal of perseverance, ingenuity and money. The city fathers of Falkirk and Edinburgh, in their wisdom, had sanctioned the destruction of key bits of the old canal's infrastructure when the canal had been closed. One canal basin on the outskirts of Edinburgh had been turned into a housing estate, and the M8 drove right through the Ratho canal basin near Glasgow. Worst of all was the ripping up in 1933 of Falkirk's magnificent flight of eleven locks, which had joined the Union Canal to the Forth and Clyde Canal.

The Falkirk Wheel, opened for the millennium, was built to replace this flight of locks. It is an amazing structure and unique in the world of engineering marvels, but I began to wonder how many people would actually use the restored canal. After mountains, rivers, Roman walls and eating rib-eye steaks, I put canals about fifth on my 'rather be doing list', and have taken my family of five children, at various stages of their evolution, on at least half a dozen canal holidays. On my 35-mile walk from Lin Mill to Kirkintilloch, I saw only four or five canal boats on the Union Canal, and saw none at all on the Forth and Clyde, suggesting the Wheel might be something of a white elephant in terms of boat usage. But it clearly draws a huge number of entrance-paying visitors and the balanced counterpoise mechanism is cannily tight on the electricity consumption. Personally, I would have preferred the old flight of locks to this giant up-ended tin opener.

The visitor centre cafe was just closing as I arrived and I took in the scene, sheltering from the wind and drizzle under a plastic lemon tree erected to promote a new sugar-laden drink

called 'Lemon T'. I chatted to the two youngsters manning the empty publicity stand, who had had a bad day because no one fancied trying a free thirst quencher on a cold wet miserable day. Their faces lit up when I accepted one, and I immediately became their best customer of the day, and was then offered a whole box full – enough for the next four or five hundred miles if only I had the strength, or the supermarket trolley to carry it in. They were nice people and I later kept them posted on the walk.

Hyped up and feeling jolly on the 'Lemon T' sugar hit I set off along the Forth and Clyde at a belting rate thinking, 'Now this is a real canal.' The first thing you notice is the canal's enormous width, for it was designed to enable sea-going vessels, with up to a 20-foot beam, to cross Scotland at its narrowest part, linking the Firth of Forth near Edinburgh and the Firth of Clyde near Glasgow. Fishing vessels could now pass from the east coast to the west avoiding the hazardous passage across the top of Scotland that had put paid to half of the fleeing Spanish Armada in 1588.

When the canal opened in 1783 it was the main highway across Scotland with a Clyde-built steamer, the *Fairy Queen*, carrying day trippers out from Port Dundas on the Clyde, with on-board dining, newspapers and a bar. What a great day out that would have been. The Forth and Clyde was built with locks, all 39 of them. The great thing for me was the expansive area of manicured grass surrounding the 72-foot-long lock chambers that make the perfect camping spots for the itinerant back packer. I camped on the grass next to Lock 13 near Allendale, after a long 21-mile day, a record so far for the Scottish part of my walk.

ABOVE: The beautiful Forth and Clyde Canal, near Kelvinhead. Opened in 1790 it was designed to take fishing boats across Scotland to avoid the treacherous north coast. Day 75.

John Muir Way follows the old Blane Valley Railway, Day 75.

DAY 75: 13 July   Forth and Clyde to Strathblane
Miles this day: **18**   Miles to date: **909**

Heading west from the lock, the towpath became quite rural in character. Overhanging trees and banks of wild flowers bordered the canal, and water lilies nudged each other in the breeze, happy to be floating around in circles going nowhere in particular enjoying the lovely boat-free canal.

I passed an old jetty at Kelvinhead, a relic from the Industrial Revolution. A noticeboard explained that iron ore had once been mined near here, and was used to produce cannons for the Napoleonic and US civil wars. I noticed that the OS map revealed a number of old mining sites around the nearby village of Banton.

Further along the canal another noticeboard told of a large number of Covenanters' bones were found in the bog whilst the canal was being dug in the 1780s. The 1645 Battle of Kilsyth was a devastating defeat for these defenders of the Presbyterian faith, at the hands of the Marquis of Montrose, and is remembered in the place names like Drum Burn, Slaughter Haw and Baggage Knowe, all marked on the OS map, on a hillside about a mile and a half to the north-west of the old jetty.

From the Falkirk Wheel to Glasgow, the Forth and Clyde runs parallel and just to the north of the Antonine Wall. A hundred or so miles to the south, Hadrian had built his wall on top of the steep ridge of the Whin Sill, but here the Antonine Wall runs next to low-lying marshy land. Modern ditches now drain this but in Roman times the marshland would have been a formidable additional defence.

OPPOSITE: The Argentina–Germany world cup
– Argentina and I both lost!

I took a short break at Kirkintilloch to celebrate the end of the canals and a long awaited change in direction towards the north, tucking into a huge rib-eye steak at Nana's Italian restaurant, followed by an over-weighty shopping spree at Tesco. Following the advice of a walking couple I had met on the Union Canal, I left the Forth and Clyde on the northern outskirts of Kirkintilloch to head north on the John Muir Way, rather than continue westwards to the formal starting point of the West Highland Way. This cut off a sizeable corner of my planned route, as well as allowing me to savour this splendid trail, that is based on the former track of the Blane Valley Railway.

The bearded naturalist, glaciologist, amateur geologist and defender of the wild places, John Muir, was born in Dunbar near Edinburgh in 1838. His family emigrated to the US when he was 11 years old and, after studying chemistry he went on to take a keen interest in the outdoors and was an early campaigner for the preservation of wilderness areas like the Yosemite Valley in California, that eventually led to the establishment of the world's first national park system. For some time now I have had my eye on the John Muir Trail that passes through the Sierra Nevada mountain range, taking in the Yosemite National Park. One day maybe, or am I perhaps now too old to be taking on the bears?

Nevertheless, the watered-down and budget-canny John Muir Way is really pretty, with sideways glimpses of Campsie Fells to the north that owe their prominence to volcanic lava flows that created the rocky landscape. It was a welcome sight for a geologist after tramping across endless miles of the Scottish Central Lowlands.

The Argentina-Germany World Cup final was in progress when I arrived at the Kirkhouse Inn in Strathblane. It was intended to be just a quick water stop before heading on to the West Highland Way and camping somewhere for the night. On arrival I foolishly got caught up with a group of outdoor instructors watching the game, all coerced fans of Germany judging by the flag painted on all their foreheads. The flag painter was a young German woman and before I knew what was happening, I was ordered to sit down to have the German flag painted on my forehead.

The beers flowed and when I made a move to head off to look for a campsite, the instructors said they could fix me up with a bed for the night back at the outdoor centre. It's a long story but the promised bed with a hint of some food and a shower didn't materialise, and I ended up putting up the tent in a field full of rejoicing midges. ●

9

THE WEST HIGHLAND WAY

After joining the West Highland Way at Strathblane, I cross the remaining few miles of Lowlands to Balmaha at the southern end of Loch Lomond.
Here, a major geological fault marks the abrupt start of the Highlands and the going gets progressively tougher, with the path now following the eastern side of the loch over wooded rocky knolls. From the head of the loch, the Way follows an 18th century military road through magnificent glens to Bridge of Orchy and then crosses the wilderness of Rannoch Moor to the head of Glencoe.
Here the walker is compelled to take in the spectacular landscape as we pass in front of Buachaille Etive Mor, the best loved of all the Munro peaks, which stands guard over the entrance to Glencoe. A steep climb over the Devil's Staircase takes us on to the high country above Kinlochleven and the start of the final run down to Fort William.

DAY 76: 14 July   Strathblane to Drymen
Miles this day: **9**   Miles to date: **918**

It hadn't dawned on me until I woke up with a hole in my head that the previous night's escapades and the well-meant lift to the outdoor centre was going to result in another hole, but this one in my Cape to Cape walk, unless I headed back to Strathblane to resume the walk where I had left off. This meant forgetting the shortcut on to the West Highland Way and backtracking to Strathblane for a good hour and a half along the road.

Arriving at Strathblane, I made for the hotel to use the loo and check in the mirror that the German flag had been completely eradicated from my forehead before having breakfast. When the sniffling waitress eventually returned, the requested soft-fried eggs had been baked rock hard on the sizzling-hot plates, doing nothing to alleviate my black mood. Over a lousy coffee I recalculated the timing of the remaining distance to Fort William, coming up with about 95 miles to cover in seven days. This, I thought, was quite doable providing I steered well clear of all future sporting events.

I joined the West Highland Way (WHW) at Dumgoyach Bridge where I met Jennifer, the first of many friendly people that I would meet along the Way. Jennifer was a job-share nurse in the Canadian Arctic, working all hours in darkness for five winter months and then taking five months off for long-distance walking and travelling the world. A neat lifestyle, I thought. She was backpacking with full camping gear but wearing tiny lightweight blue trainers that made my leather Scarpas look ridiculously large and clumsy. I stopped to help her put up her tent in the rain at a campsite at Easter Drumquhassle Farm, and then I continued on to Drymen. After piling in a fish supper at The Winnock Hotel, I found a nice £20 bunkhouse with continental breakfast called 'Kip in the Kirk'.

DAY 77: 15 July   Drymen to Rowardennan
Miles this day: **15**   Miles to date: **933**

Breakfast in the bunkhouse was communal, noisy and very entertaining. I met up with several WHW walkers whom I would see several times during the next few days. I caught up again with Charlotte and her fiancé Louis who I had met a few days earlier on the Union Canal, and then Pamela, a bubbly blonde girl from Falkirk, and her friend, Karen. I would say goodbye to them time and time again, and meet up later with big hugs. I then headed off to meet up with Jennifer from Canada in a coffee shop. After weeks of solitude, talking mostly to owls and rabbits, my social life had suddenly become very hectic.

From Drymen, the WHW winds through woodlands, a small outlier of the Queen Elizabeth Forest park, and then climbs up the aptly named Conic Hill. The hill is only 361 metres high but geologically is of interest as it stands right on the line of the Highland Boundary Fault, a giant crack in the earth's surface that cuts right across Scotland, from Stonehaven on the

The WHW on Conic Hill, marks the Southern Upland fault. Day 77.

The WHW Loch Lomond Woodland near Rowardennan. Day 77.

east coast to the island of Arran on the west. The fault has a profound impact on the land-scape and cultural fabric of Scotland, separating the Highlands to the north of the fault from the mostly flat-lying land to the south.

The ancient Dalradian rocks on the northern side of the fault started out as deep-sea muds and sands, later caught up and crushed almost to melting point between colliding continental masses. The resulting schists and slates, some of the hardest and oldest rocks in Britain, account for the rugged Highland landscapes that we treasure.

From the top of Conic Hill, on a clear day such as this was, you can clearly see the trace of the fault picked out by a chain of small islands (Inchcailloch, Torrinch, Creinch and Inchmurrin) that cut across the southern part of Loch Lomond in a south-westerly direction. A great span of Highland peaks is also visible from this vantage point, with Ben Lomond, 974 metres, some eight miles to the north-west, the most southerly of the Munros.

A long line of walkers was heading slowly down the path towards Balmaha – there were more walkers on this one small hill than I had seen in the last 250 miles. Jennifer and I joined the throng, arriving at the small loch-side village in the early afternoon. It was a lively place with a bustling holiday atmosphere, with day trippers out from Glasgow as well as other West Highland Way walkers. Everyone seemed to be heading for the Royal Oak, and we followed suit.

From Balmaha, the WHW heads northwards, keeping to the eastern, mostly wooded side of Loch Lomond. It is by no means the gentle shoreline stroll one might imagine, for in places the mountains plunge straight into the loch obliging the walker to clamber up and around rocky knolls and cliffs. Using my Routebuddy mapping software, I later calculated that the total elevation climb for the 21-mile 'lochside' section between Balmaha and the Inverarnan campsite at the head of the loch was about 1,250 metres!

The scenery mostly comprised ancient oak woodland that hid abundant chattering and whistling bird life, and became increasingly dramatic as the loch narrowed and I entered the Highlands proper. The path was now rougher due to the large amount of scree shedding off the steep glacier-cut slopes above. The rocks are varied, for the most part a metamorphosed sedimentary package, with gnarled and twisted tree roots clinging to boulders for security on the shifting slopes. The Loch Lomond area once lay under the Lomond Glacier with successive periods of glaciation carving out the present day loch. When the last ice caps melted, the sea level rose and seawater flooded into the loch until 'isostatic rebound' (i.e. floating) caused the landmass to rise with the loch reverting to a freshwater domain.

We took time off to sit quietly by the loch side, arriving at the Rowardennan hostel in the early evening. We later met up with several members of our original 'group' for a very pleasant evening, except when the barman went rabbiting on and on about the popularity of The Famous Grouse whisky, just because I happened to ask for a Bells that he didn't happen to have.

The 'Falkirk Girls' Pamela and Karen, with the Leeds lad, Mark. Day 77.

The gloaming (dusk) at 11 p.m. near Rowardennan, Loch Lomond. Day 77.

North end of Loch Lomond, Day 78.

DAY 78: 16 July   Rowardennan to Inverarnan
Miles this day: **14**   Miles to date: **947**

The next morning, the Falkirk girls told me that Jennifer had had a migraine attack during the night and was staying behind until she felt better. We all looked out for her but she never made it to the next campsite, and sadly we never saw her again on the walk. I headed off up the loch, bracing myself for a long walk in the rain on what I knew was the most difficult part of the Loch Lomond walk. I got to the hotel at Inversnaid by early afternoon to find the Falkirk girls and Mark readying to depart. After a quick chicken baguette, I set off in the rain after them.

The landscape changes about three miles beyond Inversnaid, with the path leaving the rocky shore to head up through pretty heathland and mixed deciduous woods. I stopped to look at a bothy, where a young couple sat by the smoky fire to escape from the midges. They said there was plenty of room if I wanted to stay but I wanted to push on.

By early evening I reached the campsite at Inverarnan and found Mark, the lad from Leeds, ensconced in a wooden hut. I put my tent up in the grassy field and then headed off for a long shower that only a long-haul walker can appreciate. I was feeling great, surrounded by mountains in a splendid campsite, but even better was in store as I made my way down to the cosy bar/restaurant: warm, full of chatter and the tantalising smell of garlicky food.

There was something about the lady serving in the bar that prompted me to ask where she was from. 'Spain', she replied. Switching to Spanish, Lucia told me how she had come to

Britain from Galicia in north-west Spain during the downturn in the Spanish economy a few years earlier. We talked away for half the evening between her attending the bar. I told her how, from 1987 to 1990 I had lived with my wife Bridget and our youngest son William in a small *pueblo* in Asturias, the province just to the east of Galicia in northern Spain. At the time I was running a gold exploration programme with a great team of Spanish geologists, eventually finding what turned out to be one of Europe's largest gold mines.

I said goodnight to Lucia and headed back to my tent. I could see she was missing home, but at least here she was surrounded by beautiful mountains and rivers to remind her of Galicia.

DAY 79: 17 July   Inverarnan to Bridge of Orchy
Miles this day: **19**   Miles to date: **966**

Packed up after an early breakfast, I made my way to the main block, meeting up with Charlotte and Louis who had overnighted in the bothy that I had passed the previous evening. They were sitting at an outside table and I was tempted to join them for a delicious bacon and egg bap with several free coffees. Everyone except me burst into laughter when a mangy dog came up, sniffed around and then cocked its leg on my rucksack.

The Beinn Dòrain Munro, near Bridge of Orchy, marks the start of the Highlands. Day 79.

I headed off down Glen Falloch just after 10 a.m., soon to be overtaken by Mark, the fast and light Leeds lad. The railway, the busy A82 and a major river all share this narrow glen but tranquillity is restored when the WHW enters woodland above Crianlarich. I made good progress reaching the popular tourist and walkers' village of Tyndrum after 13 easy miles at about 5 p.m.

The village is notable for several reasons: firstly, it is the only village in Britain to have two mainline railway stations. The West Highland Line splits about five miles south of here, with one branch heading west to Oban and the other following a northerly route to Fort William. The two branches pass through the village but on opposite sides of the glen, and both have stations a mile apart, but 10 miles apart by train.

Secondly, the village is renowned for its Green Welly Stop, a shop that sells just about everything, although these days it is more of a tourist trap than the vital provisioning stop that it once was. I discovered later from the Internet that it was given the prestigious *Loo of the Year* award in 2016.

Thirdly, Tyndrum has the only significant gold deposit in Britain, although plans to put it into production have been hampered by planning permissions and the scarcity of venture capital for mining projects. The deposit comprises a polymetallic vein centred on the beautiful Cononish Glen, located about two miles south-west of the town, overlooked by the splendid Munro of Ben Lui. The mineral vein was originally worked in the Victorian era for lead, attested to by the row of old miners' cottages that sit just above the Green Welly Stop. As gold deposits go these days it's pretty small, with potential to produce a total of 200,000 ounces over a 10-year mine life, a quantity of gold that some modern gold mines produce in just a few weeks. Nevertheless, the mine could produce enough gold for a new Scottish crown if needed at some time in the future, but in the meantime the Green Welly loo and two stations will keep the village firmly on the map. I caught up briefly with Mark who was planning to overnight at the 'By the Way' cabins. I was tempted to do the same but decided to press on to Bridge of Orchy.

For me this next leg, following one of General Wade's military roads, is one of the best on the WHW. The British government sent Wade, an Anglo-Irishman, to construct a network of military roads to facilitate rapid troop deployment after the first Jacobite rebellion of 1715. Today the military road makes for very pleasant walking, with the section beyond Tyndrum becoming increasingly dramatic as the conical Beinn Dòrain comes into view. I pushed on at a good rate, arriving at Bridge of Orchy just before 9 p.m. after covering about 20 miles for the day.

I made straight to the bar to try to secure some food before the dreaded last food deadline and ran into some of the people in our 'group'. Karen was in the bar with some others and went off to find Pamela, who greeted me like a long-lost friend. We had a good evening before I headed off around 11 p.m. to look for a place to camp, crossing the river on General Wade's military bridge. The midges were waiting for me, anxious to start the attack, until I got under cover.

When the family and I passed through here walking the WHW in August 1999, we had set out the lunch picnic somewhere very close to where I was now camped. Midge assaults usually start gradually until the pheromone 'come and get 'em' message gets out and the main onslaught begins in earnest a few minutes later. Within a few minutes the hordes had descended and the picnics were hurriedly stuffed back in the packs and we all ran off up the path to escape. As we hurried off, we saw that all the people in the campsite were wearing head nets and some even wore kitchen gloves.

DAY 80: 18 July   Bridge of Orchy to Kinlochleven
Miles this day: **21**   Miles to date: **987**

I took breakfast back in the Bridge of Orchy hotel and then headed off over the shoulder of a hill, following the Wade military road before going down into open country near the Inveroran Hotel overlooking Loch Tulla.

The family and I had stayed at this hotel in 1999, enjoying our stay except that I melted the lampshade of the bedside lamp trying to dry out my socks. The next morning we split up, Penny and Adrian continuing to the Kings House Hotel on Rannoch Moor, whilst Tim, William and I headed off over the Black Mountains to Glen Etive. Blessed with fine weather, we had a fantastic walk over Stob Ghabhar, Clach Leathad, Creise and Stob a' Ghlais Choire, three of them being Munros. Adrian, who had got to the Kings House Hotel several hours earlier was waiting for us down on the Glen Etive road, a bit concerned as we were well over schedule and daylight was waning.

Looking back to Bridge of Orchy, Day 80.

***

Returning, some 15 years later, I carried on past the hotel and over the Victoria Bridge, skirting around the flanks of the Black Mountains and across the western edge of Rannoch Moor, arriving at the Kings House Hotel just after 3 p.m. Mark arrived about 4 p.m. planning to overnight, but I wanted to get to Kinlochleven in order to make Fort William the next day. My second camera battery went suddenly dead as I was leaving the Kings House so sadly there is no photo coverage for the final two days of the WHW.

Approaching Kings House Hotel at the head of
Glencoe, with Munro Buachaille Etive Mòr on
the left, Day 80.

Shortly beyond the Kings House, the West Highland Way begins a zigzag climb, known as the Devil's Staircase, engineered by General Wade to facilitate the hauling of cannons and other heavy loads up over the pass. I stopped for a few minutes to take in the wonderful views from the saddle by Bienn Bheag, looking back over to Glencoe and north towards Ben Nevis, before starting the grinding five-mile descent to Kinlochleven. At the top of the pass I found a good Arc'teryx zipped top in the middle of the path, dropped by a WHW walker. I took it with me, thinking if they discovered the loss and came back, I would meet them on the way and return it. I still have it.

A mile down the track, the impressive dam wall of the eight-mile long Blackwater Reservoir came into view, an impressive feat of engineering built to generate electricity for Kinlochleven's aluminium works. Construction of the reservoir began in 1905 and was completed four years later, and is cited as the last major engineering project in Britain to be built with the help of the traditional Irish navvy. Up to 3,000 men and just one woman were employed on the project – a puzzling ratio. A small graveyard just below the dam remembers those who died in the endeavour.

Aluminium is the most abundant metal in the earth's crust but the process to liberate the metal from the ore requires huge amounts of electrical energy. The minute quantities of metal that were produced in the late 19th century, shortly after the metal's discovery, were valued more than gold, as witnessed by the aluminium tableware commissioned by Napoleon III and the aluminium crown made for King Christian X of Denmark – a bit like wearing an aluminium saucepan on your head! In the 20th century large aluminium smelters were built in countries with abundant hydropower such as Norway and Canada, and two were built here in Scotland.

At Kinlochleven, electricity was generated using water taken from the Blackwater Reservoir, the pipeline roughly following the steep route taken by General Wade and the West Highland Way. I eventually reached the aluminium works on the outskirts of the town around 9 p.m. As I passed the long shed I could hear the steady hum of the turbines that turned free water flow into free watts, but the other buildings seemed a bit forlorn. Later I found out that aluminium production here had actually ceased back in 1996 but that the turbines still turned to feed electricity into the national grid. In the meantime, the town seems to have survived the loss of its core industry that once supported 700 well-paid jobs. It has, however, secured investment in mountaineering-based tourism for which the town is ideally placed, being almost hemmed in by ten Munro mountains. The town's multimillion pound ice wall outdoor centre, opened by Queen Elizabeth II, has the world's highest indoor ice-climbing wall.

It was cold and wet when I checked in to the Blackwater campsite, after which I made a half-hearted attempt to look around for Pamela and her friend, trying the first pub I saw, called The Tailrace Inn. There were no girls and, worse still, no food.

DAY 81: 19 July   Kinlochleven to Fort William
Miles this day: **16**   Miles to date: **1,002**

After an early start and a cup of tea with a few biscuits, I was away by 7.30 a.m. hoping to find somewhere open for a decent breakfast, but I was out of luck. In the early morning the town had a 'seen better times' feeling about it, which I supposed followed the closure of the aluminium works. It must have been a blow to the local community.

Heading out of the town, the West Highland Way first follows the Allt Nathrach river to the south of The Mamores mountains. The path climbed steadily up the long treeless glen and, looking back, I spotted Pamela and her friend in the distance, advancing rapidly towards me. I took off my pack and hid in the heather pulling my black woolly hat over my head, with just half an eye open ready to jump out on them, but they spotted me first.

'Who's that, is it Jo'on? Looks like Jo'on, at least the beard does. Is it you?' or words to that effect. I pulled off my woolly hat and got the last big hug from Pamela and caught up with yesterday's events. They were in a hurry, hoping to get back to Falkirk that same evening so I let them push on. They were smashing girls, as were all the people I met on the West Highland Way and I wished them good luck, agreeing we might meet up again sometime, somewhere.

The descent into Fort William was uneventful, the drizzle increasing to steady rain the closer I got to the town. Someone had recommended the Bank Street Lodge that I found to be a great place, and after dropping my pack, I headed off to buy my train ticket to Yorkshire for the following morning. After a good shower I headed over to the Crannog seafood restaurant on the pier to celebrate clocking up 1,000 miles since starting out from Cape Cornwall. The restaurant was fully booked but by acting half-starved, (that came very easily) I managed to get a table and settled down for a superb dinner.

My mind was then turned to getting back to Yorkshire for Mum's birthday, but looking out across Loch Linnhe, with shadows now falling on to the Ardgour Peninsula, I first raised my glass to the next stage of the walk, the 'Dare to Imagine' Cape Wrath Trail.

But first there was the 100th birthday party …

A BREAK BACK IN YORKSHIRE

Before continuing on the Cape Cornwall to Cape Wrath walk, it would seem amiss not to mention something of my mum's 100th birthday party held on 26 July, the happy reason for interrupting my Cape to Cape walk at Fort William. The venue was the Coniston Hall Hotel, set in lovely parkland at the western edge of the Yorkshire Dales, just four miles from the village of Hellifield where I was brought up with my two elder sisters. The weather could not have been better and mum was on great form and almost her old self, but still adjusting to the idea that she had lived for an amazing 100 years! All she could say was, 'Crikey.'

My family was represented by my five children and nine grandchildren[1], but in total mum had all of her 10 grandchildren and her 16 great grandchildren at the party.

The event was recorded in the *Yorkshire Post* and in an interesting post-birthday development, my eldest sister received a flat parcel containing a black and white photograph of the *MV Orion* sailing under Sydney Harbour Bridge. My mum went out to live in New South Wales when she was about eight years old. Her mother was widowed when my grandfather, Private A.E. Butler of the 20th Battalion, London Regiment, was killed at Lebucquiere in March 1918 during a fierce German counteroffensive. He was just 25 at the time and my mum never really knew him.

---

1 At the last count now 10.

A wall-full of grandchildren! (and two more not shown or born), July 26.

The gentleman who sent the picture had read about the 100th birthday party and was in possession of this wonderful black and white photograph that he had bought some years earlier in an antique shop. This was the very ship my mum and grandma sailed in to Australia, departing from the Port of London and travelling out to Australia via the Suez Canal, Aden, and Fremantle, to arrive in Sydney six weeks later. A great adventure for a young girl who had not previously been beyond the bounds of London! Not only did he send the photograph but the gentleman had been able to find the Orion passenger list for the actual sailing that listed my mum and grandma.

My mother loved Australia and cried when her mum told her, about eight years later, that they were going back to England. She continually says she wished she had stayed, but then I remind her there would have been no me. 'But then I would have had other children', she says, with a chuckle. Many of her memories are starting to fade but she remembers her years in Australia with amazing clarity.

After the festivities and family catch-ups, it was time to head back to Fort William, the journey taking 12 hours following a similar 400-mile route that had taken me 28 days to walk. ●

OPPOSITE: A break back in Yorkshire for my mum's 100th birthday party, July 26.

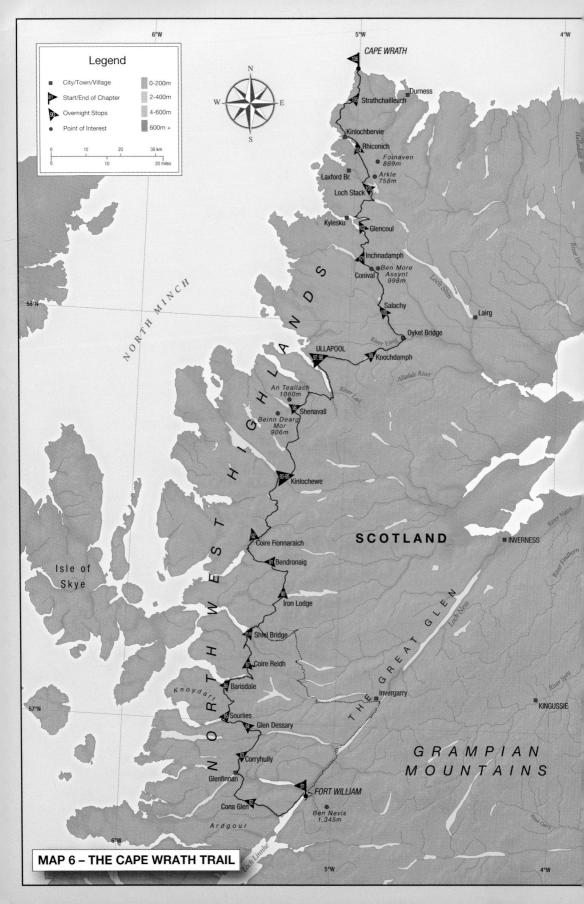

Legend

- City/Town/Village
- Start/End of Chapter
- Overnight Stops
- Point of Interest

0-200m
2-400m
4-600m
600m +

0   10   20   30 km
0   10   20 miles

N
W — E
S

CAPE WRATH

106
Durness
105 Strathchailleach
Kinlochbervie
104 Rhiconich
Foinaven
869m
Laxford Br.
Arkle
758m
103 Loch Stack
Kylesku
102 Glencoul
Inchnadamph
101 Conival — Ben More Assynt 998m
Salachy
100 Oykel Bridge
Lairg
ULLAPOOL
97,98
99 Knochdamph
River Einig
Alladale River
River Lael
An Teallach
1060m
96 Shenavall
Beinn Dearg
Mor
906m
93-95 Kinlochewe
Loch Shin

NORTH MINCH

58°N

S C O T L A N D

INVERNESS

92 Coire Fionnaraich
91 Bendronaig
90 Iron Lodge
88,89 Shiel Bridge
87 Coire Reidh
86 Barisdale
Knoydart
85 Sourlies
84 Glen Dessary
83 Corryhully
Glenfinnan
81 FORT WILLIAM
82
Cona Glen
Ben Nevis
1,345m
Ardgour

Isle of
Skye

N O R T H   W E S T   H I G H L A N D S

57°N

T H E   G R E A T   G L E N

Loch Ness

Invergarry

River Nairn
River Findhorn
River Spey
KINGUSSIE

G R A M P I A N
M O U N T A I N S

River Garry

Loch Linnhe

River Ha...

6°W
5°W
4°W

MAP 6 – THE CAPE WRATH TRAIL

10

THE CAPE WRATH TRAIL

The 250-mile walk from Fort William to Cape Wrath on the north-western tip of Scotland was perhaps the most challenging and awe-inspiring adventure I have ever undertaken, making a splendid grand finale for my 1,250-mile long walk across Britain.

My route was largely based on Cicerone's excellent guidebook, The Cape Wrath Trail, following Iain Harper's more westerly alternative. After crossing Loch Linnhe on the Camusnagaul ferry I headed across the remote Ardgour and Knoydart Peninsulas to Barisdale and then on to Loch Hourn. This was followed by a challenging walk over to Shiel Bridge, passing just below the Forcan Ridge during the surprise onslaught of Hurricane Bertha.

After pausing to allow the worst of the storm to pass I then climbed on past the Falls of Glomach to Strath Duilleach, heading over to Maol Bhuidhe and Bendronaig and on to Strathcarron. After sheltering from more stormy weather at Kinlochewe, I made my way over to Strath na Sealga and Shenavall and on into Ullapool. From there, I headed eastwards to Bridge of Orchy followed by a climb over to Inchnadamph under Conival and Ben More Assynt. Here I met up with schoolmate Bob Peckam who joined me to complete the final leg to Cape Wrath via Glencoul, Loch Stack and Rhiconich. The Cape Wrath Trail took me 21 walking days to cover the 250-mile route.

A NOTE ON THE CAPE WRATH TRAIL

Considered by many walkers to be the toughest backpacking trail in Britain, the Cape Wrath Trail is an arduous 250-mile trek through the North West Highlands, from Fort William to Cape Wrath on the north-west tip of Scotland. It is not an officially recognised UK National Trail, but rather a collection of routes that can be joined together in any number of ways, according to the preference and ability of the walker, and the weather. The walk is challenging in various respects – the distance covered, the rugged and often pathless terrain, unpredictable spate[1]-prone river crossings, the general absence of accommodation and provisioning points, and of course the dreaded Scottish midge that seems to get more aggressive as the years go by.

The walk is best undertaken with full backpacking gear, although a good sprinkling of bothies will reward the walker with some midge-free nights, providing you do not find them jam-packed full during the midges' low season. For the bothies you will still need all the usual backpackers' kit apart from the tent. Given the remoteness of the terrain the tent, however, becomes a reassuring part of mountain safety, especially for the lone walker.

In fair weather the trail is not difficult, with the route mostly winding through remote and beautiful glens that connect with the next opposing glen via lower-level passes called 'bealachs'. Bad weather will of course add additional challenges to the walk, requiring the itinerary to be flexible to allow for possible delays, such as those caused by rivers in spate. Food and fuel supplies for six or seven days are needed for some sections, adding more weight to your pack. Mine increased from the normal 'low country' weight of about 18 kilograms to around 22 kilograms.

When I called in at the National Trust field office at Morvich to enquire about the state of the gorge below the Falls of Glomach in the aftermath of Hurricane Bertha, the warden told me most Cape Wrath walkers had given up long before getting to Strathcarron, with painful blistered feet cited as the most common reason for aborting.

It would be much safer and a lot easier on the back not to walk alone as I did, with two people sharing the weight of the tent, cooking gear and fuel, as well as giving you someone to fall out with when you are battered by gale force winds and rain and the spirits start to flag, as will inevitably happen.

An ankle sprain or worse can happen anywhere, especially when carrying a heavy pack. I carried my Spot satellite-based device that can call up emergency services independently of the generally poor mobile phone coverage. It is fully waterproof and looks like it would survive a raging torrent, even if you may not!

---

1 A term used mainly in the Scottish Highlands for a flooded, and often impassable river.

The Camusnagaul ferry over Loch Linnhe sea loch to the Ardgour Peninsula – the only bit I didn't walk. Day 82.

DAY 82: 5 August   Fort William to Cona Glen
Miles this day: **12**   Miles to date: **1,015**

My departure for Fort William was delayed by an hour-long business Skype call to Australia and the delay meant I missed the 10 a.m. Camusnagaul ferry over to the Ardgour Peninsula. I passed an hour or so in Wetherspoons with a coffee and a dreadful sticky bun, followed by a Becks lager to send me off on the Cape Wrath Trail.

The half mile passenger-only ferry crossing from the town pier over to the Ardgour Peninsula takes only a few minutes, but sets you down in another world where emails, traffic, throngs of summer tourists, and the mingled aromas of street curry and haggis fritters are left behind. The next town I would come across would be Ullapool, scheduled for about two weeks' time. Until then, I would have to survive on what food and fuel I could carry, plus a couple of mailed supply drops.

Alighting at the tiny hamlet of Camusnagaul, the road heads south-west keeping close to the Loch Linnhe shoreline. The single-track road with passing places was incredibly quiet and nothing stirred for the next six miles except for two touring cyclists and a road gang out fixing some recent flood damage. In the same distance on the West Highland Way, I might have easily seen 50 walkers.

Fort William slowly disappeared from view but the rarely seen whaleback of Ben Nevis kept me company for a few hours longer. The road being essentially flat, I was able to make good progress and was feeling in excellent spirits and in great shape, except for my new Trango La Sportiva boots that felt a bit uncomfortable. Perhaps they just needed wearing in, I thought.

I stopped to eat a small Fort William pork pie, relieved to find there was not a single midge about. The road runs close to the shoreline of Loch Linnhe, one of several lochs located in the Great Glen that runs north-east from Fort William for 60 miles to Inverness. Other lochs in the Glen include the freshwater Loch Lochy and the monstrous Loch Ness.

The Great Glen follows the line of a major geological fault that formed about 400 million years ago, when the land mass to the north of the Glen (now the Highlands) was pushed to the north-east for a distance of about sixty 60 miles on what is known as a strike-slip fault. Today the Glen provides a dead straight and level 60-mile transit route to Inverness, as well as a lock-free passage for ships using the Caledonian Canal. A walking and cycling path runs along the Glen connecting Fort William and Inverness.

I cycled along part of the Great Glen Cycle Path in 1999 whilst on a home leave visit from Ecuador. I had taken my bike up to Glasgow by train and then headed across the west coast islands of Bute, Mull and Skye. Travelling to Mallaig for the Skye ferry, I came unstuck on an ungated level crossing at Morar on the Fort William to Mallaig railway line. It was chucking it down and getting dark and with my head down and spectacles awash with rain, the level crossing took me by surprise. Here the rails cut diagonally across the road and my front wheel slipped down the crack between the road and the first rail, sending me flying over the handle-bars to land with my hipbone on the adjacent rail. I have no idea how the bike and I escaped with just a good whack on the hipbone and a broken mirror.

The pain started to trouble me two days later as I was leaving Skye, and it got steadily worse, but with a train booked from Fort William to Yorkshire followed almost immediately by a daughter's wedding in Wales, I had no option but to push on with the 75-mile journey. When I reached the Great Glen at Invergarry the main road traffic was horrendous but then I spotted a sign pointing to the Great Glen Cycle Path. Pushing the bike up the first steep bit of track, I found myself on a good forestry road that basically follows a contour on the northern side of the glen. I 'limped' back into Fort William at reduced speed by keeping the pedals turning with my good leg with the other hanging down clear of the pedal. This I was able to do because the track was almost dead level and I was wearing cleated Shimano cycling shoes that allowed my good leg to lift the pedal for the power down-stroke. The last 20 miles took forever but thankfully I was able to get to the church in time to give away Amanda!

✷✷✷

With my mind still on a bicycle or half way up the Ben, I missed the turn-off to the Cona Glen and had to backtrack for some 20 minutes. For the first mile or so the track runs through riverside water meadows and woodlands belonging to the Conaglen Estate. At one point, the track pulls away from the river to pass through ancient woodland

The Cona River, lower Cona Glen. Day 82.

An adder on the hunt for frogs in Cona Glen. Day 82.

beneath the spreading canopies and twisted boughs of Scots pine, and gnarled oak trees with branches decorated with small ferns that have taken to tree climbing. I stopped to listen and record the shriek of an unseen hawk.

Once out of the woods I made my way on to a wooden footbridge to take a look at the river. The water level was low and no fish were to be seen in the peaty water, although I did see a heron that I took to be a good sign that there had been a hatch of salmon parr. Salmon and sea trout are migratory fish that return to the rivers where they hatched to spawn at certain times of the year, but their numbers have seriously declined in recent years because of infection said to be spread by the proliferation of fish farming. Their disappearance from the world-renowned Scottish waters would be a real blow to rural communities as well as a loss to river life.

Continuing, I disturbed a small adder that was curled up on the track enjoying the sun. It had an unusual dark brown colour. The glen started to narrow and then climb around a rocky knoll, and it was time to start thinking about a camping spot. My guidebook had mentioned a bothy higher up, but warned it was not always open. I got there at about 7 p.m. and found it was locked. Peering through the window, it was enviably well stocked and fitted with comfortable-looking bunk beds. A scruffy and rather ramshackle lean-to was attached to the far end of the building, apparently used by other wild creatures, but it was also open to the elements and the midges, and had a grotty floor. I decided to carry on.

A short while later I found a less boggy spot next to the river. It could have been an ancient meander, now filled with long reedy grass that I flattened with my boots to make a firmer bed to prevent my tent from sinking into the squelch. Far from perfect but with the evenings already shortening, it would have to do.

The midges were poised for the attack the moment I stopped but the tent was up in no time and I was able to settle down with a fruit tea listening to the river; a citronella stick smoking away in the tent doorway kept the midges at bay.

DAY 83: 6 August   **Cona Glen to Glenfinnan**
Miles this day: **12**   Miles to date: **1,027**

Come early morning the midges were even meaner and I stuffed the last items in my pack without my normal due care in my haste to get away. I put on long trousers for the first time on the walk and set off with my midge net on. From the safety of the net I studied the midge horde; with the slightest breeze they would get wafted away, but the moment it dropped they would drift back.

I saw no one all day and wondered if this was more to do with the midge season, with August generally reckoned to be the worst month. The terrain was now getting steeper and the river that once ran lazily over gravel now cascaded over rocky outcrops. My slow progress was watched with silent disdain by the occasional clump of ancient gnarled and twisted Scots pine. Looking up towards the top of the glen, I could now see the distant source of the river in the coire[2] under Meall nan Creag Leac.

From the end of the vehicle track, a well-defined path climbs up to the first bealach of the trip. Eventually I would cross about 12 bealachs on the Cape Wrath Trail but this one was a fairly low-level 'beginner's bealach' of just 400 metres. Even so, I remember the feeling of modest satisfaction at crossing my first one.

Once over the pass, it was an easy walk down to Glenfinnan, a small village tucked into the head of Loch Shiel and hemmed in by mountains. This beautiful spot is where Prince Charles Edward Stuart raised his standard in August 1745 after landing from France. Almost all of the 1,200 Highlanders who joined forces with the prince that day, along with many more later

---

2 Also a corrie or cirque, meaning a half-open steep-sided hollow at the head of a valley or on a mountainside, formed by glacial erosion.

Upper Cona Glen, Day 83.

volunteers who joined along the way, would be shot down with ruthless precision by the king's men at Culloden in just eight months' time; the first blow to the Highland clan system.

The village of Glenfinnan has a train station on the Fort William to Mallaig line, and crosses the River Finnan on the viaduct made famous by the Hogwart's Express that starred in several *Harry Potter* films. This 21-arch structure was built using concrete by Robert McAlpine at the close of the 19th century. As viaducts go, it's pretty ropey compared to the magnificent hand-dressed stone viaducts, built some 50 years earlier, that are scattered all over the English countryside, crowned by Yorkshire's splendid Ribblehead Viaduct.

I gave the busy tourist centre a miss and made straight for the Glenfinnan House Hotel for a feed. The hotel, built just a few years after the 1745 uprising, is a magnificent oak-panelled place. I sat on the steps of the winding staircase to take off my boots and spruced up as best I could before entering the bar, closely watched by other diners.

I got to the Corryhully Bothy, located just two miles above the viaduct, around 7.30 p.m., to find four people installed: a young newlywed couple from Georgia, USA and two young lads, one in the Merchant Navy and the other studying physics at Edinburgh. The bothy was maintained by the estate rather than the Mountain Bothy Association and had electricity supplied from the estate's small but controversial hydro plant located down on the River Finnan. The bothy had an electric meter and guests were invited to leave a tip in the tin for the electricity, but the temporary residents all suspected that the head keeper had himself put the note there to 'cover his essentials'. I got the fire going and we had an enjoyable evening sitting around and spinning yarns.

Corryhully bothy, Glen Finnan. Day 84.

Watching the fire, the lad from Georgia told us he was a chimney sweep back home, causing a temporary halt to the conversation. He said chimneys were now coming back in the US following hikes in electricity prices, and his business was booming. The first generation of American chimneys, he explained, were poorly designed and didn't draw properly, and his main job was replacing them with 'high tech' chimneys based on tested Victorian designs that actually worked.

DAY 84: 7 August   Glenfinnan to Glen Dessarry
Miles this day: **9**   Miles to date: **1,035**

After leaving a generous two pound in the tip box for 'essentials' I opened the door and almost walked into a gentleman wearing plus fours and an old tweedy jacket, who I took to be the head keeper.

'Oh', he said, 'Ah was jist comin' in tae check th' meter; ye ken some folk charge their telephain an' other things an' don't pay a penny fur th' electricity, woods ye believe it.' Assuring him I had left something in the tin, I told him everyone was still asleep and bade him good day.

Low black clouds were now threatening and I put on waterproof longs over my shorts before heading up Glen Finnan, an incredibly beautiful glen but slightly disfigured by the hydroelectric scheme. I spotted a pair of circling buzzards and wondered if these were the same birds that I had listened to in the Cona Glen. A short while later I thought I spotted a

Heading over to Glen Dessary, hiding from the midges.

deer hiding in the bracken but it stayed put, making identification uncertain.

The vehicle track eventually petered out, as did the path that replaced it, just where most needed. After a steady two-and-a-half-hour climb, I reached the top of the bealach, the summit marked by an ancient iron gate, the fence having long since disappeared. I would come across about half a dozen of these redundant gates on the trail, some still carrying a rusting enamelled 'Please Close the Gate' sign.

The rain started as I stopped for a snack, and with the midges joining in I was obliged to put on my net, which rather complicated the mechanics of eating. I had now learned that the best way to evade the midges was to put the net over the top of my hat before setting off, tucking the main body of the net under the hat when not needed, ready to pull down at the first approaching whine.

After descending some three miles, the Allt a' Chaorainn River joins the much larger River Pean, but fortunately a bridge has been provided to avoid what would be an impossible river crossing. Here I met a couple of backpackers heading back up to where I had just come from, who asked me about possible camping spots. Although we were surrounded by wide-open spaces, it is surprisingly difficult to find a decent camping spot in this peaty waterlogged mountain terrain, even worse if your tent is not self-supporting and relies on guy ropes to keep it tensioned, as the spongy ground will not support a tent peg.

Crossing the bridge, I was confronted by the extensive dense larch forests that flank the high ground of Monadh Gorm. I looked for the path marked on the map that was supposed to connect with a major forest drive but ended up climbing over the high fence to push through the barrier of interlocking prickly pine branches. Beginning to wonder just what I'd let myself in for, I came across a swampy stream that had apparently been left open as a firebreak. It seemed to head roughly in the right direction so I latched on to it, but was led into a treacherous strip of midge-infested bog. For a while I struggled, probing with my pole to find a way across. The slow-moving ribbon of dark peaty water was only about 12 inches wide but was flanked on either side by a wide strip of deceptive semi-floating mossy grass. It was the sort of place where Tom Bombadil[3] might have appeared from nowhere to guide me on a secret way to his house in the woods, where Goldberry, Daughter of the River, would be waiting with a decorated teapot, a glowing fire and a pair of slippers.

3 Characters in the *Lord of the Rings*.

A welcome sight, the A' Chùil bothy, Glen Dessarry, Knoydart, on Day 84.

Eventually, I got on to the main forest track that would take me to the A' Chùil bothy. On the way, I passed a small fenced off paddock surrounded by woodland. It looked kind of odd and, investigating, I noticed that hummocky grass had all been turned upside down. At one end, I found a small animal shelter with a small gate leading off into the forest. It was intriguing but I couldn't fathom it out until a year or so later, I read that one sporting activity offered by the Glen Dessarry Estate was wild boar hunting. I have worked in wild boar country in Venezuela and Costa Rica and, sitting around the fire in the evenings, listened to scary stories about herds of boar charging down the narrow paths, giving you just a few seconds to get out of their way or get ripped to pieces. Hopefully Scottish boars would be more civilised.

The A' Chùil bothy is set in a clearing at the edge the forest and was very welcoming, providing a safe haven from the swarms of midges. My first job after a brew was to hunt around for firewood, not easy as the surrounding woodland had been well picked over for windfalls.

Unpacking, I found the three missing mini pork pies that I had bought in Fort William. I was tempted to try them but thought the consequences of even just a mild touch of food poisoning here in Knoydart could be pretty dire. I was now a bit more cautious about eating dodgy stuff, having had a bad dose of food poisoning in Yorkshire after having eaten some expired seafood. That episode ended up with a visit to the local Skipton hospital.

I decided to put the pie decision on hold and in the meantime cooked up the usual spaghetti with Ainsley Harriott mushroom soup. This dead-safe recipe would be my standard evening meal when fending for myself along most of the Cape Wrath Trail. I then had a grand evening

Relaxing at A' Chùil, fire bucket at the ready, Day 84.

by the fire, listening to the strains of Buddha Sounds on the threshold of the Knoydart Peninsula. My last task of the day was to reluctantly[4] leave the resident mouse the three Tesco Fort William mini pork pies.

DAY 85: 8 August   Glen Dessarry to Sourlies

Miles this day: **7**   Miles to date: **1,042**

During the night, I thought I heard the mouse and possibly his entire family noisily getting stuck into the mini pies. Come morning I saw that they had made serious inroads but they seemed to have mainly gone for the pastry.

I was quite excited at the prospect of the next leg of my journey, which would now take me over a major watershed into the Rough Bounds of Knoydart, a remote land where deep sea lochs invade the mountainous terrain to create a landscape of mind blowing magnificence. On this journey I would only explore the eastern marches of Knoydart, but one day I will return for a 'final' grand finale.

From what I had read in the bothy logbook, the famous mouse at the Sourlies bothy would be waiting impatiently for my arrival and so, after a good clean up around the fireplace and burying buckets full of ashes left by other walkers, I hurried off for my first date of the trip.

My route took me first over a short stretch of open moorland before I headed back into another dense larch plantation that straddles the western end of Glen Dessary. The track runs next to a stream in places and is incredibly boggy, but when I eventually emerged from the woods I was pleased to discover that I was well on my way up to the watershed. With three giant Munros standing guard over the bealach, I was beginning to feel the sheer remoteness of this place as I pushed on into Knoydart. 'Increasingly Tolkienesque' is how my Cicerone guidebook aptly describes this next section.

The path became increasingly indistinct and progress slowed over the rocky ground. Carefully making my way down to the twin lakes of Lochan a' Mhaim, I surprised a trio of red deer that made no attempt to hurry off, content to just stare at me as if asking what on earth I was doing here. I saw not a soul that day and I was a curiosity for them, and they for me.

I reached the Lochan in the early afternoon having taken four and a half hours of hard work to cover just 4.3 miles. I attributed the slow progress to bogs and terrain rather than to old bones. Even so I was a bit surprised at the dismal rate of progress and was beginning to feel

---

4 The reader can have no idea what a painful decision that was, giving away precious food, miles from anywhere …

Looking back at A' Chùil bothy. Day 84.

Red deer in Knoydart: more heads than legs; more rocks than grass. Day 85.

Glaciated valley heading down to Loch Nevis at Sourlies, until …

… a 1,000-foot drop down to Sourlies, with rocks worn down by glaciers. Day 85.

Loch Nevis, Sourlies bothy and an abandoned shieling at the end of a long, hard slog on Day 85.

Sourlies bothy by saltwater Loch Nevis. Day 85.

Sourlies bothy is owned by a Highland mouse. Abandoned kit hanging from rafters. Day 85.

very thankful that I had stayed last night at the cosy bothy and not attempted a late evening crossing of the bealach. I had a feeling that might have been a bit of a disaster. I found the Lochan an eerie place. The water lapped at my boots as I made my way around the water's edge, and then it started to rain, making the place look even gloomier. I thought of Tolkien's tentacled Watcher lurking in the black waters, and trod carefully.

Eager to be moving on, the Lochan was followed by a flat-bottomed glacial valley where the nascent river Finiskaig meandered at a gentle pace before its final crashing descent to Sourlies. On this steep section the faint path climbed away from the river to head over tricky sloping ice-carved slabs of gneiss, and I was rewarded with my first view of the distant Loch Nevis, 1,000 feet below.

Taking care on the steep descent, I found a faint path that led me down to the steep wooded ravine of the Allt a' Ghille Chruim. Wondering how on earth I would get across the river I spotted a bridge hidden in the trees. (It is not shown on the OS map nor mentioned in the Cicerone guide but for those who might follow, it is located at NM 8791 9447). I have no idea who built this wonderful bridge but I could have danced a little jig, had it not been for the unwieldy pack and the slippery rocks.

From here it was fairly plain sailing down to the Sourlies bothy at the head of Loch Nevis. The building is set back perhaps 100 yards from the shingle and seaweed beach, with an adjoining narrow strip of once-farmed flat land between the river and the sea. Other abandoned fields and stone ruins are located just across the Finiskaig river.

Entering the bothy I found all sorts of junky stuff hanging from the rafters, including a scruffy looking sleeping bag and a number of plastic bags, leading me to believe that someone else was staying here. After a bit of detective work I came to the conclusion there wasn't and that this was all abandoned stuff. Leaving my pack near the door, I sat down on one of the red stacking chairs and within seconds a mouse appeared on the table just a few feet in front of me. I would say it was more audacious than tame, standing up on its hind legs with its nose twitching, as if to say, 'Come on then, where's the food?' At last I had come face-to-face with the celebrated Sourlies mouse!

Fumbling to get my camera, the mouse vanished into thin air, reappearing an instant later perched on top of my rucksack, right on top of the zipped pocket that held my daily stash of Tesco mixed nuts. I am not sure if he had sniffed them out or knew from his mousey experience that the top of a pack usually held the best treats.

Having had several painful experiences with mice in my mum's loft back in Yorkshire, I shooed him away. He leapt off the pack and shot into a tiny mouse-sized hole at the bottom of the wall. I left a small pile of nuts by the hole to hopefully keep him busy until I could follow the log book's advice to hang everything up from the rafter, making my plastic food bags as mouse-proof as possible by suspending them with twine.

The bothy's fireplace had been bricked up[5] some years ago, although some fires had been lit outside. There was no firewood close by and none of the usual driftwood down in amongst the seaweed. I spotted lots of mussel shells piled up by the bothy wall, which was a bit of a mystery for I found none living on the beach.

Reconciling myself to a fireless evening, I went back inside to prepare some food. It was a lovely evening and after supper I headed off to explore the north-western end of the beach where I would be heading the next morning. If I could gauge the tide right, I should be able walk around the headland, avoiding a pathless climb over rough ground. Walking along the beach, I noticed what looked like ordinary grass happily growing under several inches of seawater, something I had not seen before.

I selected a 'spare bunk' and settled down for an early night.

---

5 But later looking at a photograph I think I can just about make out a fireplace, so perhaps I am mistaken on this.

Heading off from Sourlies along Loch Nevis shoreline. Day 86.

DAY 86: 9 August   Sourlies to Barisdale
Miles this day: **9**   Miles to date: **1,051**

After a very early start, I headed outside to check the state of the tide. It was a lovely fresh morning with mostly blue sky and little wind, but the tide was still on the way out. I spent some time burying other people's[6] broken glass and other rubbish and cleaning the grimy trestle table as best as I could, before heading off around 9 a.m. close to low tide.

I managed to get around the headland with a bit of scrambling, and avoided getting wet feet. To get to the suspension footbridge at Carnoch, I first had to cross the grassy marsh flats of the Carnach Estuary. Dodging around a maze of brackish ponds with a connecting maze of rivulets and gullies made for an interesting start to the day. The suspension footbridge carried an 'Unsafe' warning but it looked OK and saved me a time-consuming boots-off river crossing.

Once across the bridge, I stopped briefly to look at the ruined homesteads, another sad reminder of the shameful Highland Clearances that took place from the time of the first Jacobite rebellion of 1715 through to the mid 19th century. Hereditary tenancies did not exist in the Scottish legal system as they did in England, and the large hereditary landowners could force the crofters off their lands without compensation. Often whole glens would be emptied and the incumbents either encouraged to move to the coastal areas or to emigrate to North America, Australia or New Zealand. Today I am told there are more descendants of Highlanders in Canada and New Zealand than in the Highlands themselves. Donald McLeod, a Sutherland stonemason, wrote[7] about the events he witnessed:

---

6 I wonder if local fisherman may have overnighted here, as most of the rubbish was not that of a backpacker, with numerous smashed whisky bottles, broken ceramic plates and mountains of mussel shells etc.   **7** Donald McLeod, 1892, *Gloomy Memories in the Highlands of Scotland*.

Squelchy ground around the point in the Carnach Estuary, Day 86.

A ruined homestead (a shieling) at Carnoch, Day 86.

'The consternation and confusion were extreme. Little or no time was given for the removal of persons or property; the people striving to remove the sick and the helpless before the fire should reach them; next, struggling to save the most valuable of their effects. The cries of the women and children, the roaring of the affrighted cattle, hunted at the same time by the yelling dogs of the shepherds amid the smoke and fire, altogether presented a scene that completely baffles description – it required to be seen to be believed.

A dense cloud of smoke enveloped the whole country by day, and even extended far out to sea. At night an awfully grand but terrific scene presented itself – all the houses in an extensive district in flames at once. I myself ascended a height about eleven o'clock in the evening, and counted two hundred and fifty blazing houses, many of the owners of which I personally knew, but whose present condition – whether in or out of the flames – I could not tell. The conflagration lasted six days, till the whole of the dwellings were reduced to ashes or smoking ruins.'

It seems that the principal underlying reason behind the Highland Clearances was financial, with the mainly hereditary landowners waking up to the idea that there was money to be made in sheep farming and crop growing. It was essentially an agricultural revolution, with the emphasis now placed on the land making a profit rather than providing subsistence living for the peasant farmer or crofter.

Particularly disconcerting are the strong undertones of ethnic cleansing in the Highland Clearances. In a letter to Sir John McNeill, Sir Charles Trevelyan wrote in 1852:

'A national effort would now be necessary in order to rid the land of the surviving Irish and Scotch Celts. The exodus would then allow for the settlement of a racially superior people of Teutonic stock.'

Feeling in great shape and excellent spirits, I set off at a good pace following a track for a few of miles until it slowly disappeared as the valley narrowed. From here on, the ground got boggy and progress slowed until finally I left the riverbank in the search for firmer ground on the valley side. Struggling through thick heather, my right leg suddenly disappeared down a 'peat crevasse', not much wider than my boot but several feet deep and concealed in the heather. As I dropped, the top of my pole and clenched fist whacked me under the chin, almost knocking my teeth out. I might easily have broken my leg with the forward momentum of my pack. Once I realised I hadn't, I couldn't help laughing. From then on I concentrated on the terrain and used my pole to probe my way through the heather until I tired of the tediously slow progress and headed back down to safer but boggy ground.

The valley continued to narrow, with the direction changing abruptly from north to north-east, possibly due to the influence of geological faults. Entering a patch of woodland, I climbed

Upper Carnoch Glen. The going now gets a tougher over pathless terrain through ravines, Day 86.

Afternoon shadows as I climb up the steep side of Carnoch Glen, Day 86.

Baridsale and Loch Hourn, Day 86.

up the valley side to bypass a ravine and waterfall. Dropping back down to the river after the obstacle I saw a distant figure approaching at a fast pace. I hadn't seen a soul now for several days and was surprised. The walker, in his mid-thirties, was from Germany and walking the Cape Wrath Trail from north to south so we were able to brief each other on our respective routes that lay ahead. I was very envious of his waterproof Harvey map of the trail that I hadn't come across before and would strongly recommend it to anyone planning to do the Cape Wrath Trail. He was in a hurry with just two days to get to Fort William for his onward journey. We shook hands and carried on our respective ways.

An hour later, I reached the point marked Carn Mòr on my 1:25,000 map, where the valley makes another abrupt change in direction from north-east to south-west[8]. This was my cue to climb up the 30-degree rough slope to intercept a high-level path that connects Barisdale with Loch Cuaich, some three miles east.

It was a well-trodden and well-engineered path. Heavy stone slabs, weighing around a tonne had been manoeuvred into place at the stream intersections for carts or possibly gun carriages, and the steeper sections had zigzags to reduce the gradient. Although not marked as such on the OS map it looked very much like one of General Wade's military roads. Thanks to this stroke of good fortune I made good progress from the bealach down to Barisdale. Arriving in the early evening, it had taken me a good nine hour slog to cover a measly 10 miles, slowed down by the rough terrain in the Carnoch Glen.

Barisdale is an inhabited estate centred on Barrisdale bay on the southern shore of Loch Hourn. Although there is no road access, it feels much closer to civilisation than Sourlies, with perhaps 50 acres of pasture and hay meadows supporting a scattering of sheep. There is a good bothy owned and cared for by the estate, which has placed an honesty box for receiving the small charge, 'to cover the essentials'. For the brave, there is an adjacent camping field that can be shared with hordes of waiting midges. Opting for the bothy was a no-brainer. Others were using this on their way to Knoydart's only village, Inverie, that has Britain's most remote pub and a ferry connection to Mallaig.

8 At NG 8969 0017.

Loch Hourn at Barisdale, and another ruined shieling from the Highland Clearances. Day 87.

DAY 87: 10 August   Barisdale to Coire Reidh
Miles this day: **10**   Miles to date: **1,061**

I headed off along the southern shore of Loch Hourn at about 8 a.m. making for Kinloch Hourn. It was a pretty walk through wooded glades and purple heathland with fine views across the sea loch. The path keeps well back from the rocky shore with a sprinkling of short steep climbs, taking me a surprising five hours for the 6.5 miles to the tearoom at the head of the loch. A geologist friend had told me about the teahouse, and the young couple that were helping out cooked me up a splendid late breakfast feast of bacon, eggs, beans and lots of toast.

I listened intently when they told me about a severe weather warning and minutes later it started to rain. My main concern was a red-flagged stream crossing that I would get to later in the day that my guidebook warned would be difficult to cross in a spate. They didn't have a bed for the night otherwise I might have been tempted to stay, and so headed off into the rain hoping to beat the spate.

Heading around the bay, I stopped at the stalkers' cottage to enquire about the river crossing but no one answered the door. I then tried the estate house where the door was opened by a pretty girl of about seven years old, with her two front teeth missing. She went off to find her mum, who then went to find her husband who was familiar with the local hills around here. He listened with interest about my trek to Cape Wrath, and said he thought I should be

Heading along the shore of Loch Hourn sea loch towards the old fishing settlement of Kinloch Hourn, Day 87.

Loch Hourn, before the hurricane. Will the last man to leave please shut the gate. Day 87.

With the onset of Hurricane Bertha I take temporary shelter at the Coire Reidh hut on Day 87.

able to still wade across the Coire Reidh River, adding that if not, the stalkers' hut would be unlocked and was big enough to sleep in. As I made ready to leave he asked if I needed anything, and pulled a bottle of Kronenberg lager out of his fishing pack. With that I headed off into the woods, grateful for the brief shelter from the now strengthening wind and rain.

The hut on the Coire Reidh is located at NG 940 096. When I got there about 6 p.m. my first priority was to check out the river, which was already a swift tea-coloured torrent. I wondered if it might still be possible to wade across, and left a marker stone to keep check on any rise or fall and then headed back to the hut, having half decided to overnight there to get out of the atrocious weather.

The hut was sound and dry, about the size of a garden hut with a bench running down one side, which was just too narrow to sleep on. It was a bit draughty and I noticed that other visitors had tried to block up some of the knotholes with screwed up paper. Cooling down after the walk, I started to feel the cold, and put on my thermal jacket. The steady rain continued and just before turning in, I went back to the river by torchlight but my marker stones were underwater.

DAY 88: 11 August   Coire Reidh to Shiel Bridge
Miles this day: **12**   Miles to date: **1,072**

I had a terrible night. Awakened by the howling wind after a few hours, I started fretting about the river crossing, and, for the first time on the walk, felt the cold despite having slept in all my cold-weather gear. From my sleeping bag I brewed up a hot tea, listening to the wind buffeting the hut, wondering if it might take off[9]. Later I would learn that north-west Scotland was taking a battering from Hurricane Bertha, with 100 miles per hour plus winds reported on the higher ground. This weather system would plague me for the next 10 days as I crossed some of the toughest terrain of the whole walk.

Some time later I got up with first light and checked the state of the river. I still couldn't find my marker stones but didn't need them to tell me the water level had risen overnight. More important, the stream velocity had also increased. I decided to give it a try, first testing the water without my pack. Feeling my way around submerged boulders with my canoeing shoes, I only managed to advance a few feet from the bank but felt unsafe and cautiously retreated to the bank.

After drying off and making a brew, I started to make an inventory of my remaining food. I knew it was getting low as I should have arrived at my Shiel Bridge food drop-off the previous evening. Option A was to overnight here again, which my food supplies would just cover.

OPPOSITE: A 6.00 a.m. brew in the Coire Reidh hut
after an all-night storm battering, Day 88.

---

9 Writing these words in the comfort of my home I reckoned it might have made a good headline,'Man washed out to sea in a wooden hut.'

Option B was to follow my guidebook's advice, which stated: 'The river here will be very difficult to cross in a spate, so you may need to try further down where it becomes wider and shallower.' I have since checked the satellite imagery and it seems this potential flood crossing is less than one mile downstream from the hut[10]. Had I known it was that close I would probably have walked down to check it out. However with water now tumbling off the hills everywhere, this option sounded counterintuitive, with every 50 yards adding yet another side stream to swell the flow. I therefore decided to head upstream towards the back wall of the corrie to walk out the river to its source.

The riverbank, if one can call it that, was cut by innumerable deep peat gullies with steep slippery sides, similar to the peat hags of the Yorkshire moors. Approaching the back wall of the cirque some time later, I counted an impressive curtain-like array of 20-plus whitewater cascades. The first one, the largest, was still impossible to cross lower down. Higher up, the stream was channelled through a steeply inclined gully cutting deeply into a rock buttress to form a narrow but scary-looking water chute. I found a place where I was able to cross, but on a wing and a prayer. The other cascading tributaries were a bit easier to cross, most being jumpable with a bit of knee bashing, and I started to shout almighty 'yeaaaahs' in defiance of the foul weather as I knocked them off one by one, even starting to enjoy myself. All in, it had taken me three hours from setting off from the hut to getting back to a point across the river just 200 feet in front of it. I felt immensely relieved.

ABOVE: Unable to cross the river by the hut, I head up towards the back-wall of the corrie, where 20 or more streams crash down the mountainside, Day 88. **OPPOSITE:** Three hours later I stand opposite the hut after multiple stream crossings. The camera now goes into a plastic bag for two days! Day 88.

It was now about midday and I had got nowhere. The track from the ford rapidly degraded to a faint stalkers' track until that too disappeared as I skirted around the western slopes of Sgùrr na Sgine. Here I was met with strong winds that started to knock me off balance as I climbed up towards the bealach, passing somewhere under the east end of the Forcan Ridge below the Easter Buttress, hidden in the cloud.

To add to my woes the display of my Satmap GPS had started to mist up on the inside of the screen.[11] My spectacles were awash with rain but I left them on to give some protection to my eyes, peering over the tops and struggling a bit with my astigmatic vision. I was wet through, cold and, for the first time on the walk, getting seriously concerned.

Onto the bealach, I could feel myself getting disorientated and in the first flush of panic, blundered off into the wrong valley[12] in my desperation to get off the mountain. Realising my mistake, and taking deep breaths to regain control, I climbed back up and set off down the pathless valley of the Allt a' Choire Choil.

Here I made a very stupid mistake and descended on the west side of the river instead of keeping to the east side where, lower down, the OS map shows a discontinuous path. Writing later, I think I can blame part of the mistake on not being able to see very much. The upper part of the valley, corresponding to the corrie back wall, was very steep, perhaps exceeding 30 degrees in places, driving my raw nail-less toes hard against the unforgiving toecap of the ridged *La Sportiva* boots. After crossing several side tributaries, the gradient then started to slacken off and, I started to feel like I had it beaten.

Gaining lower ground I then realised the full consequences of my mistake when I found myself trapped in the centre of an inverted 'Y' between the now raging Choire Choil that I had descended and the much larger Allt a' Coire Uaine that it joined in the main valley. I stood and gazed at the raging Uanie that was quite impossible to cross (although my guidebook said to cross this below the union of the two rivers where it was even more ferocious!)

---

11 Due, I later discovered, to a faulty seal. **12** Coire Mhalagain.

This was no place to camp with water running off everywhere, although I did briefly consider sticking the tent on top of a small glacial hillock. I was cold and wet through and didn't fancy it. Neither could I face retracing my steps up the Choire Choil, involving a climb of over 500 metres, and opted for the second detour of the day by heading up the Coire Uaine. I was now off my guidebook's strip map, and both the screen of the *Satmap* and my spectacles were misted up and so I had really no idea what was in store, but hoped perhaps I would find a lucky crossing place.

The river first ran in a tree-lined whitewater ravine for perhaps a half of a mile[13] with no chance at all of crossing, even in low water conditions. Pulling myself up by heather and clumps of grass, I climbed up over successive deposits of lateral moraine until I reached a break in slope with a wide accumulation of glacial boulders, a sort of boulder delta. Here the force of the river dissipated somewhat with a braided network of narrower channels that I was able to wade across, one by one, keeping on my water-filled boots. This was an incredibly fortuitous stroke of luck. The detour up and down the Coire Uaine had taken me another three hours but I was now on a good path that would take me directly to Shiel Bridge.

I got there just after 8 p.m., cold, wet through and completely knackered after what I reckoned had been my toughest day in the hills ever. The campsite was mostly inundated with flowing water but I found a sloping spot above the water level and, fumbling with cold hands, managed to get the tent up just as the torrential rain began to ease off.

A chap came out of a nearby tent and offered a hand. Then, taking measure of my situation, offered to run me to the pub for a warm up and a feed and later, Guentie and his wife Sophie, drove me to the nearby Kintail Lodge. After I had downed a mediocre steak pie and a beer, Guentie casually picked up a stack of beer mats from the table and performed some amazing impromptu magic tricks. He then pulled four small sponge balls out of his pocket and made them disappear and reappear all over the place, a bit like the Sourlies mouse. I told him he reminded me of one of the gypsies in Gabriel García Márquez's *One Hundred Years of Solitude* that I had on my e-reader.

Ensconced in the cosy bar, I couldn't believe that just a few hours before I had been battling, at my wits end, in threatening mountain conditions.

DAY 89: 12 August   In Shiel Bridge
Miles this day: **0**   Miles to date: **1,072**

Waking up late the next morning to the sound of heavy rain, I looked out to find Guentie had done another disappearing trick, taking his family and tent with him. He had left me a note near the tent door that was falling apart and barely legible. It looked like the rain was set in for the rest of the day so I decided to stay and look for somewhere to dry out. One of the worst things about continuous backpacking with a very small tent in wet conditions is that what gets wet, stays wet. After picking up my mail parcel of food

---

13 But struggling to see without my spectacles this is a guestimate at best.

supplies at the garage shop, I headed off to look out for somewhere to dry out. I was feeling very miserable.

I tried one B&B that turned out to be full but Colin, the owner, kindly offered me the use of a large open-sided agricultural shed to get out of the rain. I jumped at the offer and set to work fashioning a cosy shelter out of straw bales, and rigged up a clothes line to drip dry my tent, feeling happier by the minute.

Colin took some of my wet clothes to rinse and dry out, and then ran me up to the Kintail Lodge, where I holed up for the rest of the day, catching up with emails and enjoying the cosy warmth. After supper, I headed back to my five-star shed with its cosy bed in the hay for another long sleep.

ABOVE: After a grim night in a flooded campsite I retreat into an agricultural shed and make a wind break from straw bales. Day 89.

DAY 90: 13 August   Shiel Bridge to Iron Lodge
Miles this day: **12**   Miles to date: **1,085**

The storm had cleared overnight and the morning looked a lot brighter, so I decided to up and away and go for it. The owner of the shed had kindly invited me in for a complimentary breakfast in the B&B's kitchen with its lovely warm Aga.

My route took me past the Kintail Lodge where I caught up on a few business emails, before setting off on the 40 mile walk over to Kinlochewe past the Falls of Glomach, Maol Bhuidhe, Bendronaig and Strathcarron. I will let my photographs capture the magic of this truly awesome part of the walk.

The first leg involved a climb past Falls of Glomach, with a 370 foot single-leap drop making it one of Britain's highest waterfalls. My guidebook warned that the descent down the ravine below the falls could be treacherous in wet weather, so before heading over there I called in at the National Trust field office at Morvich to seek their advice. The warden agreed that this was not the best day to descend the gorge after all the recent rain, but his main concern was to be setting off at 4 p.m. I decided to give it a try and if worst came to worst, I could always camp for a night on the moors above the falls. I now carried plenty of food and an extra day here or there would be of no real consequence.

Leaving Morvich, I stopped to talk to a couple of chaps repairing a roof, who suggested I overnighted at Iron Lodge, a semi-abandoned lodge owned by some distant Arab gentlemen.

The walk up the glen was superb, at first passing through woods and heathland before giving way higher up to a blaze of purple heather. I met quite a few people heading back down after visiting the falls but no one was able to offer any further advice on the state of the ravine. I met one chap with his elderly dad repeating a walk they had done 40 years earlier, and then met a family of five who pointed out a large herd of red deer on the side of the valley opposite. Everyone was heading back down which I found a bit disconcerting

It was after 6 p.m. when I got to the falls, an awesome sight with the river in full flood, leaping out into space to crash down into the gorge several hundred feet below with a deafening roar, creating an updraft of smoking spray and drizzle. It made me feel slightly dizzy just watching it, an uncomfortable sensation when one is standing on a narrow slippery path above a gorge.

The path down the side of the ravine past the falls required care, as a slip or trip would have meant certain curtains. Without the pack it would have been relatively straightforward but a heavy pack has a momentum of its own, impairing the fine balance needed to negotiate awkward places. Taking the time to plan each step, I made it safely down, stopping every now and again to take a deep breath and take in the awesome views. About halfway down the ravine I woke up to the fact that my guidebook's route had me crossing the river lower down with no guidance or explanation of how to do so. It turned out to be a false alarm, for the Scottish National Trust (SNT) had built a key bridge at the crossing. By about 7.30 p.m., I was safely out of the ravine, crossing the River Elchaig on two more SNT footbridges.

The rain abates, but the rivers are in full spate. I set off over to the Falls of Glomach. Day 90.

Heading up A' Ghlas bheinn towards the Falls of Glomach. Unusual gullies on the mountainside opposite. Day 90.

River just above Falls of Glomach. Day 90.

The Falls of Glomach, Day 90.

The tricky gorge below the Falls of Glomach, where a slip would be fatal. Day 90.

Strath Duilleach at the end of Day 90.

Here I joined an estate track, stopping briefly to watch two young lads with midge nets who were trying to cook. Looking at the hordes of midges that surrounded them, I decided to push on another two and a half miles to Iron Lodge, where I arrived around 9 p.m.

As the two roofing lads had predicted, I found the door to Iron Lodge unlocked and cautiously went inside. It had clearly once been a rather nice place, but the first thing I noticed was the red fitted carpet covered with plaster from the partly collapsed ceiling. The filthy kitchen was fitted with a huge brown enamelled stove and the table was stacked with innumerable malt whisky empties, pointing to a succession of past jollities.

Upstairs was even worse. Small bats, apparently alive, hung upside down from the steps with dozens more dried and flattened bats, apparently dead, littering the carpets. The wooden banisters had been kicked in for firewood, and the toilet and bath were full of burnt paper. The three bedrooms all had fireplaces and some bedroom furniture had been smashed to fuel them.

One room was empty apart from an ironing board leaning against the wall, the solitary item that for some reason had not been smashed. It all made me very angry, but I was absolutely certain that the perpetrators had driven here and not walked.

DAY 91: 14 August   Iron Lodge to Bendronaig
Miles this day: **9**   Miles to date: **1,094**

The day started with porridge to which I added some sticky banana followed by a brew. There was one odd thing I noticed: the meths I had bought in Spean Bridge didn't seem to burn properly. Readying for the off I heard a vehicle pull up outside, and peering through an upstairs window saw two chaps with a pickup loaded with cut timber and other stuff. My first thought was that they might have come to start some much needed repair work. I watched for a few minutes, wondering what to do, surrounded by all this vandalism. Eventually, I decided to head out the door with my pack on and approach them in a straightforward way. The vehicle had been left unattended and I twice walked all round the building looking for the guys, checking out the generator shed. Strangely, there was not a trace of them.

Glad to get away from the dreadful lodge, I headed off up the glen and over the bealach and then sloshed my way over a very boggy moorland tract to the splendidly isolated Maol-bhuidhe bothy that overlooks Loch Cruoshie. The bothy setting is quite spectacular but there was a melancholic feeling hanging over the place.

From photocopies of old letters and stuff that I found inside the bothy, I learned that 100 years ago Maol-bhuidhe had been home to a family of 10. Looking out over this wild expanse, I could imagine the children running about in the heather playing hide and seek that surely must have been their favourite, if not only game. I could almost hear their laughter, the girls in bonnets and long white dresses and the lads with caps on. A copy of a letter in the bothy recalled that a gentleman, called Ian McKay, had met two men who were once part of that

Maol-bhuidhe bothy – 100 years ago, it was home to a family of 10. Day 91.

The River Ling, about a mile downstream from
Maol-bhuidhe, just visible on the left.
Wonderful countryside on Day 91.

family of 10. They were then in their eighties and had left Maol-bhuidhe in 1916 aged 12 and 13. Their father had been a keeper on the Killilan Estate and the children had had what was known as a 'side teacher' who came to stay in the cottage one week in three.

The letter went on to say *'Up to and shortly after the 1939–1945 war, there were many tramps who regularly wandered through the glens and I remember the local stalkers complaining that they did a lot of damage to the old abandoned houses by using any wood they could rip from the walls or floor for firewood.'* Nothing much seems to have changed in that regard, I thought.

The bothy was clean, neat and tidy, a timely antidote for the horrible mess that I had stumbled into at Iron Lodge. I would have loved to overnight here but it was mid-afternoon and I couldn't rustle up the right excuse. Anyway I wanted to get across the nearby red-flagged River Ling before another downpour thwarted my plans.

The River Ling drains a large expanse of lochans and boggy moorland and is already a sizable river by the time it flows out of Loch Cruoshie, just 300 yards below the bothy. The midges watched with delighted anticipation as I stripped off to my underpants and put on my canoeing shoes to wade across to the north bank, with boots and clothing strapped to the top of my pack. I crossed without too much difficulty but the debris flood-line on the far side showed how downright impossible the crossing would have been just a few days earlier. In a later bothy I read a harrowing account of a man being nearly swept away trying to cross the river here after waiting for three frustrating days at Maol-bhuidhe for the spate to subside.

My route followed the River Ling downstream for about two miles passing a couple of long-abandoned fields, and then I started the long climb up over the shoulder of Beinn Dronaig keeping a sharp eye open for the 'faint stalkers' path' mentioned in my guidebook[14]. As I climbed, I kept stopping to look back towards Maol-bhuidhe, unable to unlatch my mind from images of the seven or eight children leaping around in this wonderful school-free wilderness.

The excellent Bendronaig bothy, where I would spend the night, is maintained by the estate and has the luxury of a flushing toilet that you fill from the stream outside. At the time of my stay there was an abundant supply of redundant tar-dipped fencing posts stacked outside that burst into flames with very little coaxing.

Judging from the correspondence affixed to the wall, it looks like the estate had upset the mountaineering community by 'upgrading' a stalkers' track using a bulldozer, creating a scar over part of the remote (and of course treeless) Monar Forest. The Mountaineering Council of Scotland reported this in July 2002 as 'A Slice out of the Cheese Cake' in a reference to one of the more remote Munros called Bidein a' Choire Sheasgaich, affectionately known as 'Cheesecake' by the mountaineering community.

I cooked supper in a proper kitchen, listening to my tinpot radio, and glancing up from time to time to watch a herd of red deer from the kitchen window. After supper I lit a cracking fire, and fell asleep in front of the glowing embers.

---

14 Even a feeble path through heather on a steep hillside can be a godsend.

Bendronaig bothy, a welcome sight after a long, hard Day 91.

A splendid fire with old tar-soaked fence posts, supplied by the estate. Day 91.

DAY 92: 15 August   Bendronaig to Strathcarron
Miles this day: **11**   Miles to date: **1,105**

I woke up early, all set to go after a great night's sleep, chuffed after crossing the notorious River Ling, and believing I now had the Cape Wrath Trail licked. I was just readying for off when two muddy ladies pitched up with bikes and a dog having left home at dawn to cycle up the estate track. I stayed to chat for a while.

After heading west for about a mile and a half along the estate track, I climbed up over pathless terrain towards the Bealach Alltan Ruairidh, having failed to connect with the path shown on the OS map. From the bealach, I followed a fence-line westwards over fairly level ground past two lochans, with splendid views over to Applecross and the distant Cuillins on Skye.

Arriving at the small railway village of Strathcarron around 2 p.m. I tried the town's only hotel, hoping I might find something nice to eat but they had just stopped serving lunch. The cook overheard my pleas for food and came out into the bar. Learning that I had just walked up from Cornwall, she offered to make me something, making a recommendation that I daren't refuse: try her venison burgers. The pub also sold McEwan's beer, which I hadn't seen for many years and as I was only heading to a bothy a few easy miles away, I took a glass or two, joining a few people in the bar who had arrived early to get their weekend off to an early start. I listened carefully when one of them told me that even more bad weather was heading this way, with gale-force winds and heavy rain.

Light rain started as I was leaving the pub, but didn't detract from the splendour of the River Carron that I followed upstream through woods and heathland. The Carron is a famous salmon river and I heard the splash of a big fish but just missed the leap.

FIRST TENANT AT CORIE FIONNARAICH

Mr and Mrs K Maclennan at their wedding

In December 1913.

Note the fur worn by the bride came from a fox that was shot by the groom shortly before their wedding

After two miles, my route climbed away from the Carron valley and headed up the Fionn-abhainn river to the Coire Fionnaraich bothy. It was a cosy spot with an ancient cast iron stove and a small supply of coal briquettes provided by the Mountain Bothy Association. What caught my attention were some fascinating old photographs of a gentleman called Kenneth Maclennan of Strathcarron and his new bride, Katie May of Gairloch, taken on their wedding day on 13 December 1913. Katie was proudly wearing a fox that her husband Kenneth had shot just before the wedding.

As well as the wedding photograph there was an interesting 100-year-old letter setting out the terms of Mr Maclennan's employment as the third stalker on the Ben Damph estate. He and his new wife would have been the first tenants of Coire Fionnaraich.

COPY OF TERMS OF ENGAGEMENT AS AT WHITSUNDAY, 1913.

This wage to be at the rate of forty pounds per Annum.
Free house and liberty to cut peats.
Trenched ground of about quarter of an acre within the deer fence for potatoes or other crops.
Grazing in the Forrest for one or two [animals] if wanted, with allowance of six pounds per annum for purchase of Winter Keep.
Allowance of £2-10-0 for keep of dog for herding back sheep off the Forrest.

OPPOSITE: Coire Fionnaraich bothy, Strathblane. The heavy rains resume, and I turn back to seek a lower-level route to Kinlochewe. Day 92. **ABOVE:** The first tenants at Coire Fionnraich: Kenneth Maclennan with his new wife Katie May, who sports a freshly shot fox. Day 92.

Kenneth Maclennan's terms of engagement with the Ben Damph estate in 1914. Day 92.

> Allowance of thirty shillings per mile for upkeep of hill paths on his section
> of the ground the length being about 4 ¾ miles or £7-3-2 per annum payment.
> Vermin money per fixed scale in this Forrest.
> The position is that of third stalker and he would be under the general instruction
> and supervision of the head stalker at Bein Damph.

I wondered if Kenneth had been paid vermin money for shooting his wife's fox. The Ben Damph estate house, I later discovered, was away over at Torridon and the round trip to collect his wages would have been a 20-mile hike over very rough terrain, a challenge in summer and impossible in winter.

As I was the only guest in the bothy, I was spoilt for choice of rooms, and opted for one upstairs. It was getting cold but for once I didn't bother to light the fire and instead, got straight into my sleeping bag and thermal top snuggling down with a hot chocolate after one last look outside at the worsening weather. Sometime in the middle of the night, I was awakened by the sound of the wind battering the bothy roof and the rain lashing against the window. I couldn't get back to sleep and started to think about the weather warning that I had heard about the day before, and the route ahead. My guidebook had red-flagged several river crossings below Sail Mhor and Ruadh Stac Mor to the north of the Ling Hut. I made a brew from my sleeping bag and then tried to figure out possible alternative routes, avoiding difficult-looking river crossings. I would decide later, after looking at the cloud-base level and

Red sandstones of Corbett Fuar Tholl above Achnashellach station on the way over to Kinlochewe. Day 93.

taking a guess at a forecast. I didn't normally miss the weather forecasts, but prior warning of extreme weather would have been very useful. One day soon we will have simple satellite devices that will flash you severe weather warnings for your location, but somehow I don't think the mountains would approve.

With the help of my Satmap, I found an alternative route by heading back down to the main Carron Glen and then following the road to Achnashellach where a good track, free of major river crossings, would get me over to Loch Coulin. This was part of an alternative route detailed in my guidebook, so I would have the additional benefit of 1:50,000 strip maps in case my Satmap played up again. It sounded like a plan and feeling a bit happier, I went back to sleep for a while.

DAY 93: 16 August   Strathcarron to Kinlochewe
Miles this day: **19**   Miles to date: **1,124**

Venturing forth next morning, I saw that the cloud level had dropped almost to bothy level. It was raining heavily and the wind was up but surprisingly, the river was not yet in spate. Weighing up the odds and mindful of the weather warning, I decided to implement my Plan B. The heavens opened when I reached the main road for the four-mile walk up to Achnashellach, the rain bouncing off the road. Several cars and vans stopped with the drivers asking if I wanted a lift. One chap coming from the Achnashellach direction offered

Easan Dorcha heading over to Torran Cuilinn, Kinlochewe. Day 93.

to turn round and run me back up there. Declining the lifts, which they couldn't understand (and neither could I) I plodded on reaching the tiny Achnashellach railway halt and hamlet around midday.

The rain eased and the walk up through the woods was superb, with glimpses of the brown sandstone buttresses on Fuar Tholl, a Corbett that just misses out on Munro status. The distinctive brown-red rocks that formed the surrounding cliffs were the Torridonian sandstones deposited on a much older basement of Lewisian gneiss (known as an 'unconformity').

The rain was easing as I made my way over the low bealach to a small bothy-hut at Easan Dorcha (NH 0122 5257) known to the walking community as the 'Tea House' that stands in a spinney of Scots pine. From there I headed down to Coulin and Torran Cuilinn and skirted around the eastern shore of Loch Clair to then follow the single track A896 into Kinlochewe.

Arriving at gone 8 p.m. I checked into the bunk barn that adjoins the hotel. The place was full with a group of Munro baggers who had been rained off. After a really good rib-eye steak in the hotel I was invited to join them in the bar in the middle of a heated discussion on the Scottish referendum. I got a right telling off from one irate pro-independence lady when I innocently asked the date of the referendum. 'What de yer mean, yer dinna even know the date of the effing referendum', she chided, adding several more 'effs. Foolishly I countered that I didn't even know today's effing date, which happened to be absolutely true, earning me another severe bollocking. Sensing I was about to get a beer chucked in my face, or a punch in the gonads I backed away. They can bloody-well keep their effing Scotland, I thought.

After sheltering from stormy weather for two days, I head over to Shenavall via river Loch an Nid. A hard Day 96.

DAY 94: 17 August   In Kinlochewe

Miles this day: **0**   Miles to date: **1,124**

The heavy rain continued unabated all through the night and by the morning the river was brimming over. It was fortunate that I had opted for Plan B, as my original route via the Ling hut would today almost certainly have had me facing impassable river crossings with dwindling food supplies. The local weather forecast was for continuing heavy rain and an 85 mph wind on exposed ground.

Cancelling their planned walks because of the foul weather, the Munro baggers packed up their bags and headed home a day early. One chap apologised for the verbal onslaught I had received from the irate lady, adding she had got a bit carried away with the independence issue and assuring me she was 'actually a nice girl'.

After they all left I was thankful to have the place to myself, having decided to stay put until the worst of the weather had passed. I didn't have much option, for apart from the torrential rain, I learned that the cafe that was hopefully holding my mailed food stash was closed on Sundays and the owner apparently lived out of the village. The rain continued unabated all day.

I was feeling a bit down until a car full of cheerful French tourists pitched up and invited me to share their delicious tartiflette, an oily hotchpotch of bacon, gratin potatoes and onions – just the job to counter the lousy weather with a slug of wine.

DAY 95: 18 August   Second day In Kinlochewe
Miles this day: **0**   Miles to date: **1,124**

I overslept until about 8 a.m. and feeling a bit miserable, put on some Ornella Vanoni Italian music triggering memories of happy days in Ecuador. The river in front of the bunk-house was now an impressive raging torrent and looking at my planned route, I decided to stay another day at the bunk barn, hoping that the sky would eventually run dry, but that the pub wouldn't.

The high point of the day was collecting my food stash from the Whistle Stop cafe. The roast cod was one of the great meals of the walk, with the owner-cook and her friendly ladies chatting away to me from over the cooking range in the open-plan kitchen. Afterwards a comfortable old sofa made an ideal spot for an after-lunch doze.

DAY 96: 19 August   Kinlochewe to Shenavall
Miles this day: **17**   Miles to date: **1,141**

The weather looked a bit more settled for the day's long walk over to the remote Shenavall bothy. After following a good 4x4 track and a path for about eight miles up to Lochan Fada, I struck north-east over rough pathless moors, skirting around the south-east facing slopes of Sgùrr Dubh keeping to higher ground to avoid the flat boggy ground on the bealach summit. I found this featureless terrain strangely disorientating, struggling to match the map with the landscape. I paused for a few minutes to watch a life and death airborne contest between a hawk and a smaller bird that, by well-timed last-minute manoeuvres, managed to avoid getting nabbed for a tasty warm lunch.

Disregarding my guidebook's advice, I crossed to the east side of the river near the 300-metre contour to avoid a tricky crossing lower down. Once across, I connected with a good path that heads down the eastern side of Loch an Nid and then northwards into the magnificent valley of Strath na Sealga to join a 4x4 track that comes over from Dundonnell. Some might be tempted here to cut out the dogleg to Shenavall, but they would miss out the splendid, wildly remote bothy.

Arriving at Shenavall, I was surprised to find I would be sharing the bothy with a young Canadian couple and two young lads from an outdoor centre near Todmorden in Yorkshire, who had been tackling the Fisherfield Five group of Munros until the bad weather had confounded their plans. The lads were travelling 'fast and light' and all their kit was soaking so I gave them a hand getting the fire going, using old bones' expertise.

Warming up in front of the good blaze, the lads pulled out the last few drams of their precious Scotch that they shared with everyone, making a grand evening.

Stormy weather in Strath na Sealga approaching Shenavall on Day 96.

Shenavall bothy with Corbett Beinn Dearg Mòr. Day 96.

Beinn Dearg Mòr and Shenavall bothy, starting a 12-hour walk to Ullapool on Day 97.

DAY 97: 20 August   Shenavall to Ullapool
Miles this day: **18**   Miles to date: **1,160**

I didn't hear my alarm go off and by the time I woke up, everyone was readying for off. The place seemed suddenly empty after they had gone, but a short while later, after a bit of cleaning up, I was away myself. As I hauled myself up the steep path through ferns and heather, I kept stopping to turn and take in the wonderful panorama across towards the stunning Beinn Dearg Mòr.

The walk over to Dundonnell was straightforward but I could find no sign of the cafe mentioned in my guidebook and so pushed on to Inverbroom, a long but simple walk with just a couple of easy stream crossings.

The real challenge of the day, however, was the steep descent to Inverbroom at the head of Loch Broom. By then I was starting to feel the miles with the rain now making the path muddy and slippery. The estate had recently felled some trees and the path was barred with a tangle of trunks, uprooted gorse and brambles. I wondered if this had been done on purpose to deter people from using the path that passed a bit too close to the estate lodge, inconveniencing the paying guests. I swore several times and ended up climbing over barbed wire fences before crossing two boggy fields to the road.

I briefly debated whether to camp here in a muddy field or continue on a further nine miles into Ullapool on the dreaded A835. It was now 6 p.m. and the thought of a good supper and a place to dry out tempted me to push on.

The nine-mile slog in the downpour along the busy A835 from Inverbroom to Ullapool was unbelievably horrible, with an endless stream of articulated fish lorries sending swirls of road spray into my face as they hurtled past. The light was fading earlier than usual as I approached the town. Passing a cosy looking American-style motel that displayed a large illuminated 'VACANCIES' sign, I thought I would give it a try. I was told they were full, although something about the woman's face, as she scanned the dripping apparition in front of her, told me that they probably weren't. It was getting a bit late and I was famished after my 20-mile slog. I decided to forget the bed for the moment and concentrate on supper.

The Ferryman Inn overlooking the Loch Broom was the answer to my prayers. It was chock-a-block and with a roaring fire at one end. Leaving my pack in a corner, I found the lady who seemed to be in charge. 'Yes' she said, 'I can fit you in but you will have to order right away as its past 9 p.m.' After ordering a hake with a tiramisu to follow, I hogged the fire until I started to steam to the amusement of some of the diners.

The manageress gave me the number of the youth hostel. It was full but they had a bed for the following night that I grabbed. She then found me a number for a large hotel, that 'always had rooms' that sounded rather ominous, and yes, they had a room. With the bed now sorted, I relaxed and enjoyed the fantastic meal with a couple of glasses of Pinot Grigio.

DAY 98: 21 August   In Ullapool
Miles this day: **0**   Miles to date: **1,160**

I was up at 4 a.m. to attend to some important work stuff with another long Skype phone call to Australia. These calls were beginning to drive me nuts as I was supposed to be on an unpaid sabbatical, but the future of our struggling gold exploration company depended on the outcome. The bus-tour hotel was pretty dreadful and I couldn't wait to escape to the youth hostel. I couldn't formally check in until 5 p.m. but was able to leave my pack in the care of the warden before heading off to do my chores. That accomplished, I headed over to The Ferry Boat Inn to wait for Bob, my school and caving mate who was driving up from Inverness to coordinate where we would meet up in four days' time.

As schoolboys, Ullapool had been a favourite hitch-hiking destination of ours, with the Ullapool fish lorries providing a reliable lift back to Yorkshire at the end of the trip. I remember the British-made Fodens, Guys and ERFs, belching black smoke as they crawled slowly over Shap Fell on the A6 leaving a 200-mile-long trail of nasty fishy liquid that dripped off the back of the flat-bed truck.

In Ullapool we would camp out at an old abandoned tweed mill about two miles from the town overlooking Loch Broom. It had three floors but the upper one was in a bad state, with a hole in the roof letting in the rain and rotting part of the wooden floor. If the weather was decent, we would camp on a patch of grass in front of the mill just a few feet above the shingle beach overlooking the Loch. Stacked conveniently round the back of the mill was a

Laying up for a break at Ullapool on Loch Broom. Day 98.

pile of discarded old wooden tweed combs, about two foot length with rusting iron hooks running down one side. These served both as firewood and for impaling the mackerel to grill by the fire.

We caught the mackerel out in the loch from hired rowing boats, using multiple-hooked handlines baited with slivers of mackerel. Mackerel are shoal fish and would cruise round the loch at high speed and we would sometimes hook three or four in one hit, with the frenzied fish then jumping about in the bottom of the boat leaving a fishy tangle of lines. A freshly caught mackerel is a wonderful fish when grilled on an oak fire overlooking the sea.

✳✳✳

Bob and I met up at The Ferry Boat for a catch-up followed by a lazy lunch and a stroll around the town. We firmed up a plan to meet in four days' time at Inchnadamph, and for the second time on the walk, I had an itinerary.

That evening I returned once more to The Ferry Boat. As I waited for my meal, the setting sun broke through the clouds for just a few minutes, illuminating the sailing boats moored up for the night, promising an end to the stormy weather. After another round of halibut, the place took off with a ceilidh with lively music played on violins, guitars and a flute together, accompanied by stern recitals of Gaelic poetry, making for a very Scottish evening.

Knockdamph bothy, on the way to Oykel Bridge on the 100th day of the walk.

DAY 99: 22 August   **Ullapool to Knockdamph**
Miles this day: **12**   Miles to date: **1,172**

After all these years I still found Ullapool a lively place, but chased by my new itinerary, I was happy to be heading off back into the wilds. Culturally invigorated and only slightly feeling the wine from the night before, I set off over to Oykel Bridge, breaking the journey at the Knockdamph bothy.

The walk was very straightforward, mostly on low-level estate tracks that showed recent flood damage. A lone mountain biker caught up with me and pushed his bike alongside for the last couple of miles to the bothy, with a young German couple catching us up shortly afterwards. Scavenging around, we managed to find just enough wood for a fire, making for a pleasant evening until I decided to write up my log and discovered diary number four – covering the whole of the Cape Wrath Trail – was missing.

This sent me into a blind panic, unpacking my rucksack several times and leaving the others wondering if I was off my rocker. After calming down, I rationalised that I had probably left the diary at the youth hostel. Steve the mountain biker kindly offered to lend me his bike to collect it, but it was getting a bit late.

A double rainbow past Knockdamph bothy promises that the rains have stopped. About time! Day 100.

DAY 100: 23 August   Knockdamph to Salachy hut
Miles this day: **15**   Miles to date: **1,186**

Anxious to sort out the lost diary, I headed off early to Oykel Bridge to make some phone calls. On the way there was another trousers-and-boots-off crossing over the Abhainn Poiblidh River that the guidebook ought have red-flagged. The recent flood debris showed it would have been a corker of a crossing just a few days earlier.

A quick walk through the woods took me on to the traditional Oykel Bridge Hotel that was full of beached salmon fishermen kicking their heels: today, being a Sunday, was both the ghillies' and the salmon's rest day. Logging on to the Internet, I was over the moon to find an email from the Ullapool Youth Hostel, reporting finding the diary, with Bob later offering to pick it up on his way north. It was a stroke of very good fortune.

The young German couple caught me up at the hotel just before I headed off up the glen of the River Oykel, one of Scotland's foremost salmon fisheries. They caught me up again later on, tortoise and hare fashion. After walking together for a while we came to the Salachy anglers' refuge hut with a trestle table overlooking the river. We rested for a while but the midges were just too fierce and, checking out the hut, we all decided to overnight there. Kevin told me that he and Maggie were both studying physics at Jena University in the former East Germany, and were at pains to point out they were travelling together but were 'not *together*'.

River Oykel just above Oykel Bridge. Day 100.

Stepping out in Glen Oykel. Day 100.

Upper Glen Oykel, Conival and Ben More Assynt lost in the clouds. Day 100.

DAY 101: 24 August   Salachy to Inchnadamph

Miles this day: **13**   Miles to date: **1,199**

I had looked forward to today's walk over to Inchnadamph passing close to Conival, a ridge neighbour of the iconic Ben More Assynt. Maggie and Kevin headed off earlier but were going by a different route, over what looked like wild boggy terrain, towards Gorm Loch Mor. Looking at their map I cautioned them about the number of big river crossings.

My route continued alongside the river through heavily forested countryside past the Benmore Lodge, and then headed into wild moorland country approaching the headwaters of the Oykel River. I got the occasional glimpse of Conival and the lower slopes of Ben More Assynt, but the summits of both remained hidden in clouds. Following my guidebook's recommendation, I kept more or less to the 300-metre contour and then picked up a feeble stalkers' path that took me to some waterfalls below Dubh-Loch Mòr.

OPPOSITE: Looking south-east towards the col at Bealach Traligill, with Conival on the left in the Moine thrust zone. Day 101.

ABOVE: The famous geologists Benjamin Peach and John Horne outside the Inchnadamph Hotel, Assynt, in September 1912. *Reproduced courtesy of the Geological Society of London.*

From here I began a very steep heather-grabbing climb up to Bealach Trallgill. I was puzzled to see that the clear stream I had been following showed no sign of diminishing as I approached the watershed. I then came to the source, a spring or resurgence with the water bubbling up through a hole in the limestone.

I was now approaching what for many British geologists is considered to be the hallowed ground of the famous Moine Thrust Zone, where metamorphic rocks (i.e. rocks changed by the effects of heat and pressure) overlay a younger, layered sedimentary sequence. The Victorian gentleman geologist Roderick Murchison (later director general of the geological survey of Great Britain, who had named and claimed the Silurian epoch), believed that the metamorphic rocks were the upper and therefore youngest members of a 'normal' layered sequence – rather like in a layered cake, the icing goes on last!

This explanation was challenged by an Aberdeen University geologist called James Nicol, who pointed out you couldn't have metamorphic rocks conformably overlaying un-metamorphosed sedimentary rocks, and that the explanation must lie in the thrusting of the older rock on top of younger ones. The scale of this low-angle faulting was quite mind-boggling, with slices of the older rocks from the west being pushed laterally over the younger ones in the east for distances of up to 125 miles.

A famous geologist, Archibald Geike said in 1884, 'When a geologist finds … gneiss over-lying gently inclined sheets of fossiliferous quartzite, shale and limestone, he may be excused if he begins to wonder whether he himself is not really standing on his head.'

Geike later accepted the existence of the Moine Thrust and as director of the Geological Survey sent a crack team headed by Ben Peach and John Horne to map the area over a 20-year period, publishing in 1907 one of the finest geological papers of all times. A photograph of the elderly pair hangs inside the Inchnadamph Hotel posing in front of the hotel, just outside the bar.

Once over the bealach, the much improved path then follows the nascent River Traligill passing the limestone karst topography of the Durness Limestone to the west of the river and pale brown Cambrian screes shedding off Conival to the east.

Then, in the far distance, I spotted a lone figure looking up towards Conival. It was Bob. We should probably have camped somewhere close by but I fancied a hot shower and a square meal so we stayed the night in a very comfortable holiday cottage.

DAY 102: 25 August   Inchnadamph to Glencoul
Miles this day: **9**   Miles to date: **1,208**

The fine weather continued and with only 40 miles to go, I felt I was now on the home straight. From Inchnadamph, the route climbs up past Loch Fleodach Coire to the quartzite-littered pass of Bealach na h-Uidhe. The views from here are quite stunning, with the terrain now having a more expansive character. We sat down to take in the view and munch a few

Heading off from Inchnadamph, Day 102.

School mate Bob Peckham at Poll an Droighinn on Day 102.

nuts before beginning the steep descent to the river Abhainn an Loch Bhig, passing close to Eas a' Chual Aluinn, the highest waterfall in Britain with a clear drop of 200 metres (658 feet). What an ice climb that would be, I thought.

The walk down to Glencoul looked straightforward on the map but we found the going surprisingly tiresome on the hummocky pathless terrain. Arriving at the bothy, I was surprised to find the German couple installed. Bit by bit we learned that their walk from Benmore Lodge had been quite an ordeal, fraught with multiple big river crossings and mile after mile of boggy terrain, ending with a late night walk by headlamp to arrive exhausted at the bothy the previous night around 11 pm. Sadly they had scrapped their plans to head to Cape Wrath and were now going to stay and relax at Glencoul for a day or two before heading back to Germany, and hopefully more 'together'.

After a wander around the edge of the sea loch I came up with the bright idea of making some seafood broth. I got everyone organised with pans and down to the rocky shore and, after a short while, we had accumulated a fair quantity of small clams. Apart from abundant supplies of 'ready salted' water, we lacked most of the other basic ingredients, although I still had a smidgen of garlic paste and planned to add some mushroom soup powder as a thickener. We left the clams in the pan of cold seawater to flush out the sand whilst we headed off to hunt for firewood. Checking the cleaning progress on our return, all of the clamshells were now open and waving at us with their tiny siphons. Their ploy worked and I told the others I couldn't face boiling them alive. Neither could they so we ended up putting the clams back in the sea. I could almost hear the clapping of their shells.

Loch Beag near Glencoul, Day 102.

Hunting for firewood for clam chowder, Glencoul Bothy, Day 102.

OPPOSITE: With nerves of steel Bob Peckham dry-paddles across Loch Fleodach Coire. Magic country (in good weather), Day 102.

Looking down on Glencoul (Eas a' Chual Aluinn, Britain's highest waterfall in the distance), Day 103.

DAY 103: 26 August   Glencoul to Loch Stack
Miles this day: **15**   Miles to date: **1,223**

Bob and I said goodbye to the two Germans and then set off in glorious late summer sunshine over to Lock Stack, first climbing around the headland of Beinn Aird da Loch and then dropping down to the bothy at Glendhu, where I knocked up two cups of hot soup.

Shortly after we passed a deerstalker with a horse, packing a recently shot six-pointer stag, dripping with blood. Then there was an easy climb up the Maldie Burn to Loch an Leathaid Bhuain, where I spotted a fox trotting around Loch Fleodach Coire. I wondered what peaty prey he hoped to find out in that boggy land. Once over a shallow bealach, we passed an old shieling (stone shelter), pausing to take in the stunning views of Arkle and Foinaven.

On the way down to Loch Stack we stopped to watch a large group of red deer. Alerted to our presence, they subdivided into smaller groups, each heading off on a different escape route but stopping every few minutes to reappraise the threat. We were fascinated by their divide and scatter ploy. They would know the seasonal cull had now started and that stalkers in plus fours or their well-healed clients sporting clunky gold watches could train the telescopic sights of their high-powered rifles and on their slender necks at any moment.

We were heading for the Achadh Fairidh estate, owned by the Duke of Westminster. It is a small self-contained hamlet, almost a village. In 2008 it boasted a school with eight pupils, a post office and a black and white public phone box erected in the 1960s. When the Duke

Deer stalkers at Loch Glendhu, Day 103.

Loch Stack and the shattered quartzites of Arkle. Day 103.

Loch Stack campsite with a fire to ward off the midges, Day 103.

appealed against the proposed removal of the phone box, BT said that in all of 2008 it was used to make just three paid calls, as well as 26 free calls.

From the estate, we headed off on the A838 towards Lochstack Lodge keeping a sharp eye open for a possible campsite. This was open country, presumably well patrolled by gamekeepers and we were looking for somewhere a bit less visible, this being in one of Scotland's premier hunting playgrounds. We settled for a small wood just off the road perched on a little cliff directly overlooking the loch. Through the trees, we caught a glimpse of Arkle's massive quartzite ridge captured in the sunset afterglow. With the tents up and a fire helping to ward off the midges, we settled down, talking long into the night about the school days in Yorkshire, £5 hitch-hiking adventures in Scotland with my old green Tinker tent, and the meaning of time as well as other light matters.

Arkle with distant Foinaven, the last of the big mountains in the North West Highlands. Day 103.

DAY 104: 27 August   Loch Stack to Rhiconich
Miles this day: **9**   Miles to date: **1,232**

A visitor, perhaps a hedgehog or something larger, rattled the pans in the middle of the night and then a few fish lorries rumbled past in the early hours. After resurrecting the fire to ward off the midges, we sat eating our porridge and savouring the gorgeous morning with the sun streaming down through the trees before heading off for our last day in the hills.

For the first two miles, we walked along the road in a north-westerly direction just below the steep screes of Ben Stack. We then turned on to an estate track past the Lochstack Lodge and headed straight for Arkle's quartzite whaleback. We passed a painted cardboard cutout deer tucked into a bend in the track, presumably placed for the guest shooters to get their eye in.

After about two miles, the track swings to the north-west, following a pronounced alignment of lochs and lochans that seem to track a major geological fault that heads directly towards

Garbh Allt, a red-flagged difficult river crossing in a spate. Day 104.

the day's final destination, Rhiconich. We left the stalkers track to head over rough pathless ground along the steep shoreline of Loch a' Garbh-bhaid Mor, where progress slowed. Foinaven, Arkle's bigger sister peak that is just twelve feet short of making a Munro, was now just three miles to the east. Both look wonderful mountains and I put them towards the top of my steadily lengthening to-do list.

At the next lochan, we came to another red-flagged river crossing over the Garbh Allt. Almost disappointingly, we were able cross with just a shallow paddle, but recent flood debris warned that it would have been an exciting crossing just a few days earlier.

Just beyond that we stopped to watch a lone fly fisherman wading a fair distance from the shore, struggling to cast his fly in the strong wind. After that, it was easy going down a good path to the hotel at Rhiconich, a comfortable anglers' and walkers' hotel that overlooks the Loch Inchard inlet.

The landlady kindly washed a few clothes and then we passed a pleasant evening in the hotel with something nice to eat, but I forget what, whilst looking out over the loch and enjoying a half-decent Rioja.

Abandoned shielings at Kinlochbervie. Day 105.

DAY 105: 28 August   Rhiconich to Strathchailleach

Miles this day: **14**   Miles to date: **1,246**

After a full-works-with-black-pudding breakfast we headed off to Kinlochbervie, home of the London Stores, a higgledy-piggeldy shop that has become a famous landmark for Cape Wrath Trail walkers. We stocked up with some almost-end-of-walk celebration goodies at the Spar shop, including an end-of-walk celebration half-bottle of Famous Grouse.

From Kinlochbervie we opted for the more coastal route via Blairmore and at precisely 3.20 p.m., we spotted the tiny gleaming white speck of the Cape Wrath lighthouse on the distant horizon, pinpointed in the bright afternoon sunlight. With journey's end now just nine miles away, I tried to fathom out if I felt happy or sad. Perhaps a bit of both.

An hour and a half later the awe-inspiring panorama of Sandwood Bay came into view, the iconic landmark that I had so looked forward to since leaving Towan Sands in Cornwall on 25 April, just 24 miles into the walk.

Black clouds were forming, threatening stormy weather and so we decided to push on to the Strathchailleach Bothy, some two miles distant.

When planning the walk, I had read an account of someone's harrowing attempt to cross the half-mile-long river in spate that drains Sandwood Loch that runs into the sea at

ABOVE: London Stores at Kinlochbervie. **BELOW:** A shieling at Sandwood Loch. Day 105.

ABOVE: Storm clouds gather at Sandwood Bay. BELOW: Strathchailleach bothy surrounded by midges. Day 105.

This is not me – the late James McRory-Smith, Sandy to the locals, who made his home at at Strathchailleach for 32 years. Day 105.

the north end of the bay. Today the river was shallow but wide and we headed upstream to look for a better place to cross. As we headed upstream the river gradually disappeared, to finally flow out from beneath a low bank of shingle. It was very strange, but saved us a boots-off river crossing.

From here we headed off over bleak moorland on an easterly heading, puzzled because the bothy failed to appear on the horizon. It is very well hidden from view in the boggy Strath Chailleach valley, a lonely, eerie sort of place, surrounded by moors and guarded by swarms of unbelievably aggressive midges. Perhaps the 'buzzword' had got out that this evening was their last chance to have a go at me.

Feeling somewhat guilty, I concentrated on the cooking whilst Bob braved the midges outside and practised smashing firewood with a large rock, a technique that I had just demonstrated but which he clearly needed to practise! The saving grace of the bothy was the abundant supply of peat that we eventually managed to coax into a red glow with the help of the firewood primer, after almost choking on the first two or three attempts.

For over 30 years, the bothy had been home to a hermit, James McRory-Smith, whose primitive murals still adorn the bothy walls. James, who had served with the Black Watch during WWII, returned to Germany afterwards and later married, but then lost his wife in a horrific car accident. He first moved into the abandoned shepherd's hut in the early 1960s and enlisted the help of the Mountain Bothies Association to repair and maintain it, with part of the hut reserved for bothy visitors. The arrangement worked well until Sandy started to deny them access. He died in 1999, but his presence surrounds you in the bothy.

Settled comfortably in front of the glowing peat fire, we broke out the whisky rations for a couple of drams to celebrate the last night of the walk, and even braved the midges for a couple of hasty photographs of the splendid sunset.

ABOVE: Some of Sandy's murals at the Strathchailleach bothy. BELOW: A peat fire in the bothy. Day 105.

Sunrise at Strathchailleach Bothy. Day 106.

DAY 106: 29 August   Strathchailleach to CAPE WRATH!
Miles this day: **7**   Miles to date: **1,253**

A stunning sunrise greeted us the next morning as we set off on the final leg of the walk
followed for a short while by a cloud of midges. The recent dry spell had tamed the red-
flagged, deeply incised gully hidden just behind the bothy, but the polished pinkish-white
quartzite boulders and the tideline of recent flood debris warned that it could be a real
challenge after a spate.

There were no longer any mountain markers on the horizon to keep us on the right heading over this pathless and featureless moorland, and for the first time on the walk I found myself having to use a compass to stay on track. After about a mile and a half we climbed over the high fence and headed into the MOD firing range, taking note of the ministry warning not to touch any metal objects we might come across. This was the largest bombing range in Western Europe, and the only one that authorised the dropping of 1,000 lb bombs. Watched by a distant herd of inquisitive deer that had somehow survived the NATO exercises, we set off across the last stretch of moorland, making good progress over the walker-friendly, ankle-deep heather. I was getting excited and almost breaking into a run.

We crossed one final swampy section of moor, and climbed the last slope, watching as the long-awaited 66-foot-high lighthouse climbed above the horizon, its white paintwork gleaming in the afternoon sun. There was no crowd of people to wave me on as I crossed the finishing line of my 1,250 mile-long walk, just the wheeling seagulls that were too engrossed with their soaring and diving antics to even notice our arrival.

After passing several derelict-looking but listed buildings that once housed a Lloyds of London lookout station, we made our way past the outbuildings where the lighthouse keepers and their families lived before they were replaced by mechanical gadgetry in 1998. We made for the aptly named Ozone Cafe where we had some home-made tomato soup and a sandwich with a couple of celebratory beers. We chatted with the owner John Kay who lived on the premises with his wife and four huge chocolate coloured springer spaniels. He told us the dogs had rescued a number of people who had got lost on the featureless moorland when mist blew in from the sea.

Fully recharged and on a bit of an ozone-high, I sat alone for a while on the 900-foot-high cliffs overlooking the troubled waters. Just below me, the swirling wild Atlantic currents raced westwards to mingle with the calmer waters of the North Minch, and, from time to time, some of the treacherous eddies joined forces and gathered momentum to form short-lived, but sinister-looking whirlpools. It was as though some giant creature had just pulled out the plug on the ocean bed to suck down a passing ship; that same fate might also be waiting for me should I lose my footing and slither down the steep slope and over the cliff edge.

These ancient cliffs of twisted gneiss and layered sandstone made a very dramatic and abrupt end to my long walk. To the north lay vast cold grey seas, and somewhere beyond these, mile upon mile of creaking pack ice. Here, Mother Nature had finally run out of rock on which to shape a landscape, and there is nowhere left to walk. It was time to head home.

✳✳✳

For a few pounds the keeper of the Ozone Cafe offered to drive us the four miles to the start of the steep track leading down to the Kearvaig Bothy to the east of Cape Wrath. Before heading off we stocked up with a few cans of beer. It felt uncanny, being driven along the bumpy track after many months of legging it.

Almost there! Day 106.

Kearvaig is a very beautiful spot overlooking a golden beach. The bothy is very well maintained, apparently with the support of the MOD who use it to billet retired senior army people who, we were told, periodically came up to shoot the tame deer trapped within the MOD shooting range. It was a bit like shooting zoo animals, I thought.

After installing ourselves in the comfortable bothy, we explored the bay and later got stuck into some end of walk celebrations. The still-cold beer and some leftover salami and other nibbles bought in Kinlochbervie went down very well as we made ourselves comfortable in front of the roaring fire. The days were already shortening and the summer was drawing rapidly to a close. There was a nip in the air but the bothy had a good supply of MOD firewood. After supper we finished off the remainder of the half-bottle of Famous Grouse that we had cracked open at Strathchailleach. It made for a grand evening and a fine end to the walk.

Snuggling down for the night in my comfy sleeping bag, I let my mind drift in and out of the walk, settling on random detail here and there along the way. In coming years, I knew that the 1,750 photographs and 100 hours of digital voice recordings would help me to relive some of the walk's special moments, but there was something else I could do: I could write it all down. The blood-curdling 'Yeaaaah!' that I let rip as I crossed into Wales; the magic tricks at Shiel Bridge in the aftermath of Hurricane Bertha, and the long night spent with the Romans, on guard at Hadrian's Wall. Some of the very kind people I met along the way would get mention, including my new friend, the Sourlies mouse[15].

And then perhaps I would plan the next one: a book or a walk. Or possibly both … ●

---

15 Which reminds me, with the help of my grandchildren (after first getting it wrong), I make the answer to the cats problem on Day 3 of the walk to be 2,745.

Cape Wrath lighthouse, Day 106.

CAPE TO CAPE

APPENDIX 1: EQUIPMENT LIST
AS USED ON CAPE WRATH TRAIL, N.W. SCOTLAND

Includes seven days' iron rations, one litre fuel and one litre water, excludes boots and worn dry-weather clothing.

1. DOCUMENTS AND VALUABLES — GRAMS

Cash	
Target timeline	
Bank cards	
Driving licence, Railcard, National Trust card	
Contacts list	
House key	
Train ticket	
Notebook and pens	

SUBTOTAL: c.200

2. ELECTRICAL AND OTHER EQUIPMENT

*Satmap Active 12 GPS, case and 3 batteries	315
*Camera, Lumix LX7	455
*Leki Sherpa XL pole	300
*20 spare Energizer Ultimate Lithium AA batteries for Satmap, 3 per day	350
6 Spare Lithium AAA batteries (for Spot, Digital recorder and head torch)	65
*Cicerone Cape Wrath Trail guidebook (has 1:50k maps)	246
*Spot emergency device	133
*Sony voice recorder	75
iPhone with charger	230
Tripod-mini	51
Mini Suunto compass	10
Ebook	280
Head torch with batteries	92
Spare torch	53
Swiss knife	61
Alarm clock	34

SUBTOTAL: 2,750

3. BASIC CAMPING GEAR

*Rucksack, Osprey Aether 70 litre.	2,290
*Tent Hilleberg Soulo with extra pegs	2,510
Cord 10m	30
Plastic sheet	10
Old towel	50
Loo trowel	60

SUBTOTAL: 4,950

4. SLEEPING GEAR

*Sleeping bag, RAB Quantum 400g fill	1,031
*Silk liner, RAB	137
*Thermarest mat	419
Pillow inflatable	116
Repair kit	30

SUBTOTAL: 1,733

5. COOKING GEAR

*Trangia 1-man meths stove with 2 pans, small bottle, funnel	222
Lighter, high performance	30
Source flexible 2l water bottle	50

Titanium KFS utensils 65
Fuel bottle, MSR 33 Fl.oz (937 ml) filled with Meths 1,025
Miscellaneous 250

SUBTOTAL: 1,642

6. FOOD AND WATER
Includes iron rations for 7 days (Highlands)
Daytime water, replenished from streams, unfiltered 500
*Spaghetti, Tesco 5 minute 1,000
Soup powder 250
Porridge with instant milk and sugar 500
*Semi-dried banana (Trader Joe, Thai origin, purchased in USA) 500
*Tesco mixed nuts 1,500
Tea bags 60
Salt 50
Goodie bag with 90g Gia garlic puree, olive oil, herbs 200
Energy bars and wine gums 1,000

SUBTOTAL: 5,560

7. TOILETRIES
Towel – REI travel towel 115
Flannel 10
Toothbrush 5
Plastic tooth picks 5
Midge repellent 6
Soap solid 30
Nail clippers 20

SUBTOTAL: 191

8. MEDICAL AND EMERGENCY PACK
50 Ibruprofen 400 mg 10
Vitamins 50 35
*Hartmann Omni fix tape – for feet, 1m x 5cms 10
Scissors 20
Antihistamine 40
Tick tweezers 22
Bivvy bag, whistle, 100g Hammaro fire-lighting paper 160

SUBTOTAL: 297

9. CLOTHING
Mountain Equipment Lhotse jacket 543
*Mountain Equipment Gore-Tex Paclite trousers 289
*Mountain Equipment thermal compressor jacket but highly flammable! 424
*Arc'teryx top (found on Devil's Staircase) 296
*Macpac thermal longs 168
*Midge head net 30
Wide-brimmed hat 90
*Keen canoeing shoes (uncomfortable but needed for Highlands river crossings) ... 250
*RAB Latok Alpine gaiter 246
Gloves 155
2 Spare thick socks 200
Spare briefs x 1 32
Sleeping vest 90
Shorts (unused in Highlands because of the midges) 230

SUBTOTAL: 3,043

TOTAL: 20.32kg (44.8lb)

Note 1: Seven days' food and fuel autonomy is recommended for the Cape Wrath Trail. In less remote areas the pack weight can be reduced by approximately 3kg.
Note 2: Items that I strongly recommend are marked with asterisk.

APPENDIX 2: DAILY LOG

DATE	WALK DAY	CHAPTER	OVERNIGHT STOP	MILES		ASCENT M	OVERNIGHT	
				DAY	DAY TO DATE		POSITION	TYPE
April 21	0		**ST JUST**					
April 22	1	1	Portheras Cove	5	5	236	SW 385 358	Camp
April 23	2	1	Trevail Mill (St Ives)	9	14	702	SW 480 403	Camp
April 24	3	1	Towansands	10	24	174	SW 564 394	Camp
April 25	4	1	Porthtowan	13	37	945	SW 691 479	Hostel
April 26	5	1	Porthtowan	0	37	0	SW 691 479	Hostel
April 27	6	1	Penhale Sands	10	47	871	SW 764 575	Camp
April 28	7	1	Porth Reservoir	12	59	433	SW 863 619	Camp
April 29	8	1	Boscarne Junction (Nr Bodmin)	16	75	448	SX 042 674	Camp
April 30	9	1	Blisland	7	82	295	SX 101 731	Camp
April 1	10	1	Bodmin Moor	8	90	288	SX 181 784	Camp
May 2	11	1	Hidden Valley (Launceston)	9	99	162	SX 282 850	Camp
May 3	12	1	**LAUNCESTON**	4	103	111	SX 332 846	Hotel
May 4	13	2	Galford Down	12	115	246	SX 487 861	Camp
May 5	14	2	East Dartmoor	13	128	634	SX 663 881	Camp
May 6	15	2	Drewsteignton	7	135	282	SX 735 908	Hotel
May 7	16	2	Morchard Road	13	148	411	SX 751 048	Hotel
May 8	17	2	Witheridge	10	158	309	SS 804 144	Hotel
May 9	18	2	Exmoor	13	171	451	SS 858 289	Camp
May 10	19	2	Wimbleball Lake	12	183	524	SS 973 289	Camp
May 11	20	2	Gauldon	12	195	389	ST 115 317	Camp
May 12	21	2	Fyne Court	9	204	445	ST 222 320	Camp
May 13	22	2	Moorlinch	16	220	118	ST 398 366	House
May 14	23	2	Glastonbury	9	229	77	ST 398 366	Hotel
May 15	24	2	Glastonbury	0	229	0	ST 498 391	Hotel
May 16	25	2	St Cuthberts Swallet	13	242	329	ST 544 507	Camp
May 17	26	2	Hallatrow	12	254	208	ST 643 572	Camp
May 18	27	2	Bath	12	266	344	ST 764 640	Hostel
May 19	28	2	Golden Valley, Wick	13	279	131	ST 705 730	Camp
May 20	29	2	Alveston Common	15	294	146	ST 624 875	Camp
		2	**SEVERN BRIDGE**					
May 21	30	3	Wye Valley	13	307	355	ST 549 979	Camp
May 22	31	3	Grace Dieu Abbey	18	325	524	ST 447 134	Camp
May 23	32	3	Llangattock Lingoed	10	335	300	SO 361 201	Hotel
May 24	33	3	Llanthony Priory	8	343	503	SO 289 277	Camp
May 25	34	3	Llanthony Priory	0	343	0	SO 289 277	Camp
May 26	35	3	Bettws Dingle (Nr Clifford)	14	357	618	SO 225 462	Camp
May 27	36	3	Kington	12	369	551	SO 295 567	B&B
May 28	37	3	Hengwm Hill	11	380	617	SO 283 687	Camp
May 29	38	3	**CLUN**	12	392	528	SO 304 813	Hostel
May 30	39	4	Alcaston, Wenlock Edge	14	407	678	SO 464 866	Camp
May 31	40	4	Much Wenlock	14	421	374	SJ 622 000	B&B
June 1	41	4	Kings Wood, Evelith	11	431	251	SO 744 047	Camp
June 2	42	4	Wheaton Aston	14	446	111	SO 854 132	Camp
June 3	43	4	Wolsey Bridge, Trent Valley	16	462	168	SK 021 205	Camp
June 4	44	4	**UTTOXETER**	14	475	154	SK 093 336	Hotel
June 5	45	5	Lin Dale (Off Dove Dale)	16	492	475	SK 154 511	Camp
June 6	46	5	Sparklow	13	504	612	SK 128 659	Camp
June 7	47	5	Nr Castleton	15	520	673	SK 141 819	Camp
June 8	48	5	**EDALE**	5	524	250	SK 125 857	Camp
June 9	49	6	Crowden	16	541	818	SK 071 994	Camp
June 10	50	6	Redbrook Reservoir	11	552	653	SE 028 099	Camp

June 11	51	6	Hebden Bridge	15	567	367	SD 973 264	Camp
June 12	52	6	Ickornshaw Moor	14	581	848	SD 969 410	Camp
June 13	53	6	**GARGRAVE**	13	594	513	SD 932 542	Home
June 22	54	7	Horton in Ribblesdale	21	615	1,013	SD 808 727	Bunk B
June 23	55	7	Hardraw	16	630	539	SD 864 916	Camp
June 24	56	7	Tan Hill	14	645	934	NY 897 064	Hostel
June 25	57	7	Middleton-in-Teesdale	18	663	782	NY 922 262	Camp
June 26	58	7	Dufton	18	681	562	NY 688 251	Hostel
June 27	59	7	Gregs Hut	9	690	911	NY 691 354	Bothy
June 28	60	7	S of Slaggyford	15	706	302	NY 685 516	Camp
July 29	61	7	Greenhead	11	717	371	NY 659 654	Hostel
July 30	62	7	Milecastle 39	8	725	365	NY 760 678	Camp
July 1	63	7	Bellingham	15	740	537	NY 841 834	Bunk B
July 2	64	7	Byrness	15	755	496	NT 764 028	B&B
July 3	65	7	Cheviots – Clennel Street	14	769	773	NT 872 160	Camp
July 4	66	7	**KIRK YETHOLM**	11	780	497	NT 826 283	Hostel
July 5	67	8	Blindswell Plantation	13	793	499	NT 694 236	Camp
July 6	68	8	St Boswells	13	806	290	NT 591 307	Camp
July 7	69	8	Melrose	6	812	269	NT 547 341	B&B
July 8	70	8	Three Brethren	11	824	665	NT 423 318	Camp
July 9	71	8	Peebles	16	839	515	NT 237 424	Camp
July 10	72	8	Pentland Hills	15	854	580	NT 121 574	Bothy
July 11	73	8	Union Canal	17	871	182	NT 082 763	Camp
July 12	74	8	Forth and Clyde Canal	21	892	176	NS 791 787	Camp
July 13	75	8	**STRATHBLANE**	18	909	88	NS 520 804	Camp
July 14	76	9	Drymen	9	918	111	NS 474 886	Hostel
July 15	77	9	Rowardennan	15	933	290	NS 359 993	Hostel
July 16	78	9	Inverarnan Campsite	14	947	963	NN 321 186	Camp
July 17	79	9	Bridge of Orchy	19	966	775	NN 296 397	Camp
July 18	80	9	Kinlochleven	21	987	930	NN 189 620	Camp
July 19	81	9	**FORT WILLIAM**	16	1,002	770	NN 104 739	Hostel
Aug 5	82	10	Glen Cona	12	1,015	259	NM 948 723	Camp
Aug 6	83	10	Corryhully Bothy, Glen Finnan	12	1,027	438	NM 913 844	Bothy
Aug 7	84	10	A' Chùil Bothy, Glen Dessary	9	1,035	601	NM 944 924	Bothy
Aug 8	85	10	Sourlies Bothy	7	1,042	370	NM 869 951	Bothy
Aug 9	86	10	Barisdale Bothy	9	1,051	619	NG 872 043	Bothy
Aug 10	87	10	Coire Reidh Hut	10	1,061	982	NG 940 096	Bothy
Aug 11	88	10	Shiel Bridge	12	1,072	892	NG 938 186	Camp
Aug 12	89	10	Shiel Bridge	0	1,072	0	NG 938 186	Camp
Aug 13	90	10	Iron Lodge	12	1,085	824	NH 043 294	Bothy
Aug 14	91	10	Bendronaig Bothy	9	1,094	574	NH 014 388	Bothy
Aug 15	92	10	Coire Fionnaraich bothy, Strathcarron	11	1,105	417	NG 949 480	Bothy
Aug 16	93	10	Kinlochewe	19	1,124	551	NG 028 619	Bunk B
Aug 17	94	10	Kinlochewe	0	1,124	0	NG 028 619	Bunk B
Aug 18	95	10	Kinlochewe	0	1,124	0	NG 028 619	Bunk B
Aug 19	96	10	Shenavall Bothy	17	1,141	873	NH 067 810	Bothy
Aug 20	97	10	Ullapool	18	1,160	963	NH 131 941	Hotel
Aug 21	98	10	Ullapool	0	1,160	0	NH 131 941	Hostel
Aug 22	99	10	Knockdamph Bothy	12	1,172	370	NH 286 954	Bothy
Aug 23	100	10	Salachy, Glen Orchy	15	1,186	358	NC 331 072	Bothy
Aug 24	101	10	Inchnadamph	13	1,199	504	NC 252 217	Bothy
Aug 25	102	10	Glencoul Bothy	9	1,208	698	NC 270 305	Bothy
Aug 26	103	10	Loch Stack	15	1,223	964	NC 291 417	Bothy
Aug 27	104	10	Rhiconich	9	1,232	258	NC 255 523	Hotel
Aug 28	105	10	Stathchailleach Bothy	14	1,246	446	NC 249 658	Bothy
Aug 29	106	10	**CAPE WRATH**	7	1,253	218	NC 292 727	Bothy
			TOTAL		**1,253 miles**	**48,015m**		
			AVERAGE PER DAY	**12.7 miles**		**485m**		

A GPX file of the route followed is available at www.johnsutcliffe.net

ACKNOWLEDGEMENTS

Sincere thanks to my family and friends who spurred me along the way; to the many kind people that kept me supplied with drinking water, cups of tea, superglue, cakes, a bed for the night, hen eggs, the loan of a pub garden, an agricultural shed, complimentary breakfasts or just a friendly chat. And thanks to my old school mate Bob Peckham who risked joining me at Inchnadamph for the last 54 epic miles to Cape Wrath, by way of Arkle, Foinaven and Sandwood Bay. A special thanks to geologist friend Roger Ellis who planted the seed-idea for an end-to-end walk over a game of scrabble in a dusty tent in a snake-infested walnut grove somewhere in the Zagros mountains of south-east Iran, some 40-odd years ago!

A special thanks to my daughter Amanda who gave up many hours of her busy life to create the superb pen and ink illustrations for the chapter headings. Amanda and her daughter Fiona made valuable suggestions during the early drafting and editing process. Ali Hull helped enormously, knocking the first manuscript into shape, as well as offering very valuable advice throughout the whole book-writing process. I am sincerely grateful to Louisa Keyworth of Lovell Johns for the six beautiful geo-referenced route maps. Many thanks also to Mick Borroff who helped with the editing of the maps and photographs, and set me up with GPS mapping for the next long walk! A special thanks to Jon Barton and his accomplished team at Vertebrate Publishing, especially the editor Camilla Barnard whom I bombarded with changes right up to the last minute! Finally, thanks to Ryder Design for the book's excellent and very professional design. The book's splendid cover photograph was taken by another Hadrian's Wall walker, who, like many others I passed along the way, must remain anonymous.

Many thanks, then, to everyone who helped me on and off the route – and to the reader for purchasing (or borrowing!) a copy of this book. I hope this small adventure might inspire some of you who have not yet explored Britain's wild places to get some gear together and do so, heading over the horizon to join the rabbits, curlews and rustling creatures of the night. But a word of caution: if you do, it might just change the way you think about everything …

John Sutcliffe